BECOMING A
TECHNICAL
LEADER

AN ORGANIC PROBLEM-
SOLVING APPROACH

D1024454

BECOMING·A
TECHNICAL LEADER

AN ORGANIC PROBLEM-SOLVING APPROACH

GERALD M. WEINBERG

FOREWORD BY
KEN·ORR

Dorset House Publishing
3143 Broadway
New York, NY 10027

Library of Congress Cataloging in Publication Data

Weinberg, Gerald M.
    Becoming a technical leader.

    Bibliography: p.
    Includes index.
    1. Leadership. I. Title
HD57.7.W45   1986   658.4´092   86-71049
ISBN 978-0-932633-02-6

Portions of this book have previously appeared in *Australasian Computerworld, bit* (Japan), *Computerworld* (USA), and *Datalink* (UK).

Cover design: Jeffrey Faville, Faville Graphics

Printed in the United States of America

Library of Congress Catalog Number: 86-71049

ISBN 978-0-932633-02-6

*To all of us
who have ever played
all-Y's*

Preface

When Banzan was walking through a market he overheard a
conversation between a butcher and his customer.
"Give me the best piece of meat you have," said the customer.
"Everything in my shop is the best," replied the butcher. "You
cannot find here any piece of meat that is not the best."
At these words Banzan became enlightened.

—Paul Reps
"Everything Is Best"
from *Zen Flesh, Zen Bones*

This is a book about enlightenment, both mine and yours. Mine is
still incomplete, but so far has taken rather longer than a walk through
the market. This book, for instance, has been at least fifteen years in the
making.

It started around 1970, when Don Gause, Dani Weinberg (my
wife), and I spent a summer in Switzerland. Don and I were writing a
book on problem solving (*Are Your Lights On? or How to Figure Out What
the Problem Really Is*), and Dani was continuing her anthropological
research on Swiss peasant communities. Over the years, Don and I had
been studying successful and unsuccessful problem-solving efforts,
particularly computing projects. Dani had been studying the ways in
which new technology had been introduced into peasant communities.
Comparing notes, we dreamed of a workshop that would have the
maximum possible leverage on the successful introduction of new
technical systems, but where was that leverage?

When we compared successful and unsuccessful systems, we
quickly realized that almost all of the successes hinged on the perfor-

mance of a small number of outstanding technical workers. Some of them were consistent sources of innovative technical ideas, some were interpreters of other people's ideas. Some were inventors, some were negotiators, some were teachers, some were team leaders. What distinguished them from their less successful colleagues was a rare *combination* of technical expertise and leadership skills. Today, we would say that they were high in innovation, but with sufficient motivational and organizational skills to use in making ideas effective.

These leaders were not the pure technicians produced by the engineering and science schools, nor were they the conventional leaders trained in the schools of management. They were a different breed, a hybrid. What they shared was a concern for the quality of ideas. Like the butcher, they wanted everything in their shop to be the best. We called them *technical leaders*.

Don, Dani, and I designed a new leadership workshop, called "Technical Leadership in Computer Programming," which was first given in Australia at the invitation of Dennis Davie. Fourteen out of fifteen participants rated it "the most profound educational experience I've ever had." The other one said it was merely "*one* of the most profound educational experiences I've ever had." We realized we had found our leverage.

In the years that followed, Daniel Freedman and a few others joined our team, and the workshop was given to hundreds of would-be technical leaders all over the world. A few electrical and mechanical engineers slipped in, as did some trainers. Except for some technical material, these newcomers found everything directly applicable to their work. As a result, we gradually dropped technical material and broadened our audience. We also broadened our vision of what was possible.

For one thing, we discovered that this technical leadership style was applicable to many problems that have nothing to do with technology. We began to hear stories from workshop graduates who had applied it to situations other than those arising from their technical work.

These people had transformed themselves from ordinary technical supervisors into problem-solving leaders with the power to make things happen. Many of them didn't understand their own transformation. It seemed as if one day they were supervisors and the next they were leaders, like Banzan in the marketplace. But if leadership were only attained through a sudden, mystical enlightenment, how could one learn to become a technical leader?

Over the years, the biggest lesson we have learned from our workshops is that becoming a leader is not something that happens to you, but something that you do. Often in a workshop, someone seems to attain a sudden enlightenment, but we have no more to do with that than the butcher had to do with the moment that completed Banzan's lifelong conversion. Our workshops do not teach people to become leaders; they merely give a boost to each person's unique experiential process of self-development. This book takes the same approach: Consider it as your personal leadership workshop.

From working with systems, I have learned that the process of change is always organic: It's never possible to change just one thing at a time. Each of my behaviors is the solution to some problem from my past. To learn, I add new behaviors to serve alongside these valuable old ones. Yet, like a seed, I already have all the behaviors needed to grow, so I merely need to cultivate them selectively.

I believe that leadership involves a nurturing process, not taking charge of people's lives, so this book is a guide to the process of taking charge of your own development. Its methods, like the methods of our workshops, are organic, designed to fit with the unique system that is you in a way that is gentle, realistic, and fun.

Nevertheless, the process of change won't always *feel* like fun. Because change is often difficult, the book is also designed to provide emotional support. I offer models of leadership, so you'll have an opportunity to let go of some old myths that may block your path. I offer models of change, so you'll understand better what's happening when old ideas fall away. I quote other people's remarks about their feelings as they've become technical leaders, so you'll know you're not alone. I know you will find your own unique enlightenment, and I hope this book will be a welcome companion on your walk through the marketplace.

April 1986   G.M.W.
Lincoln, Nebraska

Foreword

Jerry Weinberg tells a story about an astronomer giving a talk at a garden club. The astronomer is describing the "big bang" theory of how the universe began. At the end of the talk a woman in the back of the room speaks out, "Young man, that's not the way it is. The world is actually supported on the back of a large turtle."

The astronomer, somewhat used to unusual theories, replies calmly, "And what is that turtle resting on?" The woman responds just as calmly, "On another turtle, of course." Now the astronomer is sure he has her. "And what is that turtle resting on, pray tell?" The woman smiles serenely and says with absolute confidence, "Oh, no, you don't, it's turtles all the way down!"

Jerry Weinberg's books are often like his stories—turtles all the way down. His books are difficult to read at one sitting because each of his chapters, like his anecdotes, has multiple levels of meaning. Over and over I found myself stopping and thinking—thinking about what Jerry had just said, thinking about what I thought about what Jerry had said, thinking about what I was thinking about. . . you see what I mean. So the reader is forewarned: Jerry's approach to writing often induces serious thinking.

On one level, *Becoming a Technical Leader* is an extremely down-to-earth, how-to guide. On a second level, it is a set of parables, full of analogies that stick in the mind—the art of management taught through stories about pinball, tinkertoys, and electric blankets. On yet another level, this is a book about the philosophy and psychology of managing technical projects.

As much as I liked the book, there are some things wrong with it. The first thing is that it is too long. Jerry packs so many ideas and so many rules for thinking and managing into each chapter that if you are asked to read it quickly, as I was to write an Enlightened Foreword, you simply can't do it. The second thing that's wrong with this book is that it is too short. Just when you think Jerry is going to tell you how to solve all the world's major problems, you have finished the book and have discovered that what Jerry has really given you is the recommendation that you think for yourself.

In retrospect, I think I was misled by the title. I suppose you could say the book does have to do with becoming a technical leader. But in reality, this book is ultimately about what all Jerry's books are about: how to think, and how to think about what you're thinking about while you're thinking. Turtle by turtle, Jerry points out that most of the obvious solutions to the real problems of managing and working with people tend to miss the mark. So he proposes simple, but radically different, ways of looking at things we all thought we knew.

Fortunately for us, Jerry Weinberg has made unraveling the complexities of technology and management his life's work, in particular, the curious mixture of the two that occurs in modern organizations. Everything he says touches home. Over and over, I found myself laughing and being embarrassed at the same time.

One final point. No self-respecting Foreword is complete unless the Foreworder recommends the book of the Forewordee to a specific audience. I have given this some thought. In doing so, I came to the conclusion that the only people to whom I could honestly recommend this book are those who (A) manage people, (B) are managed by people, or (C) live around or know people in category A or B. If you, by some chance of fate, fit into category A, B, or C, this book is a must for you.

June 1986   Ken Orr, President
Topeka, Kansas   Ken Orr & Associates, Inc.

Contents

Preface vii
Foreword xi

PART ONE: DEFINITION 1

1 **What Is Leadership, Anyway?** 3

The reluctant leader 5
Facing the leadership issue 6
A conventional but flawed view of leadership 7
Contrasting models of the world 8
Explanation of an event 9
Definition of a person 10
Definition of relationships 10
Attitude toward change 11
An organic definition of leadership 12
Questions 14

2 **Models of Leadership Style** 15

Motivation 17
Ideas 18
Organization 18
The MOI model of leadership 19
What technical leaders do 20
Faith in a better way 22
Questions 23

xiii

3 **A Problem-Solving Style**   25

Understanding the problem   27
Managing the flow of ideas   29
Controlling the quality   31
Questions   33

4 **How Leaders Develop**   35

Practice makes perfect   37
The great leap forward   38
Falling into the ravine   39
Growth in the real world   40
How growth feels   42
The metacycle   43
Questions   45

5 **But I Can't Because . . .**   47

I'm not a manager   49
I'm not the leader type   51
I'll lose my technical skills   52
I'm in grave danger of growing   53
I don't want that much power   54
Questions   56

PART TWO: INNOVATION   59

6 **The Three Great Obstacles to Innovation**   61

Are you aware of what you had for dessert?   63
Self-blindness: the number one obstacle   64
No-Problem Syndrome: the number two obstacle   65
Single-solution belief: the number three obstacle   68
Summary   71
Questions   72

7 **A Tool for Developing Self-Awareness**   73

A test of your motivation   75
Your initial reaction   75
Your personal journal   76
        What to write about   77
        What the journal does   78
Questions   81

8 **Developing Idea Power**   **83**

The problem-solving leader's central dogma   85
Creative errors   86
Stolen ideas   86
Corrupted stolen ideas   87
Copulation   88
Why ideas seem wicked   88
Questions   90

9 **The Vision**   **91**

The career line   93
The events don't matter   95
Can success breed failure?   96
The central role of the vision   97
Why the vision creates an innovator   98
Finding the vision in yourself   99
Questions   101

PART THREE: MOTIVATION   103

10 **The First Great Obstacle to Motivating Others   105**

Testing yourself   107
An interaction model   108
The manifest part of an interaction   109
The hidden parts of an interaction   109
Satir's interaction model   110
Understanding why communications go awry   114
A way to start clearing communications   115
Questions   117

11 **The Second Great Obstacle to Motivating Others   119**

An unpleasant task   121
    Lessons from a task-oriented style   122
    Is a people-oriented style better?   123
Weinberg's Target   124
Planning and the future   124
The second great obstacle   125
The leader as a person   126
Questions   128

12 The Problem of Helping Others   129

   Help should be natural   131
   Trying to be helpful: an exercise   132
   Some lessons about helping   134
   Helping and self-esteem   137
   Questions   139

13 Learning to Be a Motivator   141

   Always be sincere (whether you mean it or not)   143
   Survival rules   144
   Meta-rules   144
   Transforming rules into guides   145
   Becoming genuinely interested in other people   149
   Why and when you should read Dale Carnegie   150
   Questions   152

14 Where Power Comes From   153

   Power as a relationship   155
   Power from technology   156
   Expertise as power   157
   Keeping power   158
   Questions   160

15 Power, Imperfection, and Congruence   161

   A mechanical problem   163
   Mature patterns of behavior   164
   Dealing with your own mechanical problems   165
       I must always be natural and spontaneous   167
       I must always be perfectly effective   168
   The payoff for being congruent   169
   Questions   172

PART FOUR: ORGANIZATION   173

16 Gaining Organizational Power   175

   Converting power   177
       Edrie's examples of power conversion   179
       Collecting points   180
   Using power   181
   Questions   183

17 Effective Organization of Problem-Solving Teams   185

A spectrum of organizational forms   187
       Individual scores and voting   188
       The strong leader   189
       Consensus   189
Mixed organizational forms   191
Form follows function   192
Appendix: scoring the ranking   194
Questions   195

18 Obstacles to Effective Organizing   197

First obstacle: playing the Big Game   199
Second obstacle: organizing people as if they were machines   200
Third obstacle: doing the work yourself   201
Fourth obstacle: rewarding ineffective organizing   202
Organic organizing   203
Questions   205

19 Learning to Be an Organizer   207

Practice   209
Observe and experiment   210
Look for incongruence: they're doing the best they can   211
Look for crossed wires   212
Legitimize differences   213
Use yourself as a model of the team   214
Change as you succeed   215
Questions   216

PART FIVE: TRANSFORMATION   217

20 How You Will Be Graded as a Leader   219

The professor's first day of class   221
       The fatal question   222
       Multiplicative grading for leaders   223
A strategy for improvement   224
Can teaching and leading be learned?   224
Grading on the first day   225
A possible solution   225
Questions   228

21 Passing Your Own Leadership Tests   229

A top executive test   231
The ability to withstand tests   232
How to handle an intruder   232
    Arnold's Approach   233
    Ramon's Approach   235
What's the right way?   235
Using and abusing tests   236
Questions   238

22 A Personal Plan for Change   239

An experiment   241
The mental climate for change   241
A personal achievement plan   242
Can it make a difference?   244
Elements of a plan   245
Questions   247

23 Finding Time to Change   249

Staying on target   251
Doing two things at once   253
The cheapest tuition   255
Questions   257

24 Finding Support for Change   259

A support system   261
Technical resource support   262
Support through criticism   263
Support for growth   263
Support for recovery   264
Emotional support   265
Spiritual support   266
Support to maintain leadership   266
Questions   268

Epilogue   269

Bibliography   275

Index   281

BECOMING A
TECHNICAL
LEADER

AN ORGANIC PROBLEM-SOLVING APPROACH

Part One
DEFINITION

Leadership is familiar, but not well understood. If it were less familiar, there wouldn't be so many leadership myths. If it were better understood, there wouldn't be so many misconceptions. The job of these first five chapters is primarily to clear away some myths and misconceptions.

There is also some construction to do, construction of models that will then make it easier to describe just what needs to be done to become a technical leader. These models will describe leadership in general, a particular style of leadership that is characteristic of technical leaders, and also the process by which people become leaders. The models will set the structure for the remainder of the book.

Finally, one chapter will confront the most common reasons we hear from people who say they cannot, or will not, become leaders. After we've disposed of these reasons, we'll be ready to tackle the task of becoming a technical leader.

1

What Is Leadership, Anyway?

If you are a good leader,
Who talks little,
They will say,
When your work is done,
And your aim fulfilled,
 "We did it ourselves."

—Lao-Tse

Leadership is like sex. Many people have trouble discussing the subject, but it never fails to arouse intense interest and feelings. If you have trouble discussing the subject of leadership, this book is for you.

Everyone says you should enjoy sex, so whom can you talk to when it doesn't work right? If you find leadership messy, embarrassing, and sometimes painful, you are not alone, though it may seem that way. Between these covers, you'll find understanding, help, and sympathy.

People who look really sexy are often great disappointments when it comes to actual performance. It's the same with people who look like leaders. They believe they're supposed to do it well by instinct, not by practice—and certainly not by reading books. If you are disappointed in your own performance as a leader, this book brings you a simple message of hope: It doesn't have to be that way.

THE RELUCTANT LEADER

According to Freud, our prejudices about sex are formed in early childhood. I think it's the same with our feelings about leadership. If you have always felt there was something slightly wrong about one person telling another person what to do, perhaps your experiences were like mine.

In grammar school, I was one of the smart kids. In the teachers' eyes, this made me a leading student, but in the students' eyes, it made me a ratfink. Whenever the teachers singled me out in class, the students punched me out in recess—if I was lucky. If I was unlucky, they wouldn't play with me at all. With that kind of training, I soon learned about the dangers of being a leader.

Although school taught me that every good citizen is supposed to lead, the schoolyard taught me to be ashamed of any desire to lead. I learned to try *not* to become a leader. If leadership was thrust upon me, I always put up determined resistance. Whenever possible, I dealt with the question of leadership by pretending it didn't exist. And to make doubly sure I would never have to deal with leadership questions, I chose a career in computer software.

It didn't work. Whenever I did a reasonably good technical job, my co-workers learned to respect me a bit more. Because they respected me, they looked to me for advice, for leadership. If I'd been smarter, I might have isolated myself from them, refusing to give or receive information. But I was naive and besides, I liked to be asked.

Sometimes I was asked to teach courses—a form of leadership. I was asked to sit on technical review committees—leadership again. I was put in charge of a project team, then a larger team. I had ideas I wanted to share even further than my own office, so I wrote papers and books—more leadership. Each time I realized what was happening, I backed off. Sometimes I was violent.

Nobody was going to make *me* into a leader, so I was snared in a paradox. The more I struggled against becoming a leader, the more I was setting my own direction—and the more I was becoming a leader. After all, isn't a leader someone who isn't satisfied with taking the direction set by others?

I grappled with this paradox for several years by withdrawing from anything that might lead other people. This withdrawal was like dealing with sex drives by pretending they don't exist. The leadership was still there, but I wasn't determining its direction. Sometimes the direction was random, but most of the time I was easy prey to manipulators. In the end, I had to face the leadership issue, no matter how embarrassing it was.

FACING THE LEADERSHIP ISSUE

I have a curious way of dealing with difficult issues. Whenever I want to learn about something, I arrange to teach a course on the subject. After I've taught the course enough to learn something, I write a book.

After twenty years of running leadership workshops, I think I've learned enough to attempt a book. Although I still have many unanswered questions, I have learned that I'm not alone. There are others out there who are tortured by leadership questions in their own lives:

- Are leaders really as stupid as they sometimes behave?
- Can I be a leader without becoming like those other people?
- How can I be a leader and keep up my technical skills at the same time?
- Is there a place for a leader in high-tech society who never had any technical skills to begin with?
- How much of my technical expertise do I have to sacrifice?
- What will I get in return?

- If I'm a leader, will I have to boss people around?
- Can I learn leadership from reading books?
- What else can I do to learn?
- Why do people see me as a leader, when I don't feel that way?
- Why don't people see me as a leader, when I feel quite capable?
- What if I don't want to assume leadership responsibility?
- What is leadership, anyway?

These are hard questions. Perhaps the last is the hardest of all. What *is* leadership, anyway?

A CONVENTIONAL BUT FLAWED VIEW OF LEADERSHIP

Psychologists and management theorists have dozens of models of leadership, with a typical one of their texts offering this explanation:

There are two principal ways to identify the leaders of a group:

1. asking the members to identify which members they regard as most influential in directing the group, or
2. asking observers to name the most influential members, or to record the frequency of effective influencing actions.

Although they appear to be scientific, these models are based on the *opinions* of the members or the observers, and on their ability to observe "effective influencing actions." Over the years, I began to see some flaws in that approach.

For instance, a company recently retained me to help a group of computer programmers improve their problem-solving techniques. The company was losing thousands of dollars of sales each passing day because of a subtle error in its software product. Until the programmers could find the error, the product was useless. To help the group, I videotaped them as they struggled to find the error.

In one hour of observation, the "effective influencing actions" of the four programmers involved looked like this:

Arnie   112 actions
Phyllis   52 actions

Weber	23 actions
Martha	0 actions

Martha's actions were easy to record. She sat like a zombie through the entire hour, studying the printout of the erroneous program. She said nothing, made no gestures, and didn't even smile or frown. Without question, she had no influence on the group whatsoever.

After consuming an hour with their effective influencing actions, the other group members were no closer to solving the problem than when they started. All of a sudden, Martha lifted her eyes from the listing, pointed a finger at one line, and said, ever so quietly, "This word should be '87AB0023', not '87AB0022'." Then Arnie, Phyllis, and Weber resumed their agitated discussion. They terminated the meeting ten minutes later, after they had convinced themselves that Martha was indeed correct.

When I asked the group who had been their most influential member, they all said, "Arnie." Then I played the videotape, asking them to be especially alert to the method by which their problem was solved. After watching the tape, Arnie, Phyllis, and Weber changed their answer to "Martha." Why? Because in terms of solving their problem, the table of effective influencing actions should have read

Arnie	0 actions
Phyllis	0 actions
Weber	0 actions
Martha	1 action

Without Martha's contribution, the meeting would have gone nowhere, yet non-programming psychologists would have probably missed Martha's role entirely. When such nontechnical psychologists observe our workshops, they are consistently befuddled by the dynamics of the teams as they solve technical problems. It's as if the psychologists were watching people from another planet, people whose culture and language look and sound superficially like ours but are entirely different.

CONTRASTING MODELS OF THE WORLD

In order to recognize leadership in a group, you must have a *model* that somehow matches the group's culture. For instance, if their model of "problem solving" is too simple, psychologists will have trouble understanding leadership in *technical* environments. Someone once said that the central dogma of academic psychology is that there is one and only one correct solution to every problem—and the psychologist knows it. Any psychologist who believes that simple model will have trouble defining leadership in a way that works in real-world situations. For one thing, such a person would certainly never recognize Martha as a leader.

There are many models of how people behave in the world. Even within the discipline of psychology, there are dozens of major models and hundreds of minor variations. The sociologists' models differ from those of the psychologists, as well as from the anthropologists, the economists, the executives, and the janitors. The reason there are so many models is that each of them is useful, but only in some contexts. The problems arise when we try to apply a model that doesn't match the situation in front of our eyes.

In this book, I will use and develop a number of models for understanding that slippery phenomenon we sometimes call "leadership." To be an effective leader, you will have to have many models at your disposal, and be able to switch appropriately from one to another as the situation demands. Most of the models I favor may be considered *organic* models, in contrast to *linear* models, but there are times when I can be quite appropriately linear.

Organic models can be contrasted with linear models on several dimensions: the way events are explained, the way a person is defined, the way a relationship is defined, and the attitude toward change. Let's compare the two types of models on each of these in turn, then see how they affect the way leadership is defined.

Explanation of an event

Linear models get their name from the assumption of a linear relationship between events; that is, one effect stems from one cause, and vice versa. Organic models may be characterized by "systems thinking": the belief that event X is the outcome of hundreds of other factors, including the passage of time.

The strength of linear models lies in the large number of events that can be well understood in terms of a single cause. Their weakness arises from events of greater complexity, which include, unfortunately, most critical events involving people.

The *threat/reward* model is an example of a linear model with morality added; there is one and only one right answer, and anyone who cannot see it must be either dumb or bad. When we use this model, we tend to feel stupid and ashamed in the face of events we don't immediately understand.

The strength of organic models, by contrast, is that they enable us to be comfortable in complex situations that we don't fully understand. When we use these models, we're able to open our minds to dozens of possible explanations (many of which can be true simultaneously) until we have sufficient information to make an appropriate choice.

One weakness of organic models is that they may prevent us from acting at all. Effective leaders often have to act even when they don't understand all possible factors. In order to use organic models, you must be able to live with the occasional error.

Definition of a person

Linear models tend to place individuals in categories. Organic models define people in terms of their uniqueness, that is, their sameness plus their differences.

The useful side of the linear approach is that it allows us to deal with people quickly and efficiently. We can order a cup of coffee in the morning without considering the waiter in his full-blown individuality.

The useful side of the organic model is the way it allows different people to find a common basis for working together in complex situations. People who abide by the organic model tend to see other people as sharing the same life force, the same spiritual base, and the same kind of relationship among their unique individual parts. They don't compare people to some standard, so they are not tempted to shape people to some ideal image. Such people tend to see the job of a leader as getting people in touch with their own inner harmony.

Linear models become less useful when they slip over into defining people in terms of what they *should* be. If people differ in their thinking, feeling, or acting from this ideal, they may be "treated" with attempts to cut them down to size, or stretch them out. The threat/reward model is a linear model that says people's actions are completely defined by the threats and rewards confronting them. When we operate out of the threat/reward model, we tend to see the leader's job as issuing threats and doling out rewards.

When we hold to the threat/reward model, we tend to have low feelings of self-worth and the worth of others. We give ourselves—and others—messages such as "I don't work hard enough," "I talk too much," "I'm too fat," and "I can't get people to do what I want." These messages often lead to feeling frustrated, angry, and unworthy, though if asked, we will deny these feelings.

Definition of relationships

Linear models tend to define relationships in terms of roles rather than people: the boss rather than the person actually exerting influence. The organic model tends to define relationships in terms of one unique person to another unique person.

One useful side of linear models is that they allow planning of large-scale operations, where it would be impossible to consider each relationship in its full glory. Linear models are less useful when they are extended to one-to-one relationships, where individuality becomes critical in understanding the interaction.

People who adhere to the threat/reward extreme tend to see power as existing in the role, rather than the relationship, so they put great store in titles as a way of defining relationships. When things get tough, they are likely to invoke their "authority," or yield to someone else's. Although this view of power can be useful statistically, it falls apart when applied to one-on-one situations. In love, or teaching, or leading, it's not too useful to think in terms of one person always on top and the other always on the bottom. When we do think this way, we tend to experience emotions of fear, anger, aggression, guilt, and envy toward the other person.

The usefulness of organic models is most clear in one-on-one situations. The two persons, regardless of their roles in the current situation, are presumed equal in life significance. Organic models lead toward problem solving in which everyone benefits. When we act this way toward other people, our most common emotion is joy of discovery. Sometimes, however, we get so wrapped up in this joy that we fail to get the job done, if there is a job to do.

Attitude toward change

When we examine the processes of change, linear and organic models are in stark contrast. Linear models tend to see change as an orderly, one-thing-at-a-time process. Underlying organic models is the fundamental idea of systems thinking: "It is impossible to change just one thing at a time." Linear models tend to be most effective in relatively stable situations, but when things start changing, they get us into trouble.

One kind of trouble is that when change doesn't fit our model, we try to stop it from happening. When faced with change, we may feel paralyzed and helpless. People holding to organic models need security just as much as anyone else, but they obtain their security by taking risks and by tolerating ambiguity.

Under the influence of the threat/reward model, we may try to assure our security by struggling to keep all people and relationships forever the same. If we do feel the need to change, we usually direct it at someone else. And we usually try to change them by "removing" their "bad" behaviors.

Organic models expect and accept change as a normal part of the universe. Some organic models go even further, and welcome change as an opportunity to go into the unknown and grow. They have faith that growth is a natural process by which our wonderful potential is realized, in the same way a seed must grow to realize the wonderful potential of the flower. We'll sometimes refer to such organic models as *seed* models.

AN ORGANIC DEFINITION OF LEADERSHIP

That's a very rough sketch of the difference between linear and organic models, a sketch we will elaborate upon as the book unfolds. Obviously, no person uses either type of model one hundred percent of the time, and that's one reason why the definition of leadership is so hard to pin down.

Linear and organic models lead to contrasting ideas of what constitutes leadership. In the extreme cases, the threat/reward model of leadership may be characterized by the words "force" and "judge," and the seed model, "choose" and "discover." In the seed model,

Leadership is the process of creating an environment in which people become empowered.

For example, before Martha made her observation, Arnie, Phyllis, and Weber were getting nowhere with their problem-solving techniques. After her observation, the environment changed so that the same techniques became powerful.

But Arnie, Phyllis, and Weber were also exercising leadership, in a surprising way, by creating an environment in which Martha was free to work in a style that was powerful for her. Some people in groups simply cannot tolerate one member not "participating," by which they mean doing a lot of talking. Talking wasn't Martha's style, and the others knew it so they left her alone. That's also leadership.

Instead of leading *people*, as in the threat/reward model, organic leadership leads the *process*. Leading people requires that they relinquish control over their lives. Leading the process is responsive to people, giving them choices and leaving them in control. They are empowered in much the same way a gardener empowers seeds—not by forcing them to grow, but by tapping the power that lies dormant within them.

Leadership in the seed sense is creative and productive through other people. It is an organic definition, because it works through creating an environment rather than confining itself to a few focused actions—threats or rewards—in a few specific instances to create a few specific results.

To people ensnared by linear models, this organic model of leadership may seem vague and wishy-washy, but it actually lends itself to more precise quantification than the more conventional models. It's especially useful in technical work because, unlike the more linear models, it allows us to take innovation into account.

Innovation is concerned with redefining a task or the way the task is done. Linear definitions of leadership assume that observers have a perfect understanding of the task. Such definitions filter out innovations that the observer hasn't seen before or doesn't understand. Such blinded observers obviously cannot see the possibility of leadership through innovation. In an age of high technology and discovery, such constraining definitions are practically useless.

The organic model of leadership covers all sorts of work, especially the highly technical. It does not offend technical workers, and can actually be used to measure innovative contributions such as Martha's. Psychologists might not agree with my approach, but I have found it a practical way to describe technical leaders and technical teams.

CHAPTER 1: QUESTIONS

1.   Observe someone you consider a leader. How is this person's life different from yours? Which of these differences are a result of being a leader? Which of them are a *cause* of being a leader?

2.   How would you expect your life to be better if you increased your leadership skills? Which of these improvements will arise from your changed behavior, and which from recognition of the changed behavior of other people?

3.   How would your life change for the worse if your leadership skills increased? Will these changes be worth the rewards? How can you change, yet behave in such a way that these changes do not affect you so adversely?

4.   Make a list of situations in which your presence seems to increase the productivity of others. Alongside this list, identify situations in which your presence seems to *decrease* the productivity. How can you characterize the differences between these situations? (For example, increases in productivity might involve working with people you know well, or working on a problem that is new and different. Or perhaps just the reverse is true for you.) What do these lists tell you about yourself and the environments that empower you?

5.   Based on the two lists from the previous question, are you statistically an asset to groups, or a liability? Do you seek out situations in which your leadership will be positive, or do you more often look for situations in which you can learn to do better? Do you, in fact, learn from these situations, or do you just keep repeating yourself?

2

Models of Leadership Style

If a particular behavior is considered important by a culture, nearly every normal individual can attain impressive competence. . . .

—Howard Gardner
Frames of Mind

The organic model says that leadership is the process of creating an environment in which people become empowered. When people are empowered, they are free to see, to hear, to feel, and to comment. They are also free to move about, to act, to ask for what they want, to be creative, and to make choices.

The organic model also tells us that each person is unique, and so we can expect many different leadership styles. If you don't believe it, spend ten minutes observing two people in a group. You will see dozens of different leadership actions, differing in myriad personal and technical details. How, then, can we hope to generalize about leadership in a way that will be helpful to you in developing your own leadership style?

In this chapter, I'll develop a model, which I call the MOI model, to help you understand your own distinctive style of working with other people. To lend reality to the model, I like to start with personal experience. Like everyone else, though, I have difficulty being clear about the source of my own leadership abilities. As a substitute, I often use my pinball abilities because I can trace my pinball career back many years without embarrassment.

MOTIVATION

As a kid, my pinball skill was one of the few things I was proud of, but my mother didn't like the idea of my playing pinball. In the days before video games, pinball machines were found in pool halls and bowling alleys, iniquitous hangouts where I ran the risk of growing up too fast. So, my father got a machine called Five-Ten-Twenty and put it in our basement, hoping to keep me safely at home for a few more years.

Naturally, I would have stayed home to play free pinball, but my parents were afraid I wouldn't learn the value of money if I could play for nothing. So, my father made me pay my own nickels to play; it was five balls for five cents in those days. Sometimes I played at home, and sometimes I went to the pool hall.

Another kid in the neighborhood, Ormond, also had a pinball machine, but his parents seemed less confused. Ormond could play all day for nothing, though he made his friends use nickels. How I hated Ormond. How I envied him. It gave me great satisfaction to beat him regularly at his own game, even though I had to pay a nickel for the privilege.

Ormond was easy to beat; he was the worst pinball player in the neighborhood. Looking back, I think his parents did him a disservice by letting him play for free, because Ormond had no motivation, no push, to learn to play better. If he wasn't doing well, he just reset the machine and started another free game. I, on the other hand, had a nickel of my own money invested in every game, so I was determined to get my full penny's worth out of every ball.

When I got older—and richer—my pinball prowess hit a plateau for many years. It didn't matter much whether I spent five cents or five dollars for an afternoon's entertainment, so there was no push to improve. Then, all of a sudden, pinball began to purify its besmirched image. You no longer had to play in the privacy of your own home. Pinball had become wholesome, and you could even win trophies. Trophies have always appealed to me, and my game took a sudden turn for the better.

Although there were two different reasons to improve my game— pride and money—they really amounted to two sides of the same coin. Whether I learned to win a trophy or to stay out of financial trouble, without some sort of pull or push, I would have been like spoiled Ormond, and nothing would have changed.

IDEAS

As a result of my improved play, I became something of a hero to the kids hanging out at Pinball Pete's and at the Red Baron. They had all the raw skill and enthusiasm of youth, but they couldn't understand how such a grandfatherly type could whip them so consistently.

Their respect felt good. It was a lot like my early days as a programmer. If you could perform, you became the leader. These kids wouldn't listen to their own parents, but they listened to me. They wanted to know my secrets, and I soon found myself running an informal clinic.

I had many easy coaching triumphs. The kids really wanted to learn, they had quick hands, and most of them could see the ball without glasses. All I had to do was watch a kid for a few minutes, then drop in a little idea about a different approach. It was like dropping dandelion seeds onto a new bluegrass lawn.

My biggest secret, of course, is that older folks have to take a more cerebral view of pinball than kids do. My eyes are dim, my legs get tired, and my hands are a lot slower than they used to be. Without ideas, I wouldn't stand a chance of winning.

ORGANIZATION

But some of the kids didn't seem to learn even when I told them very clearly what to do. Take Herbie, for instance. No matter how often

I told him, Herbie would always take one hand off the flippers to brush his hair out of his eyes. About every third time, the ball would shoot pass his immobilized flipper.

Or take Vaughn. One of the basic techniques of pinball is to flip the two flippers in sequence, but in spite of being told a hundred times, Vaughn would invariably get so excited that he punched both flippers at once.

Or Alfred. You can't play winning pinball if you won't bang the machine in a few crucial situations. Poor Alfred was just too timid to give the machine a good bump, even if it was going to cost him a free game.

On the other hand, there was Alfred's sister, Wendy. To beat a pinball machine, you have to keep your cool. I explained this principle to Wendy, but she couldn't resist venting some deep frustration on the machine by banging it as hard as she could. She didn't restrict her venting to the machine, either. After every game, Wendy managed to give the machine a swift kick in the coin box. This was harmless enough at first, but then she started taking ballet lessons—and learning to kick higher. After a particularly low score, she managed to put her heel through the back glass of Fireball and became the only female ever banned for life from Pinball Pete's.

In spite of my flawless coaching, Herbie, Vaughn, Alfred, and Wendy never improved the quality of their play. They all lacked an orderly base on which to build a better game. They didn't lack push, for they did want to play better. Their lives just weren't sufficiently organized to learn anything that required a nontrivial effort.

THE MOI MODEL OF LEADERSHIP

In order for change to occur, the environment must contain three ingredients:

- M: *motivation*—the trophies or trouble, the push or pull that moves the people involved
- O: *organization*—the existing structure that enables the ideas to be worked through into practice
- I: *ideas* or *innovation*—the seeds, the image of what will become

Leadership can also mean preventing change. If you want to stop some change from occurring, you must do one of three things to the environment:

- M: *kill the motivation*—make people feel that change will not be appreciated; do everything for them so they won't feel the need to do things for themselves; discourage anything that people might enjoy doing for its own sake
- O: *foster chaos*—encourage such high competition that cooperation will be unthinkable; keep resources slightly below the necessary minimum; suppress information of general value, or bury it in an avalanche of meaningless words and paper
- I: *suppress the flow of ideas*—don't listen when you can criticize instead; give your own ideas first, and loudest; punish those who offer suggestions; keep people from working together; and above all, tolerate no laughter

Whether used to foster or prevent change, the MOI model gives us a gross model of leadership style. In French, moi means "me," and we can characterize a particular person's approach to leadership in a specific instance by classifying that person's actions as motivational, organizational, or innovational.

A person whose actions are almost totally motivational might be a sales superstar or a charismatic politician who could sell any idea—if only she had one to sell. Someone whose actions are almost entirely organizational might be an incredibly efficient office manager who keeps things super-organized—for last year's staff and last year's problems. A person whose actions are all directed toward innovation would be a genius—full of ideas but unable to work with other people, or to organize work for others.

In order for a leadership style to be effective, there has to be some balance among motivation, organization, and innovation. I like the MOI model because it emphasizes that we all contain the ingredients for leadership. In each of us, some elements are better developed than others, but anyone can improve as a leader simply by building the strength of our weakest elements. Mr. Universe doesn't have *more* muscles than I do, just better developed ones.

WHAT TECHNICAL LEADERS DO

In consulting assignments and workshops, Dani and I have observed thousands of technical people attempting to solve problems— programmers, administrators, engineers, travel agents, nurses, designers, builders, doctors, systems analysts, architects, and many others.

We have observed many leaders who create an environment in which people are empowered to solve problems.

Some of these leaders are good motivators, but some couldn't motivate a dog to chase cats. Some are excellent organizers, but some can't find a matching pair of socks in the morning. *All* of the most consistently successful technical leaders empower people by the value they place on innovation, on doing things in a better way.

If we look more closely at how technical leaders emphasize innovation, we find that they concentrate on three major areas:

- understanding the problem
- managing the flow of ideas
- maintaining quality

These functions are the ingredients that characterize what we call the *problem-solving* leadership style. This is the style that characterizes the best technical leaders.

Of course, individual leaders accomplish these three functions in different ways, depending upon their personal skills in motivation, organization, and innovation. Introducing a new measurement tool to improve quality involves creating the tool (an I-strategy); teaching people to use it and convincing them to try it (M-strategies); and creating a structure for supporting those who use the tool (an O-strategy).

Setting up a brainstorming session to increase the flow of ideas involves selecting an effective variation of the brainstorming technique (an I-strategy); scheduling a time, place, and people (an O-strategy); as well as teaching the technique and perhaps actually facilitating the meeting (both M-strategies).

You undoubtedly have preferred approaches to leadership, just as every cook has preferred recipes. To become a problem-solving leader, you don't have to abandon your strengths. In fact, you shouldn't even consider it. People improve their performance not by amputating their old behaviors, but by adding new ones.

To become a problem-solving leader, you don't need some sudden religious conversion. You merely need to examine those ends/means combinations where you lack strategies, then fill in the holes, one at a time. With each new approach you master, you'll have another available choice, which increases your chances of being a positive influence on the problem-solving environment. Eventually, you'll notice that in some mysterious way, the teams on which you work have become more productive.

FAITH IN A BETTER WAY

In spite of all their differences in style, problem-solving leaders have one thing in common: *a faith that there's always a better way.*

Where does such faith originate? Bertrand Russell once said that faith is the belief in something for which there is no proof. Though problem-solving leaders may be logical people, they cannot support their faith with logic. Perhaps it originates with some early success in life: A child with a bright idea succeeds in transforming an unpleasant situation into a happy one. This success reinforces the child's faith in ideas. Armed with this faith, the child is more likely to try solving the next problem with a clever idea. Practice makes perfect, success produces even greater success, and a new problem-solving leader is made.

This self-reinforcing cycle doesn't work for everyone. Many children have never known the ecstasy of having one of their ideas heard, let alone used to solve a problem. After a while, they stop trying to work with ideas. Some of them grow up trying to stop others.

According to the threat/reward model, the number of ideas in the world is limited, so for each person who succeeds as a problem-solving leader, a hundred others must fail. For one to be on top, many others must be on the bottom. Perhaps that is why so many people are warning us of the dangers of high technology. If progress through innovation is only for the few at the expense of the many, then problem-solving leadership would hardly be a model for society to cultivate.

My own faith says that there really is a better way, a way that can be learned and practiced by one person without harm to others. I also believe that all people can learn the problem-solving leadership style, even if they were discouraged as children or adults. That's the problem I'm working on, and that's why I've written this book.

CHAPTER 2: QUESTIONS

1. How would you characterize yourself in MOI terms? What were you like five years ago?

2. How much are you willing to do to change your MOI profile? What specific actions do you have planned for the next five years? next year? next month? tomorrow? today?

3. Can you think of specific events that triggered an agreeable change in your MOI profile? Do these events have anything in common? What can you do to increase the frequency of such events?

4. Do you have a different MOI profile at work than you have in your life outside of work? What does this tell you about yourself?

5. Is your current leadership style contributing to your happiness? to the happiness of the people around you? to making the world a better place for everyone?

6. At the moment, does your principal motivation for change come from promise of reward or fear of punishment? Is this the best mode for you? If not, what can you do to get more of the other kind? How about some other kind of motivation entirely, such as an increased sense of self-worth?

3

A Problem-Solving Style

"Would you tell me, please, which way I ought to go from here?"

"That depends a good deal on where you want to get to," said the Cat.

"I don't much care where—" said Alice.

"Then it doesn't matter which way you go," said the Cat.

"—so long as I get *somewhere*," Alice added as an explanation.

"Oh, you're sure to do that," said the Cat, "if you only walk long enough."

—Lewis Carroll
Alice in Wonderland

Successful technical leaders employ a general style that we call problem-solving leadership. They focus on the process of innovation, and they do so in three major ways:

- understanding the problem
- managing the flow of ideas
- maintaining quality

In this chapter, we'll look at actions in each of these categories, and how leaders may use motivational, organizational, or informational means to accomplish, in the end, a better way of solving the problem.

UNDERSTANDING THE PROBLEM

There are many technical workers who enjoy wandering so much that, like Alice in Wonderland, they don't much care where they go, so long as they get somewhere. Computer programmers call this process "hacking." Sue is a technical worker who is obsessed with ideas, but she lacks any sense of connection between her work and the world outside. She doesn't especially want to understand the problem at hand; her only goal is to explore interesting things. If she hacks long enough, she is sure to find *something* interesting.

Hackers like Sue can make some of the best problem-solving team members—as long as they hack within a limited environment, one in which all participants clearly understand what they're trying to accomplish. Without that limited environment, there's a lot of hacking, but things get done only by accident. Here are some specific actions we commonly see that create the kind of environment in which everyone understands the problem.

Read the specifications very carefully. Success or failure often turns on minuscule differences in problem definitions. Although it's necessary to have an overview of the problem, the big picture often turns on one critical detail. Problem-solving leaders recognize this and pay attention to such details. Hackers, by contrast, become bored and want to rush on to something else the instant they have a solution that seems to work. To the worst type of hacker, the ultimate user of the solution is merely a nuisance.

I recall a bid for a computer system that called for 99.9 percent availability, a difficult and expensive requirement to meet. One of the design engineers, however, noticed that the company's definition of "availability" was not quite what the engineers had believed. It proved to be acceptable to bring the system down if the company was notified at least an hour in advance, which enabled the engineers to design an error-detection scheme, rather than an error-prevention scheme. The difference was worth about four million dollars, but two of the engineers still wanted to build the error-prevention system because it was a more interesting technical problem. They had no idea who would pay the extra four million dollars, and they didn't really care.

Encourage teammates to read the specifications very carefully. Reading specifications is clearly informational, but encouraging others to do so is leadership by motivation. No one pair of eyes is sufficiently reliable when a few words may make a four million dollar difference. In our work with technical reviews (special meetings organized to catch technical errors), we have seen tens of thousands of specification errors detected by effective group work. Effective problem-solving leaders know how to organize the environment so that all eyes are operating at full power.

Resolve arguments by referring back to the original problem. Unless and until all members of a team have a common understanding of the problem, attempts to solve the problem are just so much wasted energy. Most prolonged arguments are not over the relative value of the solution, but over different understandings of the problem. Problem-solving leaders are able to read the signs that tell whether an argument is based on a difference in problem definition or a difference in solution method.

Seek clarifications and additional information about the specifications from the customer. No worthwhile project is ever described fully and correctly, even in a written document, but some people would rather plunge right in with what they have than interact with other people. Sometimes a trivial interaction can truly pay off; last week, my travel agent phoned to find out if I really needed a specific departure time on a complex itinerary. Because she wasn't afraid to take one minute to ask, she got a special fare that saved me more than $450.

Refer back to the specifications after work has proceeded for a while, when the implications of some of the requirements can be better understood. Complex problems are never understood right from the beginning, but we often think they are, which is a sure road to disaster. That's why we must encourage constant re-examination of assumptions about the problem. A builder saved $33,000 on an apartment building by noticing the word "equivalent" in the specifications for finishing materials. A doctor saved a life by rereading the record of a physical examination and noticing a symptom that seemed irrelevant at the time. Effective leaders build continuous testing of their own understanding into their work. They are self-confident, but realistic about their own intellectual limitations.

MANAGING THE FLOW OF IDEAS

Ideas are at the center of problem-solving leadership; they are the method by which we go from a definition of the problem to a high-quality solution. Too few ideas means no solution at all; too many ideas means chaos. Without leadership to manage the flow of ideas, two technical experts in the same room make an argument, three make a crowd, and four make a mob. With effective management of ideas, any number makes a successful problem-solving team. Here are twelve typical actions that problem-solving leaders use to manage the flow of ideas.

Contribute a clever idea to the team. Although this is the most obvious leadership action, and although new ideas are sometimes critical, there are actually very few truly new ideas. Several thousand years ago, Aristotle said, "It is not once, nor twice, but times without number that the same idea makes its appearance in the world." In three decades of working with high-tech organizations, I've seen fewer than ten truly original ideas. Virtually all of the new ideas underlying computer software technology, for instance, were put forth by Charles Babbage more than a century ago. More important than the clever new idea is creating an environment where the right idea for solving the problem will be recognized when it comes along.

Encourage copying of useful ideas. Problem-solving leaders are inveterate copiers, though some do not like to admit it. The best ones not only admit it, they cultivate it as a fine art. As Aristotle understood, most "new" ideas are actually copies of ideas from other contexts, and problem-solving leaders are constantly searching other contexts for ideas they can use. The best teachers never cease to study the texts, lectures, and exercises of their colleagues. The best computer programmers never write a new program when they can use an old one for a new job. The best circuit designers know what designs already exist, and whether they can be used in different situations. Problem-solving leaders are not interested in doing again what has already been done well, by themselves or someone else.

Elaborate on an idea that a teammate contributed. No idea is perfect when it is first formed; even copied ideas must be adapted to new circumstances. Most problem-solving leaders devote a hundred times more energy to perfecting ideas than to proposing them. This is what Edison meant when he said, "Genius is one percent inspiration and ninety-nine percent perspiration."

Drop one's own idea in favor of an idea the team wants to develop, and *Refuse to let an idea drop until everyone understands it.* These are the yin and yang of solving any complex problem. Large problems require the joint effort of many people working in harmony. However, the need for teamwork produces enormous pressures to go along with the majority, which can prove disastrous if the majority is stuck on an incorrect idea.

It's relatively easy to let all your ideas drop, or to refuse to drop any of them. What's hard is to strike a balance: to let go when you're merely being egotistical, but to hold on when the rest of the group is plunging ahead with a fatal mistake. I particularly remember one landscape architect, part of a development team, who graciously let go of his favorite playground design concept when it didn't fit with the rest of the project. My first impression was that he was weak and wishy-washy, but later he objected to a particular slide. Although he was one against seven, he persisted until someone else finally understood why the slide would be dangerous to children.

Resist time pressure, and take the time to listen when other people explain their ideas. The landscape architect's teammates deserve credit for taking time to understand why the slide was a safety problem. Under time pressure, most ideas get dropped before they're actually understood, even though some of them would save enough time to pay for trying to understand the bad ideas a hundred times over. Even if this weren't so, people tend to lose their dedication to a project when their ideas are dropped for the wrong reason. In the end, projects go faster in an environment where people listen to all ideas, even if the ideas turn out to be inapplicable.

Test ideas contributed by other people. In any given situation, the vast majority of ideas are not useful, but which ones are useful? High-tech companies like IBM and General Electric maintain large research laboratories, but few of their products originate in the research from their own labs. The researchers' principal job is to stay on top of developments in their field, critically analyzing each one for its potential benefit to the company. When an idea looks good, they then are prepared to seize it quickly and make it better.

Withhold quick criticism of teammates' ideas, in order to keep the ideas flowing. Although testing is crucial, few ideas are so dangerous they can't be allowed to live for the few moments it takes to reconsider our initial reaction to them. Criticism is one thing; quick criticism is another. High-tech companies often reject important ideas, several times even, before some smaller company proves they can work in practice. In 1948, for example, IBM decided not to enter the computer business because the market was too small. What has made IBM the dominant force in the computer business today was not being first, but being able to reconsider early rejections after testing by others proved the ideas viable.

When you must criticize an idea, make clear that you are criticizing the idea, not the person who offered the idea. Problem-solving leaders are well aware that not every idea is useful for every problem, but they are even more aware that every *person* is useful. They know that remarks like "that's a stupid idea," or "you can't really believe that," tend to discourage further contributions, so they offer their criticisms in a caring way. This means that they pay attention to their choice of words, and criticize only ideas, never people.

Test your own ideas before offering them. The popular image of the problem-solving leader is a bright young person pouring out bright young ideas at two hundred words per minute. Such people may score high in leadership as measured by counting "acts of influence," but they are rarely the true problem-solving leaders. Quite the contrary. When asked why they talk so much, these babblers will often remark, "Well, nobody else had anything to contribute." This is nonsense. Nobody is bright enough to have all the good ideas, and a constant babble of your own unconsidered ideas is an excellent way to discourage other people's ideas.

When time and labor are running short, stop working on new ideas and just pitch in. There comes a time in every project when you have to actually do the work, because if you don't have enough ideas by then, you won't finish the project anyway. Some would-be leaders have such an inflated image of themselves that they cannot stoop to mere implementation work, but even God quit thinking up new species after six days.

Encourage the team to drop ideas that had succeeded earlier, but cannot be extended to the new situation. It's hard enough to let go of your bad ideas, but your good ideas are your stock-in-trade. Yet every great idea has its limits. Even banana cream pie gets tiresome if you have to eat it three times a day.

Revive a dropped idea later, when it has value for another part of the problem. Actually, there are no bad ideas, only ideas in the wrong place or at the wrong time. Sailing vessels disappeared when steamships took over, but as energy costs rise, sails are making a comeback. Old ideas don't wear out; a problem-solving leader has a terrific memory and an even better sense of timing.

CONTROLLING THE QUALITY

Cheshire-Cat told Alice that if she walked long enough, she was sure to get somewhere, like a hacker who has no goal, and thus no way to measure quality. But "somewhere" isn't good enough for a problem-solving leader. Once a goal has been defined and accepted, the problem-solving leader is never willing to accept a defective solution.

The leader controls the environment for quality with actions such as the following.

Measure quality as the project proceeds. The ability to reexamine the specifications does not mean the ability to compromise on quality. Understanding the problem helps only if you're actually creating what is specified. All great chefs taste the food during preparation, and effective problem-solving leaders never compromise on quality. They realize that any problem is trivial if you don't have to solve what you were given.

Design tools and processes to measure quality as you build a solution. Manufacturers don't meet schedules and specifications by accident, or by telling people to work harder. The implementation process in high-tech industries is itself a high-tech product, requiring the best in problem-solving leadership. Measuring true progress and quality sometimes seems a burden during a project, but good tools create an environment that makes quality control seem natural.

Measure the speed of implementation, compare it to the schedule, and be prepared to change the solution procedure. Time to accomplish the task is always part of the specification, and must always be compared with true progress against the original specification. Coming to market only a few months late has literally put many a high-tech company out of business.

Step back from the project to refresh your perspective and to assess its viability. Sometimes the best measurement tool is a fresh perspective on what you're doing. In the software business, more than half of all projects that begin implementation are never delivered. The earlier a doomed project is abandoned, the more money is saved. Problem-solving leaders are able not only to see when a project is doomed, but also to persuade others to accept doom before pouring more effort into a hopeless cause.

Check ideas with the customer before implementing them. In the popular image, a problem-solving leader is a solitary genius, but the true leader prefers to produce a success. Although the customer may not always be right, the customer is the one who pays, and a leader knows it's not a success if the customer won't pay for it. Fewer projects would have to be abandoned if their leaders built in some form of continuous checking with the customer.

Restore morale when an idea collapses. Problem-solving leaders are unwilling to accept failure and know how to keep things moving in the face of setbacks, especially when dedicated workers take setbacks as a personal tragedy. In the hands of an effective leader, though, failure is actually a release from bondage to a fruitless idea, a release that renews the idea cycle and makes the process more productive than ever.

CHAPTER 3: QUESTIONS

1. Observe someone you consider a leader. Make a list of this person's activities when working with others, and see how many of them fit into the categories of understanding the problem, managing the flow of ideas, and controlling the quality. Are there activities on this list that you never do? Why not?

2. Observe someone you don't consider much of a leader. Make a list of some simple opportunities for exercising leadership that this person misses. Do you miss these same opportunities? Why?

3. Do you ever have trouble getting people to pay attention to your ideas? How do you react to their ideas?

4. What techniques do you use for gaining perspective on what you are doing when you are working in a group? when you are working alone? How might you improve your ability to see your own actions?

5. Next time you work with a group, list all the things you do to exercise leadership. If you don't have at least ten items, do the assignment again, and keep doing it until you get a list of ten things out of one activity. When you have your list, put the items into the categories of understanding the problem, managing the flow of ideas, and controlling the quality. Does your style tend to favor one category over the others? Which of your actions don't fit into any of these categories?

6. Overall, what new actions would you need to practice to strengthen your style as a problem-solving leader?

4

How Leaders Develop

Year after year beheld the silent toil
        That spread his lustrous coil;
        Still, as the spiral grew,
He left the past year's dwelling for the new,
Stole with soft step its shining archway through,
        Built up its idle door,
Stretched in his last-found home, and
        knew the old no more.

Build thee more stately mansions, O my soul,
        As the swift seasons roll!
        Leave thy low-vaulted past!
Let each new temple, nobler than the last,
Shut thee from heaven with a dome more vast,
        Till thou at length art free,
Leaving thine outgrown shell by life's unresting sea!

—Oliver Wendell Holmes
"The Chambered Nautilus"

Leaders are leaders of change—change in other people, change in working groups, and change in organizations. Above all, leaders are leaders of change in themselves. To become a leader, you have to understand how change happens; yet it's difficult to see change in yourself. Now that we have a simple model to help us understand what leaders do, let's develop another simple model to explain how leaders *develop*.

The model has two major alternating stages, slow growth and fast growth, which we call *plateaus* and *ravines*, respectively. They form a cycle, so we cannot say which comes first. We can start describing the cycle at any arbitrary point. Following Holmes, I could use the nautilus to illustrate the process in biology. Or I could use training on Nautilus equipment, to illustrate it in physiology. But since I'm a better pinballer than a body builder, I'd like to stick with that example. The question to ask, then, is, How does one improve at pinball?

PRACTICE MAKES PERFECT

My father could always beat me at pool, but at pinball, I had the advantage. I wondered how he had gotten to be such a good pool player, and he wondered why he couldn't beat me at pinball. I still play a pretty fair game of pinball, better than any of my kids. But at video games, they leave me in the dust. They can't figure out how an old coot like me can be a silver ball wizard, and I'm baffled when I can't win at Gorf or Snerg.

If you tested my skill at pinball at selected points over the past forty years, it might look like Figure 4.1. A line connecting the points would appear to be pretty steady progress; and looking back, I can't recall any particular moment when I began to play significantly better. So from this point of view, the answer to the question of how you improve at pinball would be this: By practicing every day for forty years, you steadily improve your pinball skills.

This answer has a lot of appeal for us old pinball players. It says that because we misspent our youth, the young whippersnappers are never going to catch up. But once in a while, one of them *does* catch up, like that little twelve-year-old with zits who took the city championship from me a couple of years ago. Maybe simple practice isn't the whole story.

37

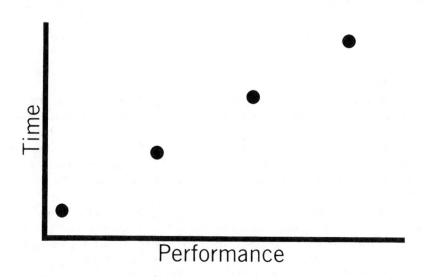

Figure 4.1. GMW's skill at pinball over forty years.

Practice is part of the slow growth stage, and there's no doubt that practice helps, but there's more to the story, even if we don't remember it. (I'm always a bit suspicious of my memory, especially over a forty-year period.) Perhaps a shorter time span, with a more accurate record, would reveal some other factor.

THE GREAT LEAP FORWARD

Whenever a new machine is brought into the neighborhood, I feel compelled to master it. Figure 4.1 could also be a plot of my scores on a single new machine over a period of a few weeks. Again, it looks like steady practice equals steady progress, but when I plot more precise data, I get a rather different picture. Figure 4.2 shows my average daily scores on the Black Knight from when I was a novice until I captured the local record with a score of 3,568,200.

Most of the growth seems to come in sudden leaps from one plateau to another. Although there is slow, steady growth between the leaps, it accounts for only a minor part of the total growth pattern.

The really big progress comes from just a few breakthroughs. In the case of the Black Knight, these weren't better flipper work or box bumping. They were different *ideas* about how the game could be played better. For instance, if you get things set up just right, the Black Knight will put three balls on the playing field at the same time; and while the three balls are in play, any score you make counts triple! One of my

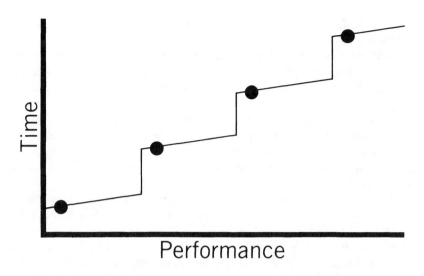

Figure 4.2. GMW's average scores on the Black Knight.

great leaps forward was realizing how fast the score could mount in the three-ball situation.

Without a certain amount of practice, though, I never would have experienced the three-ball situation. Until I had mastered some of the Black Knight's little tricks, there was little probability of getting the right setup, so the steady improvement *on* the plateau was ultimately essential to getting *off* the plateau and onto the next one.

Figure 4.2, then, suggests a more sophisticated model of growth: Practice makes perfect, but when you begin to feel you're really getting good, start looking for some conceptual breakthrough. In other words, spend some time mastering tactics, but don't forget to look for a better strategy.

FALLING INTO THE RAVINE

It's easy to say, "Look for a better strategy," but it's not so easy to do. You may have an idea that playing three balls would be better, but perhaps if you try for that setup, you'll fall into one of the machine's traps. To find a better pinball strategy, you have to test your idea in practice, but to do that, you have to deviate from the strategy you already know how to do so well.

Figure 4.2 shows my average progress on the Black Knight, but Figure 4.3 shows the same progress without averaging out some of the details. In front of each plateau is a ravine. Whenever I tried to improve,

I didn't experience a great leap forward until I had experienced a small stumble backward.

For example, once I had mastered the three-ball strategy, my scores leapt to a new plateau, which made me feel pretty good. I could now beat all the regulars at the Red Baron, though I still wasn't earning enough free games to play all day for free. As I slowly improved on my plateau, I began to suspect that I was missing something. Although my scores mounted quickly when three balls were in play, once in a while, when trying to keep all three balls going, I lost all three at once. It happened only about one time out of four, but it meant I had lost one of three precious turns.

I wondered what would happen if I stopped trying to keep all three balls going and concentrated instead on being sure that one of the three was retained on the playing field. When I tried this new strategy, my scores immediately fell, into the ravine. In fact, I was playing against a pretty fair kid at the time, and he started beating me. Unable to face defeat, I went back to my old strategy and put him in his place.

Later, though, when I didn't have an audience, I tried the new strategy again. Once again my scores dropped, but I noticed I wasn't losing a turn so frequently, perhaps only once in five times when I played three balls at once. Steadily, with practice, I improved my ability to ignore the other two balls and keep at least one ball on the playing field. I didn't score so heavily each time there were three balls in play, but my overall scores got larger. I also got to play longer for my quarter, which is one of the major objectives of the game. In fact, I started winning enough free games to play for several hours on one quarter, which is the real objective of the game.

Figure 4.3, then, represents an even more refined theory of growth. There are plateaus, but you don't really leap, you climb. In order to climb, you must leave the sure footing, letting go of what you already do well and possibly slipping downward into a ravine. If you never let go of what you already do well, you may continue to make steady progress, but you'll never get off the plateau.

GROWTH IN THE REAL WORLD

How general is the ravine-plateau model of growth? Does it apply to anything besides pinball? The smooth curve of Figure 4.3 suggests the model is a bit oversimplified. Real growth generally looks more like Figure 4.4, which represents what my Black Knight scores looked like without averaging. Pinball, like life, has a good share of randomness for which no theory can account.

The part of growth we experience most directly is the randomness, which obscures the other patterns. When a lucky shot raises my score by

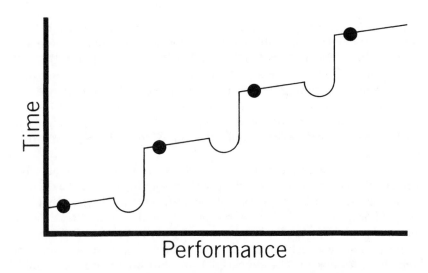

Figure 4.3. GMW's pinball skill as ravines and plateaus.

350,000 points, I suddenly feel a great surge of confidence. When an unexplainable tilt drops me below a million, I start to believe I'm getting old, and slipping. It's hard to see the climate when you're experiencing the weather.

But masked by the noise of many real growth processes, there is a ravine-plateau pattern. Entire nations follow the pattern, as do industries, organizations, and teams of all sizes. So do individuals.

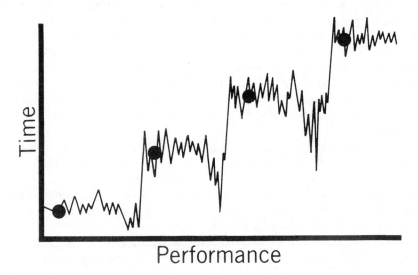

Figure 4.4. GMW's Black Knight scores without averaging.

I value my uniqueness, and I resent people who tell me I am merely part of a large invisible pattern. I would never say that anyone is "merely" part of a larger pattern; it implies lack of free choice. Besides, people cannot be "part" of a pattern because the patterns are not real. They are devices to help me communicate a lifetime of experience in a few chapters. Understanding the experiences of others expands our choices. By understanding these patterns, problem-solving leaders can make better career choices—quite the opposite of being "part of a pattern."

In the following chapters, we'll look in more detail at what happens to people as they become problem-solving leaders. To do this, neither models nor descriptions will be sufficient to tell you what you need to know about your *own* development. Models and other descriptions can tell what happens on the outside, but not how it *feels* when it happens—like how exhilarating it feels to be on top of a plateau, how frightening to look up at the next plateau, and how painful to tumble into the ravine.

No matter how high and mighty you get, you never forget the very real pain of those ravines. Without the hope of something better, however, the pain would turn you back before you got started. So before you embark on your next climb, you'll want to have an idea of what it will feel like when you reach the crest.

HOW GROWTH FEELS

The only way you can know how it feels to grow as a leader is through your own experience and through other people's autobiographical accounts. Feelings are much more reliable than factual details. Though I can't recall a single technical detail, I can still remember how splendid it felt to be the best IBM 650 programmer in San Francisco, more than a quarter-century ago. This is the typical feeling in the middle of the plateau stage—smug satisfaction. You've survived the difficult ascent, but you're still learning, so nobody can tell you that you're stagnant.

But *events* can tell you. Although I was master of the IBM 650, there was a bigger, more powerful machine on the horizon: the IBM 704. I moved to Los Angeles to work with 704 programmers who couldn't care less about my skill at placing instructions in optimal locations on the 650's main memory drum. That's how the plateau stage begins to crumble—with the introduction of some foreign element. My first reaction was typical: I tried to reject the foreign element. I argued that drum memory was superior to core memory, that decimal coding was intrinsically superior to binary. I still remember how I felt when they laughed.

To protect my feelings, I tried learning about the 704 in secret, and promptly fell into the ravine. It took me days to write a simple 704 program that I could have constructed in ten minutes on the 650. I was unable to predict how long it would take to write, how long it would take to run, or even whether it would run correctly. I felt shaky and jumped at any slight excuse to return to the 650.

In the midst of this chaos, there were a few glimmers of a new awareness. I discovered neat techniques available on the binary 704 that were not available on the decimal 650. I began to appreciate the abundant storage (in modern terms, about 36,000 bytes versus about 10,000 bytes) and high speed (12 microsecond memory access versus 120 milliseconds).

I kept all this new knowledge a secret, but it began to color my perceptions of the world. Then one day, I encountered a client with a computing problem that simply could not be done on the 650. I remember the moment when I saw clearly that the 704 was quite literally made for problems like this. From that moment on, I was a convert, rather self-conscious, but a true believer awkwardly walking the slight upward grade of a new plateau.

THE METACYCLE

One of the awkward steps in my trek to the 704 plateau was mastering octal notation. Later, when the IBM 360 came along, I had to let go of octal and embrace hexadecimal, along with an entirely new machine language vocabulary—another ravine, but not quite as traumatic as the first one. I felt the same shakiness, the same urge to pull back, but somehow I felt more confident that I could survive. I even felt a trace of excitement.

A few years later, I was forced to jump from assembly languages to higher-level languages; this was a great sacrifice, because by that time I'd written an extremely popular book on assembly language. I could have savored the assembly language plateau for a few more years, perhaps even longer. But by this time, I was confident that I could handle the change, and I looked upon it more as a creative challenge than a trial to be endured.

The plateau-ravine model describes a cycle, but it also describes a metacycle—a cycle of cycles, a spiral, like the chambered nautilus. Each time I mastered another ravine, I not only jumped to a new plateau, but I ascended another few steps along a metaplateau, mastering the growth process itself. I was learning new computer languages, but even more, I was *learning how to learn* new computer languages. My metalearning showed most clearly in my emotional reaction to new languages.

Instead of feeling anxious, defensive, and worthless, I felt excited, creative, and capable of coping with almost anything.

To achieve this kind of metalearning, you have to survive the first ravine. Not everyone has sufficient motivation, or can take the emotional shock. Some of my old friends are still back there on the first plateau, constantly refining their assembly language coding, and doing quite well for themselves. But most of them have climbed like me to other technical plateaus, with a growing sense of ease and comfort.

Even so, our technical metalearning was of limited help when we tried to become leaders. Some tried to avoid the ravine by being appointed boss, but most of them broke their backs when they fell back into the ravine. I tried a more gradual climb to leadership through teaching and leading small groups; even so, I was frequently racked with anguish. Then, little by little, metalearning took over. Now, when I approach a new small group, I enjoy my anxiety, and easily convert it to excitement. Like the chambered nautilus, my growth seems to be a spiral in which each chamber grows nobler than the last.

A few years ago, I tried my hand at managing my own company. The company was successful, but that mansion was a bit too stately—for me at that moment in time. I succeeded in making everyone miserable, including myself, until I left that outgrown shell. Nobody said that every ravine leads to a plateau. Some are just ravines.

At least I learned, though, and the knowledge that I had survived two other metacycles gave me the courage to start yet another company. It's not been easy, but so far I seem to have benefited from meta-metalearning.

CHAPTER 4: QUESTIONS

1.   Do you have some skill, like playing pinball, lifting weights, or building model oxcarts, that you have improved over a long period of time? Can you plot your progress, and can you apply your methods of learning to that of learning to be a better problem-solving leader?

2.   Can you describe a plateau you are now occupying? Are there signs that you may be approaching the ravine? Are you trying to stay out of the ravine, or to learn what you can from tumbling in?

3.   How long has it been since the last time you climbed to a new plateau? Are you still enjoying the feeling of being on the flat? What are you doing to get ready for the next one?

4.   In the course of your life, what have you learned about learning?

5.   Set yourself some small personal achievement that you can practice for fifteen minutes every day for a week. Keep a record of your progress. Next week, pick another achievement.

5

But I Can't Because . . .

. . . ideas are the symbols of relationships among real forces that
make people late for breakfast, that take away their breakfast, that
make them beat each other across the breakfast table . . .

—Rebecca West
Black Lamb and Grey Falcon

T his is a book about growth, but before we examine the details of growing, there is one more step we must take. For me, growth has brought some painful moments, and whenever I'm faced with new possibilities of pain, I look for some excuse to avoid it. If you're like me, you may have some such excuse in mind. To get your full participation in the rest of the book, I'll need to dispose of some of the most common excuses for avoiding the pain of becoming a technical leader.

I'M NOT A MANAGER

Probably the most widespread and pernicious myth about leadership is that only Leaders can lead, where the capital L indicates that someone has been *appointed* to the position of Leader. Just now, I'm looking at the cover of Michael Maccoby's book *The Leader*. With a title like that, one would think it is about all kinds of leaders, but in fact it's only about *managers*—appointed leaders. The subtitle of the book is *A New Face for American Management*.

It's only in threat/reward models that leadership and managership are synonymous. There are, in fact, *many* more potential leaders than Leaders. Problem-solving leadership especially concerns leaders, as well as Leaders; so if you concentrate on the appointed kind, you're not going to understand how to become the problem-solving kind. You may have a title like Group Leader, yet not be leading; or you may have no title at all, but be the one who makes your group start to function in new and more effective ways.

I'm reminded of the story of the village idiot whose antique watch stopped running. He pried it open and found a dead cockroach inside. "No wonder it doesn't work," he said, "the manager is dead."

Organic models say that any working group is a system and can't generally be understood by disassembling it and giving each piece a title. To take a more technical example, suppose a programmer has just built an operating system that wasn't performing too well under higher-than-average load. And suppose the programmer's manager says, "Just replace the module that contains the inefficiency. Then it will run faster." Because it's an operating *system,* inefficiency under load is likely to stem from interactions between modules, not from individual modules behaving inefficiently.

Few software managers are *that* misguided about the nature of operating systems, but many are when it comes to systems involving people. If the team isn't productive enough, the manager decides, "Just replace the person who's not providing the leadership. Then the team will work faster." Sure it will. And if we just put in a live cockroach, the watch will start running again.

Such fallacious ideas persist because sometimes systems *are* linear. With a mechanical system such as a watch, we can often find one broken part. Operating systems are more complex than watches, but *sometimes* we can still identify one module that when rewritten, produces a striking increase in efficiency. A novice programmer might succeed at such a replacement two or three times and conclude that there is always one module that "contains the inefficiency." But with experience, this fallacious notion will soon disappear.

Not so in the case of working groups. Sometimes, replacing one member produces a striking gain or loss in productivity, but not always. Not usually, in fact, but managers tend to ignore their changes that don't work. After a period of time, their selective memory contains many tales of striking individual "leadership."

We shouldn't be so hard on managers. All of us do this sort of selective forgetting when the facts don't fit our favorite model. What is the number one all-time favorite model of a manager? of any manager? Well, suppose you asked the mainspring what was the one essential part of a watch?

If you ask appointed leaders what is the one essential part of an organization, you won't be too surprised if you hear,

"The appointed leader is the mainspring of the group."

This, of course, is the myth of the appointed leader.

There is another explanation for the persistence of this myth. If you ask a mechanic why your sports car's engine sounds so awful, the response is likely to be, "Have you checked the spark plugs?" Experience says that if anything is failing, it's most likely the plugs. It's easy to slip from this observation into the fallacy that the spark plug is the critical component in an engine.

Similarly, in working groups, if any one member breaks down in an obvious way, the appointed leader is likely to be the one. As with mainsprings and spark plugs, it's easy to slip from "weakest" link to "most critical" link and start believing the myth of the appointed leader.

Why is the appointed leader the one most likely to break down? Paradoxically, it's because so many people believe in the myth of the appointed leader. The boss believes; the workers believe; even the appointed leader believes. Thus, when matters get a little out of hand, everyone turns to the appointed leader to put them back in order. The increased load on the appointed leader makes matters even worse.

If the pressure leads to a breakdown, it's the appointed leader who breaks. Even if the leader averts a breakdown, everyone can see that the appointed leader was the most active person during the crisis. Thus, the myth of the appointed leader becomes a self-fulfilling prophecy.

In a well-designed engine, there is no weakest link. If spark plugs are truly the weakest link, then a superior engine design eliminates the spark plugs altogether, giving us the diesel engine. Or, if you can't think how to eliminate spark plugs, at least you make them easily inter-changeable.

In the same way, the best-designed working groups are those in which leadership comes from everybody, not merely the appointed leaders. Therefore, you need not wait—you should not wait—for an appointment.

I'M NOT THE LEADER TYPE

Perhaps you simply cannot think of yourself as the type of person who is a leader. I can certainly appreciate your difficulty. Whenever I hear the word *leader,* my first image is of Teddy Roosevelt leading the charge up San Juan Hill. Of course, Teddy was way before my time, but because he and I have the same birthday, I've always had a special interest in his exploits. As a little boy, I tried to be a leader by imitating Teddy's gung ho approach—leadership through motivation. Unfortunately, whenever I tried to lead my schoolmates in a charge, I found myself charging alone across the playground.

As I grew older, I studied Teddy's later career, as President. I learned that as leaders grow older, they often add a second type of leadership to their repertoire. Instead of simply charging out at the head of the troops, they *organize* the troops so that when the time comes for battle, they'll charge off by themselves. I tried to adopt this leadership style, but learned that it required even more of the motivational kind of leadership necessary to accomplish such organizational changes.

My inability to become another Teddy Roosevelt probably soured me on the idea of being a leader, and made me suspicious of all those I identified as leaders. I didn't notice that I myself had *become* a leader, because the type of leader I had become didn't match my Teddy Roosevelt image. I was surrounded by people who followed my lead because they saw that I could solve technical problems that nobody else could solve. If someone had asked who was leading, I would have replied, "Nobody's leading. We are simply doing the best possible job, given the problem we are trying to solve. We don't care who supplies the ideas, as long as they work best."

This is neither leadership by motivation, nor by organization. It is leadership by *innovation*, by adding new techniques to the group's ways of getting things done. It explains how I could sell millions of dollars worth of computers, when I couldn't even sell women's shoes. It explains how I could organize the team that designed and built the space tracking computer network, when I couldn't even be captain of my sandlot baseball team. It also explains why it took me thirty years to recognize my own leadership ability.

Leadership by innovation can be quietly exercised by people like me—and perhaps like you—who lack the charisma and organizational skills that characterize the world's Teddies. It can even be exercised by people who are positively obnoxious, as long as their technical skills are sufficiently great to overcome their disagreeable behavior. A few people even measure their technical competence by the degree of offensive, or at least idiosyncratic, behavior that they can exhibit without losing their support. When I worked in space tracking, I started the beard that I have to this day. Within IBM at that time, growing a beard without getting fired was an indisputable mark of technical genius.

In the IBM context, the beard probably helped me compensate for my lack of motivational skills, earning me the undivided attention of more than one executive. Because they can't reliably identify problem-solving leaders by their technical skills, executives often employ extraneous outward signs, like beards or bare feet. If you can't grow a beard, or if you get cold feet, you need not despair of becoming a problem-solving leader. Had I possessed even a small measure of the other styles of leadership, I probably wouldn't have needed the beard.

Becoming a successful problem-solving leader does require more than the ability to think innovatively and grow hair on your face. Whether you're bearded or not, you'll need at least some motivational and organizational skills to be identified as a true problem-solving leader. Conversely, the power to lead by motivation or organization can be enhanced by a small measure of leadership through innovation. This is a lesson that anyone can learn by studying how to become a problem-solving leader, whether or not you think you're the type.

I'LL LOSE MY TECHNICAL SKILLS

One of the hardest choices for technical stars who become leaders is losing touch with the latest in technology. In my own career, I've definitely had to sacrifice some of my technical currency to improve my interpersonal skills. I don't know whether I could reverse that decision now, even if I wanted to. Like many problem-solving leaders who have evolved from the one hundred percent innovation position, I'd like to believe I could get back into the technical mainstream at any time, but that may not be true.

Climbing is always strenuous, but letting go is brutal. Most problem-solving leaders create their first success in a single field, often a highly specialized subfield. They may have other problem-solving successes in related fields, but they always retain at least a sentimental attachment to their origins. In one recent week, I visited two executives—one the head of a large software services company, the other the director of research for a computer manufacturer. Each had a large corner office with a couch and a coffee table covered with a neat array of papers and magazines. Each had *Fortune* and *The Wall Street Journal;* but one had two journals in numerical mathematics, while the other had three journals in high energy physics. I doubt that either of these executives reads their technical journals, but it would have been impolite to inquire.

Besides, it's not important. It's not even important if they were *ever* superstars in their original fields. Both of these men have transcended their specialized fields and both now master technology in a generalized way. They can talk with technical specialists in dozens of fields, and easily separate the wheat from the chaff. That's the kind of technical skill their jobs require. In MOI terms, this means an evolution toward a balance among the three factors, toward an increase in motivational and organizational abilities, paid for by a decrease in innovative skills. It's an inevitable tradeoff, and perhaps the hardest one they've had to make.

I'M IN GRAVE DANGER OF GROWING

Even though this tradeoff is a perfectly justified career decision, I hesitate to use the names of these two executives. I think they might be hurt to see in print that they are not technical superstars—and perhaps never had been. To the problem-solving leader, at whatever stage of metamorphosis, the purely innovative leader remains the culture hero.

I know it's extremely painful for me to admit that my technical skills have waned. I may be rich and fat and famous, but I often dream of being young again, accepting the admiring remarks of my team as I track down the latest obscure bug in the Project Mercury Monitor System. Sometimes, when the climb is especially devastating, I swear that I will never change again if I'm not forced to by circumstances.

Don't get me wrong. It's not bad to postpone change until circumstances force it upon you. No style is better than another, except insofar as you have some goal you're trying to accomplish. If you have no particular goal, or if you're accomplishing what you want to accomplish, don't try changing your leadership style just because somebody else wants you to. You'll be especially unhappy if you do, particularly if it's to obtain a promotion to some type of boss position. Once again, you don't have to be a boss to be a leader.

Like everyone else, you do possess a leadership style, even if it's currently low in all three categories. At any moment in your career, you can choose to stick with what you've got. This avoids the pain, like my father's choice to stick with pool or mine to stick with pinball. My models tell me quite clearly what I have to relinquish to become a video master, but I don't *want* to make that particular effort just now. I'm too good at pinball to need to learn video games, just as I was too good a programmer to need to learn to be an effective leader. No doubt, I'll despise video games until the last pinball machine is locked away in a museum. Then I'll be in grave danger of growing again.

I DON'T WANT THAT MUCH POWER

We now know that problem solving is not restricted to a high-tech environment. It's true that this style of leadership first came into prominence in high-tech situations, but that's only because of the enormous economic power of technical ideas. High-technology isn't the only area where ideas have power, and economic power isn't the only kind worth reckoning. Today we realize that technical leader is but one type of problem-solving leader.

In our high-tech, money-driven society, it's easy to forget the fundamentals and miss seeing the obvious. When we first started teaching the problem-solving leadership style, it was but a small part of a highly technical workshop. After dozens of students told us that they could transfer the technical leadership style to nontechnical areas of their life, we began to realize that we were on to something more fundamental. We even noticed that *teaching* in the workshop was affecting our own leadership styles.

Curiously, when I began to realize how wide-ranging problem-solving leadership was, I began to worry that we might be giving too much power to a small group of people. Even more curiously, some of our students expressed the same doubts about themselves. "We don't *want* to be that powerful," they sometimes said.

Will the world of the near future be shaped by a different style of leader? I doubt it. Technical leaders possess great power in our society, but they are neither demons nor gods. They are ordinary people who happen to possess an effective approach to problem solving, an approach based on leadership through innovation. Even without any technical background, other ordinary people can empower themselves and others by mastering some elements of this approach.

For the foreseeable future, we ordinary people will still have to contend with charismatic religious figures, iron-jawed generals, smooth but tricky politicians. Perhaps most of the impact of the problem-solving leadership style will be as it has always been—through the considerable impact of technology. Or perhaps it will touch that creative seed in each of us, that seed that tells us there must be a better way.

If it does, then we will enjoy many new leadership choices. The threat/reward model may say that change comes from the top, but my experience tells me that change starts with what we choose to have for breakfast. Besides, there's more to life than large organizations. You may find it empowering to apply this quieter style to such everyday problems as life, liberty, and the pursuit of happiness.

CHAPTER 5: QUESTIONS

1.   Do you know someone whose leadership style you particularly admire? Try to create a short career biography of this person, characterized in MOI terms. If possible, interview the person to check your perceptions.

2.   When was the last time you made a major change in your career? Which do you remember best, the factual details or the feelings?

3.   How did you react the last time someone you know well made a major career change? What else does that tell you about yourself?

4.   What change in your career have you made that you still don't fully accept? don't fully admit to others? to yourself? Can you now let go of it? Why?

5.   Can you remember the first major decision point in your career? Can you still recall your feelings? Were you afraid to take the step? Was your fear justified? Was it worth it anyway?

6.   What are your choices for the next major decision point? What happens to your body as you contemplate each possible alternative? What messages pop into your mind?

7.   Have you ever been appointed Leader of anything? Did people begin to assume that you, as Leader, would now handle situations that they could perfectly well handle themselves? How did you deal with these situations? Were you so taken with your new status that you tried to handle them yourself, rather than delegating them where they belonged? How did your actions affect the group's later reactions to you as Leader?

8.   Next time you are appointed Leader of some group, keep a list of situations in which people assume that you as Leader will come up with the crucial ideas, but in which you exercise leadership by changing the environment so as to encourage *them* to do it. Keep going until you have at least ten items.

9.   Have you ever felt when appointed Leader that you were essential to the group? What did the group do when you were not around? What did they do when you eventually left? Could there have been some sort of self-fulfilling prophecy in operation?

10.   For some group you work with, consider how much of your influence in that group derives from your appointed position. How much comes from your idea power? How much from

enhancing the idea power of others? Are you satisfied with this mix?

11.   Tomorrow morning change your traditional breakfast in some way. Notice if your day changes.

12.   For the next two weeks, change your breakfast each day according to some new idea each day (such as fewer or more calories, faster or slower preparation, more or less wholesome, more interaction with other people, less interaction with others, more appealing to look at, thirty minutes later, thirty minutes earlier, in a different place, using different utensils, hot instead of cold, cold instead of hot, more liquid, less liquid). Note what, if anything, is happening to you, and summarize the effect at the end of the two weeks.

13.   Tomorrow change the way you interact with some person you see frequently. Try to do it in such a way as to improve your interaction. Note the results.

Part Two
INNOVATION

Technical stars are innovators—that's how they got to be stars—but their skills as individual innovators often obstruct their climb to a leadership plateau. When they're not aware of their own innovative processes, they may lose their powers when they assume leadership responsibilities. If they don't understand the sources of innovation, their own attempts to innovate may destroy the creative environment for others.

In the following chapters, we'll explore the major obstacles to innovation and how they can be overcome, both in yourself and in others.

6

The Three Great Obstacles to Innovation

Even in her childhood she extracted from life double enjoyment that comes usually only to the creative mind. "Now I am doing this. Now I am doing that," she told herself while she was doing it. Looking on while she participated.

—Edna Ferber
So Big

Enough of theory: What are you actually doing that either makes you creative or blocks your brain? Can a new model of leadership really work for you, or is it only as useful as the latest diet fad? The *theory* of dieting is simple enough: All you have to do is achieve a balance between input and output. According to the balance theory, I shouldn't have this bulge around the middle, but look at me.

Theories are like that. I can give you all sorts of techniques for developing your problem-solving or leadership abilities, yet find that you're making no progress. In this chapter, I'd like to explore the most common obstacles to progress toward problem-solving leadership, starting with the question of why I sometimes put on pounds without knowing why.

ARE YOU AWARE OF WHAT YOU HAD FOR DESSERT?

Keeping trim is important to my business, because people pay more attention to what you do than what you say. As a consultant who's supposed to help streamline organizations, I make a poor model if I'm not exactly streamlined myself. At one such organization, Dani and I were looking for the source of diminished productivity. After we spent the day observing and interviewing, Shirley, the manager of the systems analysis sections, invited us home for dinner.

Shirley and her husband, Harrison, lived with their three sons in a busy but attractive neighborhood, which seemed well matched to Shirley's temperament. When I raided Shirley's refrigerator for a pre-dinner snack, I was surprised to find evidence that she was struggling to control her weight. There were low-cal foods inside, calorie charts on the door, and a box of appetite suppressants on top. As she prepared supper, we discussed our common problem.

"I must have a metabolic problem," I said.

"Me, too. I used to have trouble with snacks, but I've controlled that, yet I still can't lose weight."

"Maybe it's eating out. You know, Dani and Harrison have already promised the kids we'll go out to Swenson's after dinner. I'd rather stay home because I can't resist their ice cream."

"Well, *I* can resist," Shirley boasted. "I'll just have a cup of coffee."

"Maybe if I eat a full supper," I said, "I won't have any appetite for dessert." But there wasn't much conviction in my voice.

I ate a full supper, but at Swenson's I wasn't able to resist ordering a dish of raspberry sherbet. Dani had a small marshmallow sundae, Harrison had a large banana split, the two oldest boys had special children's sundaes, and the youngest had a chocolate chip cone. Only Shirley resisted, righteously and vocally ordering a cup of coffee. I noticed, though, that Shirley took cream in her coffee. And sugar.

Then when Buddy's cone arrived, Shirley seemed quite concerned that it was going to fall or drip. "I'll just trim off the extra," she announced, and proceeded to reduce Buddy's scoop to half its original size. Somehow, the excess went into her mouth.

In the meantime, Harrison offered her a "taste" of his banana split. "Just a taste," she said, but he insisted that she taste each of the three delicious flavors, plus each of the three syrups, some of the whipped cream, a bit of the banana, and both cherries. Before long, the dish was resting halfway between them, and she was using her coffee spoon to continue her "tasting."

She also sampled the other two children's sundaes, nobly eating the parts they didn't like. To wash all this down, she ordered a refill on coffee, then another, both with cream and sugar. Somehow, there seemed to be a food magnet in her mouth, irresistibly attracting all loose food on the table. I found myself compelled to offer her some raspberry sherbet, but she was busy finishing one of the decorative cookies.

Later that evening, with the kids tucked into bed, we four adults sat around having a nice chat. Around eleven, Shirley asked if anyone was hungry. None of us were, but she slipped into the kitchen anyway. When she returned with a plate of cheese, fruit, and nuts, she announced to nobody in particular, "Well, you guys all had ice cream, and I didn't have any."

"But you *did*," I observed, regretting it immediately.

Shirley regarded me with a puzzled look. "No. Don't you remember? I didn't order any ice cream. Just coffee." True, she hadn't *ordered* any ice cream, but didn't she realize that she'd *eaten* at least twice as much as anyone else at the table?

SELF-BLINDNESS: THE NUMBER ONE OBSTACLE

For many people, work is like Shirley's eating. They waste time pursuing dead ends, dragging out phone calls, or getting involved in useless arguments, yet never realize why they don't accomplish anything. Writers, for example, throw away many false starts, or sit staring at a page for hours without typing a single word. Many programmers, stuck in some fallacious argument, search for a single error long past the point where they should seek help.

I know that other people do those things (Dani and I watch them all the time), but I'm sure that *I* don't do them—not very often, anyway. Wouldn't I remember if I did?

In fact, I wouldn't remember, any more than Shirley could remember what she had for dessert. Like everyone else, I'm quite unable to see myself in action, particularly when I'm exhibiting my least productive behaviors.

Whenever I watch someone like Shirley not watching herself, my consciousness is raised, for a few days anyway. I snack less and lose weight. But soon I stop watching again, and my spare tire starts to inflate. What I need is a consultant, someone to watch me eat and report to me what I can't see for myself. The same is true for all of us. The only way we can see ourselves is through other people.

This inability to see ourselves as others see us is the number one obstacle to self-improvement. The great majority of would-be problem-solving leaders are stuck on this one obstacle. To surmount it, they must recruit others to help them. Probably the best way to get someone to watch you is by making a pact to watch that person in return. Even a mutual observing relationship is a rather delicate one, so it may take some time to develop a relationship that works well.

Whatever you do, keep it mutual. Don't ever volunteer your observations about people as I did with Shirley, no matter how helpful you think it would be for them. Shirley was nice enough not to punch me, but I was lucky.

Even when people ask for your observations, they won't always like what you have to say. I once asked Dani to watch my eating patterns. As an anthropologist, she's an expert observer—so good, in fact, that it almost broke up our marriage. It's just not much fun to be watched all the time, so whatever you do, don't pick your spouse as your watching partner.

NO-PROBLEM SYNDROME: THE NUMBER TWO OBSTACLE

On the same trip that we visited Shirley, I encountered an example of the second obstacle that interferes with every effort to become a more effective problem solver. I call it the No-Problem Syndrome. I was in Sacramento, addressing the local chapter of the Data Processing Management Association. I began my address by talking about a previous visit to Sacramento, twenty-five years earlier. It was my first business trip as a new employee at IBM, a visit I'll never forget.

The State Legislature had just passed a law allowing letters as well as numbers on license plates. Opponents of the law had argued that certain combinations of letters might prove offensive. The bill's backers promised to cull all offensive letter combinations from the plates, but they had no particular plan as to how to go about this. Somebody told them that a computer would be a big help, so they called IBM. That's where I came in.

I was a fresh young IBMer, all suited up and ready to purge the world of dirty words with a whiz-bang computer program. Unfortunately, the people from Motor Vehicle Registration had at least three requirements that I couldn't possibly satisfy:

- Some "offensive" words weren't words in English but only *looked like* words in English. To understand this problem, drop one letter from your favorite four-letter expletive. Sometimes the new word is innocuous, but other times it's as offensive as the original.

- California had many ethnic groups speaking many different languages. The program was supposed to get rid of anything that might be offensive to *anybody* speaking Spanish, Chinese, Hebrew, Yiddish, Greek, French, Armenian, and a few others I can't remember.

- We also had to remove words that *might someday* be offensive to anybody speaking any of these languages or any languages of anyone who *might someday* visit California.

I told the license plate story to kick off a discussion of what makes problems difficult to solve. Then I distributed a set of problems for everyone to try. As I circulated through the room to see how everyone was doing, I noticed one man sitting conspicuously with his arms folded tightly across his chest.

"Have you finished already?" I asked him.

"No," he said, "I'm not doing them. Why waste my time? Why don't you just hurry up and tell us what it is you're trying to tell us?"

"I can't tell you," I said, "because I want you to *feel* the frustration of trying to do certain kinds of difficult problems. Telling you just isn't the same."

"Well, you might as well tell *me*," he countered, "because I can solve any problem you can give me. In fact, your 'unsolvable' license plate problem is actually trivial."

"Trivial?" I asked.

"Absolutely. With modern technology, all you need is a big dictionary. You pass the combinations of letters against the dictionary and eliminate the ones you don't want. It's just no problem."

My first instinct was to argue. I might have asked him how he was going to get a dictionary of words that hadn't been coined yet. Or why you would bother with a computer, once you had constructed a dictionary of offensive words. Then I realized that the poor man was suffering from a severe case of "No-Problem Syndrome," or NPS for short. I had suffered from this disease myself, so I had nothing but sympathy for the poor man. I don't get any kicks out of attacking the handicapped, so I simply smiled and walked away.

Perhaps you've never heard of NPS? I haven't checked this with any neurophysiologist, but it seems to be a condition in which the ears are not properly connected to the brain. The sounds enter all right, but they trigger a stereotyped response that has nothing to do with their meaning. One person describes a terribly vexing problem, but the other merely responds with a callous, "No problem."

No-Problem Syndrome isn't the same as deafness. In fact, deaf people couldn't have NPS because the response has to be triggered by the key word, "problem," reaching the ear. Once that word registers, the ears become *selectively* deaf, the first stage of the syndrome. The second stage seems to be the mental retrieval of some favorite solution method, which is immediately presented to the talker, even if it's necessary to interrupt the problem description. My Uncle Max had NPS, and his favorite solution had to do with restoring the practice of beating children in the public schools, much as he beat his children at home. If the economy was down, it was because they don't beat kids in school any more. If crime was up, or the weather was bad, it was for the same reason.

Like most kids, I didn't understand the heartbreak of NPS. I used to laugh at my uncle, never dreaming that NPS might be hereditary. Because I lacked self-awareness, it wasn't until after my first visit to Sacramento that I found out the tragic news: I had NPS myself!

It was the license plate problem that revealed my terrible secret. The Motor Vehicle people *told* me about their requirements, but evidently their words never registered in my brain. Before they had finished talking, I had assured them that there was no problem. Before I understood what their problem was, I had managed to write a program to solve it.

You can imagine what a blow it was to a young IBMer when a bunch of civil servants rejected all his brilliant work. On the other hand, you can imagine what a blow it was to them when a young IBMer, not even listening to their requirements, told them they didn't really have a problem. It may be terrible to have NPS, but it's even worse to be in contact with one of its victims.

I used to think that computers emit some nerve-damaging high frequency sounds, because NPS seems to affect a large percentage of computer professionals. Whenever they hear the words "problem" and "computer" in the same sentence, they launch into a diatribe that would put old Uncle Max to shame. And it always starts with the words, "No problem."

As I grew older, however, I realized that computers themselves do not actually cause NPS. Perhaps it's the fast pace of the industry, which reduces the likelihood that problem solvers will take time to be aware of what they're doing. Besides, I've noticed that NPS afflicts people in all high-tech industries, so it can't just be computers. It also affects quite a few people in low-tech industries, or people not in industries at all.

My own symptoms have abated a bit with age, so perhaps the problem is simply a manifestation of the youthfulness of the computer industry. Other than senility, though, I don't know of any cure for NPS. I wish I could help these poor handicapped souls, but bitter experience has taught me that I'd have more success going to Sri Lanka to cure lepers.

People who have problems for others to solve should be better informed about the perils of NPS. Because it can't be cured, they had better learn to protect themselves through my four-step plan for early NPS detection:

1.   You describe your very difficult problem.

2.   The respondent says, "No problem!"

3.   You say, "Oh, that's terrific! *Could you please describe my problem that you're going to solve?"*

4a.   If the respondent then describes your problem, even erroneously, it's not a case of NPS but only a case of Enthusiasm.

4b.   If the respondent describes a proposed *solution* to your problem rather than the problem itself, then sadly it's NPS. The kindest thing you can do for all concerned is smile and walk briskly to the nearest exit.

Sometimes the four-step detection plan can be used for self-diagnosis, but if the NPS is too far advanced, it won't work. To detect your own NPS, you have to be able to hear yourself say, "No problem!" or at least hear yourself giving solutions before you've confirmed that you understand the other person's problem. But, alas, terminal NPS patients can't hear other people very well; and they can't hear themselves at all. They're not only self-blind, they're self-deaf.

SINGLE-SOLUTION BELIEF: THE NUMBER THREE OBSTACLE

We could characterize NPS as the unshakable belief in your own master intelligence. This definition makes it clear why NPS is the number two obstacle to becoming an innovative leader. The Chinese say that the first step to knowledge is a confession of ignorance. If you already know everything, how will you ever learn anything?

Even though you shouldn't believe you know everything, it does help to know *something*. Nobody denies that good problem solvers have to be intelligent, but lack of intelligence isn't one of the three big obstacles. We all know many high-IQ people who aren't good at solving real-life problems. Perhaps we ought to be more skeptical about the procedure by which psychologists identify "intelligence."

Recently, a science magazine ran a "Mind Benders" column prepared by Mensa, an organization of people who score in the top two percent on standardized IQ tests. Among the Mind Benders were the following two questions, which bent my mind in a direction perhaps not intended by Mensa.

1.   All the secretaries in my office are under 21. All the young ladies in my office are very beautiful. My secretary has long blond hair and blue eyes.

Which statement(s) below can be justified by the information given?

a)   My secretary is under 21.

b)   My secretary is a beautiful young lady.

c)   Neither of the above.

d)   Both of the first two.

1.   In a certain field there are both horses and men. There are 26 heads and 82 feet (or hooves) in the field. How many men are there? How many horses?

Here are the answers:

1.   The "correct" answer is given as (a) my secretary is under 21. What's supposed to trip you up is the assumption that all secretaries are female, which isn't stated. But what about the assumption that my secretary is in my office? It doesn't say that, but then it doesn't say my secretary is female. Depending on which set of assumptions you choose, all four answers are possible. Although I've never personally had a male secretary, I have worked in situations where my secretary was in another office, even in another city. Does this make me less intelligent than the psychologist who posed the question?

2.   By simple algebra, you get the official answer (15 horses and 11 men) if you assume that each horse has 4 feet and each man has 2. I don't know much about horses, but I read this test after watching a Veterans Day parade. It was obvious to me that one possible solution is 16 horses and 10 men, one of whom is a Vietnam veteran with no legs. Of course, there are lots of other solutions along this line, if you're not a psychologist.

Any intelligent being who has been exposed to this sort of testing has experienced the same frustration: You can think of several possible answers, but you know the psychologists want only one; and you're not allowed to ask questions. It's not so bad when the questions are in a magazine just for fun, or even in the Mensa admission test.

But what if you want to get into college? or get a job? or get into a favored track in the second grade? The psychologists hold the power to keep you from getting what you want, and their power is unquestionable.

Quite possibly, academic psychology is the most arrogant profession of all time. In Chapter 1, we already encountered the central dogma of academic psychology: There is one and only one correct solution to every problem—and the psychologist knows it. This dogma applies equally to tests for people or mazes for rats. Any rat who displays a modicum of suspicion for the psychologist's setup runs the maze a little slower and is labeled "less intelligent." To me, anyone who *fails* to be suspicious of psychologists' experiments should be labeled "less intelligent."

The central dogma is damaging enough to the individual person or rat trapped by the psychologist, but its long-range effects on society may be even worse. Schools and employers reward people whose thinking happens to match the thinking of psychologists, so people either learn to think that way or find themselves out in the cold. After a while, we find people in problem-solving situations who literally believe that every problem has one and only one solution, a solution so inevitable that they will recognize it when they find it.

For a would-be problem-solving leader, belief in the central dogma is a debilitating disease and the third great obstacle to becoming a star problem-solving leader. Infected designers rarely consider an adequate number of alternative designs, and never consider testing the design other than by their own intuition. Infected programmers are powerless in the face of a bug that deviates in any way from the obvious answer. Managers infected by the central dogma act like psychologists; they assign work to their subordinates and expect to have it done in one right way—their way. Before long, they create another generation in their own image.

SUMMARY

They're worth summarizing, these three great obstacles to innovation:

1. self-blindness, concealing your own behavior, so you have no chance of changing
2. No-Problem Syndrome, convincing you that you already know the answer to all problems
3. belief in the central dogma of academic psychology, blinding you to alternative solutions, even ones you could generate without help from anyone else

These deeply imbedded obstacles form a closed system, standing in the way of their own removal. People who are self-blind might read this list and nod their heads in agreement, but about other people. People who suffer from NPS will not even read the list in the first place. People who believe the central dogma will already be on what they consider to be the one and only path to success.

So let's bid those people goodbye and concentrate on those for whom there is still some hope. Let's stick with you creative people who know the double enjoyment of watching what you're doing while you're doing it and laughing at yourself while you watch. To you, I offer the following chapters on how to overcome some lesser obstacles in your path to becoming a leader through innovation.

CHAPTER 6: QUESTIONS

1. Knowing what you had for dessert is an application of general self-awareness to the question of health. How aware are you of your own health and how it affects your leadership style? How do you feel right now? Take an inventory of your physical condition, and describe how it currently affects your performance as a leader.

2. Poor health is an obstacle to innovation and just about everything else. How has your long-term health affected your career? What is your health going to be like in the future? If you have a hard time answering that question, what makes you think your health is not under your own control? What are you doing to keep it under your own control? How will it affect your career in the future?

3. In answering the previous two questions, did you respond that your health was "no problem"? What does that tell you about yourself?

4. Do you know your IQ? Do you let other people know? Does knowing your IQ affect your ability to lead? How?

5. Do you like to take tests? If you knew you were assured of doing well, would you like to take a test? What if you were assured of doing poorly? What if you had to take the test, but were never to find out how well you did? What do these questions have to do with leadership style?

6. Find some multiple choice quiz and go through it in the following way: Instead of picking one answer, take each answer in turn and give a good reason why that could be the answer. Then give a good reason for some answer that isn't among the choices.

7. Next time you're in a meeting and several ideas are brought up, apply the technique of the previous question. That is, make sure you give a good reason to the meeting's participants to explain why each idea could be the solution you're seeking. Then offer at least one more.

7

A Tool for Developing Self-Awareness

Q. How many psychiatrists does it take to change a light bulb?
A. Only one, if the bulb really wants to change.

Are the three great obstacles to innovation really so debilitating that there is no hope for change? For some, yes. For others, there is hope *if* there is a desire for change. I know because I have witnessed some remarkable transformations.

In this chapter, I want to suggest the single best tool that you can use by yourself. It can help you overcome self-blindness, which stands in the way of overcoming the other obstacles. As a way of convincing you to try it, I'd like to share with you the words of some people who used this tool to help them see themselves more clearly.

A TEST OF YOUR MOTIVATION

If this tool is so wonderful, why would you need convincing? According to the MOI theory, you'll need three things to succeed at transforming yourself into a more effective problem-solving leader: motivation, organization, and ideas. As an author, I can supply you with *ideas* and with suggestions for *organization,* but concerning your motivation, I am powerless if, like the light bulb, you don't really want to change.

I *can* give you a test, however, so you can discover for yourself if you have sufficient motivation to succeed in your own transformation. The test is simple, and it not only measures whether you are ready to change, but also gives you ideas for change and some organization for structuring those ideas. Here's the test:

Starting now, and continuing for three months, spend five minutes each day writing in a personal journal.

YOUR INITIAL REACTION

Pause now, get a piece of paper, and write down your initial reaction. This reaction is an important part of the test. Not only that, but what you wrote on that piece of paper is your first journal entry. If you didn't write it, you're already in trouble, but you're in good company. Many of our clients have had that reaction, like Birgitt:

"When Jerry suggested this test, the first thing I thought was that writing about anything was distasteful, but writing about myself

75

was revolting. Yet, the test is to write for five minutes a day, and I spend that much time brushing my teeth. So I thought that if I can't do that for three months, perhaps I don't want to be a problem-solving leader after all."

Peter initially rejected the idea:

"I just couldn't see the point of having another burden to add to my schedule, so I never really considered doing it. Four months later, on New Year's Day, I was watching the bowl games when the idea popped into my head again. During a light beer commercial, I calculated that the test asked me for less time over three months than I was spending on the Fiesta Bowl, Rose Bowl, and Orange Bowl in one day. I decided to give it a try—for *one* month."

These were their first entries and you'll read later what happened to Birgitt and Peter, but for now you can see how they passed the test. They were serious enough about their leadership goals to risk wasting five minutes a day. If they hadn't been that serious, then anything else I suggested to them would have been a waste of *my* time.

YOUR PERSONAL JOURNAL

If you decide to go ahead with a personal journal, you'll soon have a great many loose pieces of paper, so I suggest getting a nice, bound book and a comfortable writing instrument, or a word processor. These may seem unimportant, but they aren't. You'll need every aid and incentive to be faithful about recording.

If you do decide to use a computer, though, don't go back and revise previous entries. Later, when you want to review what you've written, you'll wish you had your original impressions. Instead, get a printed copy and paste it in a notebook, preferably hardbound, with dated pages.

If you feel inhibited about keeping a diary, perhaps because of an unhappy childhood experience with a sibling or parent reading it, be sure to keep your journal secure from curious eyes. This doesn't mean that you can never share parts of your journal with others, but only that *you* must be the one to control access. This is especially important so that you are completely honest about your feelings, and that you present an unbiased picture of yourself.

It's not important what time of day you choose to write, or even that you write at the same time each day. What *is* important is that you find some method that ensures you write your five minutes each day. Nadia had to try several things before she found one that worked:

"Because I used the word processor, I had to do my journal at work. But at work my time was often controlled by other people—which was my first good lesson from keeping the journal. So I made a sign for my door that said WOMAN WRITING—DO NOT ENTER. That worked pretty well, but didn't solve my problem of writing on weekends, so I bought an old-fashioned notebook.

"At home, I still had trouble finding a time I could count on to have five uninterrupted minutes at the same time every day. I tried writing just before going to bed, but sometimes I was too sleepy. Besides, sometimes my husband didn't like it. Eventually I found I could write after feeding the dogs, and before breakfast. For me, it's a good activity for easing into the day in the right frame of mind—though I suppose each person will have to find something that works right for them."

For Peter, writing was like a workout:

"I made the mistake of thinking that if five minutes was good, ten minutes was better. I tried to stretch my time every day, and eventually I was getting to dread my writing period. Now I set a timer for five minutes. When the bell rings, I can continue if I want, but I know it's all right to stop. The time is my assurance that I'm not asking too much of myself.

"If I want to write in my journal at other times, that's terrific. I write all I want whenever the spirit moves me. But no matter how much else you have written that day, you must still honor your regular five-minute period. Otherwise, it's like breaking training."

In other words, it's important to write when the spirit moves you, but it's even more important to write when the spirit doesn't move you. If you can't find a regular pattern of some time for self-observation, your leadership development program is in serious trouble.

What to write about

The testimonies of Nadia and Peter both illustrate that even if you get nothing else out of keeping the journal, you'll learn about how you react when you try to change your behavior. If you want to be a problem-solving leader, you'll need to know this about yourself. At the very least, you'll begin to appreciate how other people will feel when you ask them to make a simple change.

What do people write about? I like the way Nadia puts it:

"I've read many rules about what to write about, but only one is crucial for me: *Write about yourself*. The subject of my journal is me—what I'm like, what I do each day, how I feel about it, how I see others reacting to me."

Mavis has a different way of expressing what she writes in her journal:

"I stick to three things: First, I write down what happened, as descriptive as I can make it without labeling or judging. Then, I describe how I reacted to it—what I thought about, if it made me angry, if I dreamt about it. Finally, I put down what, if anything, I learned from it. Most of the time, I don't learn anything, until much later when I read the entry again."

Many of our clients follow this "facts, feelings, findings" formula, but Juan had a different view:

"I wasn't impressed with all that human relations garbage—feelings and dreams and fantasies. What impressed me most was when Jerry said that professional engineers and scientists doing laboratory work all kept journals. So what I wrote about was my ideas—new tricks and designs—and what happened when I tried things out on the system. I would write about the bugs I had, and how I tried to fix them."

Perhaps Peter represents the majority position when he says,

"I keep a journal to learn about myself. If I was the same as everybody else, I wouldn't need to keep a journal. I'm unique, so how can anyone else tell me what to keep in my journal. So what do I write in my journal? What does a nine-hundred pound gorilla write? I write whatever I want!"

What the journal does

I recommend the journal as a *first* step to becoming a technical leader because it is such a little commitment that there really is no valid excuse for not doing it. You can also learn about yourself in leadership workshops, but a good workshop will generally require at least a week of your time, plus travel, and might cost a thousand dollars or more. I've always found a good workshop to be worth every minute and every cent, but if you've never had the experience, you might be hesitant to take such a risk. Besides, not every workshop is a *good* workshop, and even if you get your money back, your time is lost forever.

What can you learn from just doodling in a little book? One great advantage of the journal method is that unlike a book or a lecture, everything in it is relevant to *you*. Because each person's learning is personal, I can't tell you what you'll learn, but I can guarantee you'll learn *something*. You can take the following testimonials as typical examples:

Birgitt: "Even if I had learned nothing else, I found out that my inhibitions abut writing had earned me a reputation for not documenting my programs and not answering letters from my users. I decided that I wasn't a mental defective who couldn't write, and that I was being really childish because of some unpleasant experiences in the fourth grade. Some leader! I asked my company to send me through a technical writing class and they were delighted. Now I've removed one more barrier to becoming a problem-solving leader—a barrier I'd erected myself."

Peter: "Reviewing my journal at the end of that month, I realized that I had a consistent pattern of using my busy schedule as an excuse for not stepping back and looking at what I was doing. Some of the people I work with were getting short shrift from me, their supposed leader. The journal gave me a chance to get outside the trap of all-important work once in a while and see life in a different perspective. I still watch a lot of football, and I've extended my journal writing to the full three months—with two instant replays (rereadings) so far."

Juan: "The bug reports I kept eventually showed me a pattern in my own behavior that was really counterproductive. I would waste many hours searching for a bug before I finally gave up and asked someone for help—at which point we usually found the problem in a few minutes. My pig-head was getting in the way of my doing a good job. That one insight really paid me back for keeping the journal."

Nadia: "I thought I was writing about myself, but after a while, I saw that most of my entries were about other people: Charlie made me look bad in a meeting; Greg caused my project to go out with a serious error; Mary screwed up my calendar. I was always spending a lot of energy blaming somebody else for my problems, energy I could have spent solving the problem or avoiding the next one. The journal has helped make me less of a blamer, and people have remarked that I'm easier to work with."

Mavis: "The biggest single thing the journal has done is make me realize how seriously I take everything, at the time it happens. Reviewing an event in my journal after a week, I can't imagine why I got so worked up about it. Most of the time, it actually seems funny. I think that now I'm more easy-going. I know I laugh more and have fewer stomach pains."

In other words, each of these journalists learned what they most needed to learn about themselves. I don't know what you need to learn about yourself, and chances are you don't either. That's no excuse for not keeping a journal. In fact, it's the best reason to keep one.

CHAPTER 7: QUESTIONS

1. How many reasons have you thought of already for not starting a learning journal?

2. If you have a journal or any other writing you did in the past, take it out and review it. What do you notice first? What personal changes does it measure? Are you depressed or elated that you've changed so much, or are you depressed or elated that you haven't changed very much? If you don't have any records of your own past, aren't you sorry you can't measure your progress?

3. Once a day for the next week, do some familiar task in the following way: As you do each step of the task, say to yourself (out loud, if possible), "Now I'm doing such-and-such." For instance, you might say, "Now I'm opening the drawer to get a pair of socks. Now I'm choosing a color. Now I'm matching the one blue sock with its partner. Now I'm closing the drawer. Now I'm sitting down close to my shoes to put on my socks. Now I'm putting on my right sock." You may pause at any time to ask yourself questions such as, "Why am I putting on my right sock first?"

4. Which shoe—right or left—do you put on first in the morning? Promise yourself a five-dollar present if you can put the other one on first tomorrow. Put a note on the breakfast table so you'll be reminded to check your bet after your shoes are on. Keep doing this until you succeed.

5. What are your legs and feet doing *right now?*

6. Set some personal development goal for yourself for the coming year. Note in your journal your reactions as you set this goal, and note your progress toward that goal in your journal.

7. Read at least one autobiography of someone you admire. Note in your journal those parts that are particularly surprising to you, and those parts that move you most.

8. As you read this book, write the answers to these questions in your journal.

8

Developing Idea Power

When a teacher, parent, therapist, or other facilitating person permits the individual a complete freedom of symbolic expression, creativity is fostered. This permissiveness gives the individual complete freedom to think, to be, whatever is most inward within himself. It fosters the openness, and the playful and spontaneous juggling of percepts, concepts, and meanings, which is part of creativity.

—Carl Rogers
On Becoming a Person

S elf-awareness is obviously essential to all kinds of leadership styles, but problem-solving leadership is leadership through ideas, so you also need strategies to help develop your idea power.

One strategy is to look for opportunities to practice what you're trying to learn—to solve problems. Try this one, for instance:

> A man hires a worker to do seven days of work on the condition that the worker will be paid at the end of each day. The man has a seven-inch bar of gold, and the worker must be paid exactly one inch of the gold bar each day. In paying the worker, the man makes only two straight cuts in the bar. How did he do it?

The "right" answer to this problem is supposed to be that the man cuts the bar into lengths of one, two, and four inches. By making change, he can pay the man exactly one inch per day—a very clever solution. Being an old binary machine person, I found this solution right away. I felt awfully intelligent as I watched other people struggle with it.

THE PROBLEM-SOLVING LEADER'S CENTRAL DOGMA

I no longer felt so intelligent when several people came up with another solution. The problem says nothing about bending the bar, so they had the man form the bar into a figure S. Then with two cuts, you get exactly seven pieces, and make a dollar sign, to boot.

This case is typical. Problem-solving leaders love to violate the central dogma of academic psychology. No matter which problems I offer them, and no matter what *I* believe is the "right" answer, they invariably come up with something better. It could be that I'm just stupid, but I'd like to believe there's a different explanation.

My experience with problem-solving leaders tells me that the best of them operate on a central dogma different from that of academic psychology, namely

> Any real problem has one *more* solution, which nobody has found—yet.

They may not be able to find it, or find it right now. It may not be worthwhile finding under the present circumstances. But it's there.

85

Why do problem-solving leaders have faith that there is always another solution? I think the question is probably backward. People who believe the central dogma of academic psychology never *attempt* to find additional solutions, so naturally they seldom find them. They never become effective problem solvers, so they certainly never become problem-solving leaders. The innovators are the ones who never *learned* that there was only one solution, and consequently they see new solution ideas wherever they look.

CREATIVE ERRORS

To anyone who isn't blinded by the threat/reward model, the world is overflowing with ideas. In fact, every mistake is a new idea, if seen by a mind prepared to use it. Becquerel discovered x-rays because he accidentally spoiled some film, but others had spoiled film before Becquerel without discovering anything. Freud started a revolution in psychology by noting slips of the tongue, but millions of other people had heard slips of the tongue and made nothing whatsoever of them.

In some sense, the only truly original ideas come from mistakes. I get many ideas from typographical errors. Once I typed "chance" for "change," and triggered a whole chapter in *An Introduction to General Systems Thinking*. Another time, I caught a client writing "turkey system" for "turnkey system." This mistake gave me the opening I needed for a lecture on the perils of off-the-shelf systems.

STOLEN IDEAS

Even so, creative errors are relatively rare sources of ideas. Or perhaps we rarely take advantage of our errors because a lifetime of schooling has taught us to avoid error at all costs. Or perhaps we don't bother looking at errors because it's so much easier to steal new ideas. By "stealing," I include both taking ideas from one person (which is called "plagiarizing") or from many (which is called "research"). I especially like to use creative methods of doing my research, so that other people can do all the work.

As a columnist, for example, I have thousands of readers all working on good ideas for me. Once in a while, one of them reads a column and says, "Well, that's not bad, but my own thoughts on the subject are much better. I think I'll write to Weinberg and tell him what he really should be thinking." When I first read such a letter, it touches my NPS nerve: "How can this person possibly know something that I, the great author, don't already know?" Not all of these letters are as brilliant as their authors think they are, but every one of them has turned out to be more brilliant than I first thought they were. If I wasn't aware of my NPS, I'd be unable to steal these ideas, so I'd have to supply all my own material, which would be a lot of extra work.

As a consultant, I get many of the same benefits. Each client I visit seems eager to tell me all the new ideas they're putting into practice. After I've seen just a few clients, I've got more sensational ideas than I could use in a year of visiting other clients. Moreover, I don't feel guilty about "stealing" their ideas, because I always give them many other ideas in return. If I believed the central dogma of academic psychology, I wouldn't be making these exchanges. I'd be so busy battling to show that *my* idea was *right*, I'd never even hear *their* ideas.

Just so I won't lose any clients, I should make it clear that I'm not talking about "stealing" any of my clients' proprietary ideas. I never reveal anything about which there is the slightest doubt concerning my client's wishes, but the ideas they're worried about are usually not worth stealing. The good ideas to steal are usually "trivial" ideas that the client takes for granted, or doesn't even classify as "ideas." Like plants, ideas that are trivial in one environment may bloom into major breakthroughs when transplanted to more fertile soil.

CORRUPTED STOLEN IDEAS

Another factor in my favor is my ability to misunderstand. When I steal an idea, I often introduce an error, and sometimes the error turns out to be the most creative and valuable part. Sometimes I even feed the transformed stolen idea back to its original owner, who now finds it worth a fortune.

For example, one group of managers told me they were planning to use their large computer to compile programs for some new micro-computers. I honestly thought they said they were going to use the micros to compile programs for the big machine, at least to enter the programs and perform some operator assistance and error checking. When I mentioned that approach to another group in the same company, they went wild with enthusiasm and decided that they too should have a micro for each programmer's personal use. Inasmuch as they were exceptionally poor typists, this approach freed them from the bottleneck imposed by the large machine.

Eventually, they did even better. I learned that the organization was using microcomputers to train data-entry clerks on simulated terminals. I naively asked why they didn't use the same software to train some of their programmers to be better typists. Eventually, I convinced them to use this idea, mostly by pointing out that it wasn't mine, but theirs. A year later, I returned to discover that the original group had stolen back their corrupted idea and had now given a microcomputer to each programmer, for data entry and for training.

COPULATION

This latest example also illustrates the value of copulation: putting together two ideas to form a new one that's better than either of its parents. Actually, most good ideas, like most good people, originate from copulation. You may like eggs, and you may like sugar, but you'll just *love* a good meringue. In fact, I love a meringue even though I detest eggs.

Those leaders who understand the value of copulation are well equipped to resolve conflicts that arise out of a belief in the central dogma of academic psychology. When two members of a group are arguing over whose idea is better, the alert leader tries to find a third way, one resulting from a coupling of the other two.

One of my clients was trying to improve the quality of their software, but in a meeting, two of the programmers got into a fight over which they should install first: a system of technical reviews or a formal test planning system. Their manager defused the whole argument by asking if it wouldn't be possible to conduct formal reviews of test plans. Both programmers got behind this idea, which they each believed was their own.

WHY IDEAS SEEM WICKED

It's not an accident that error, theft, and copulation are the three great strategies for developing ideas. Their fundamental nature is shown by the role they play in the genetics of living systems, but I need not go into detail about how your mother and father happened to combine their genetic ideas to produce the wonderful person that is you. Suffice it to say that this combining process is regarded by many as the most pleasant part of the whole genetic cycle; but alas, some people are actually disturbed by the *symbolic* expression of this idea.

Perhaps this aversion explains why I sometimes have trouble coming up with good ideas. When I was in school, the threat/reward people taught me an entire litany of wicked things that I mustn't do, or even speak about. High on this list were error, theft, and copulation—the very things that generate ideas.

When I turned in papers for grading, I learned that mistakes are punished with bad grades. When I tried to avoid mistakes by copying from the textbook or from another student, I found that I had merely escalated the scale of penalties. For a spelling or punctuation error, I might lose ten percent of my grade. At worst, I might have to stay after school and write the correct answer on the blackboard a thousand times. But for copying, I became a "cheater" and was sent down to the principal.

If I'd been caught copulating, or even reading a book about copulating, the punishment would have made the trip to the principal's office seem like a trip to Stockholm for the Nobel Prize. To the threat/reward crowd, the more effective the method for generating good ideas, the more severe the punishment.

Don't get me wrong: I'm not one of those lily-livered liberals who don't believe in the efficacy of punishment. Punishment is one of our most effective teaching methods. It teaches us to avoid punishment. People who are repeatedly punished for error, theft, and copulation are unlikely to generate great ideas. They won't even think they're *capable* of generating ideas.

By this time, you may have noticed the relationship between the three great idea generators and the three great obstacles to innovation. Lack of self-awareness means that we never notice our errors, so we cannot capture them and convert them to something wonderful. Belief in our own master intelligence means that we would never think of copying the work of someone else, so we cannot benefit from creative theft. And knowing that there is one and only one right solution to every problem makes combining ideas seem foolish, so copulation is ruled out.

The three great strategies can be expressed humorously as error, theft, and copulation, but there's nothing funny about schooling that teaches us that these are terrible strategies. Wrongly interpreted, schooling can teach us lessons that prevent us from being effective problem solvers. The emphasis on not making errors can create self-blindness as a tactic for self-protection. The emphasis on competition, where cooperation is labeled "cheating," can create individuals who believe that it's desirable to be the smartest, and the emphasis on tests can inculcate the idea that there is one and only one right answer to everything.

I know that I made many errors in school. I developed into a blind little perfectionist who would rather not acknowledge his mistakes. I also cheated a bit now and then, which has to this day left me overly squeamish about building on the work of other people. To my good fortune, though, I was so afraid of girls that I never gave my teachers a chance to catch me copulating. Consequently, I never learned to fear putting two good ideas together to make one great one. That tactic has saved me from a life of boring poverty.

So here's my advice to anyone who would like to become a problem-solving leader: Live a clean and wholesome youth—or at least don't get caught and punished! If your youth has already been ill-spent, there still may be hope, as the next chapter tries to prove.

CHAPTER 8: QUESTIONS

1. What's the biggest mistake you ever made? How much did you learn from it? How does the cost of this learning compare with the cost of other parts of your education, such as attending courses or reading books?

2. What part did leadership or absence of leadership play in your biggest mistake? What kind of training or previous experience would have helped you to increase the quality of leadership you exercised on that occasion? What difference would it have made?

3. Can you list at least ten different sources of new ideas that you have used in the past month? Can you list ten more that you're not now taking advantage of?

4. What happens to most of your ideas? Are most of them implemented? How many die from lack of motivation? How many die from lack of a supporting environment?

5. How do you feel about *symbolic* expression? What is your reaction, for example, to "ridiculous" suggestions, such as someone in a brainstorming session offering the idea that you burn down the building?

6. Brainstorming is a structured method by which a group of people increase their idea power. If you've never read about brainstorming, get a book about it and study it. How does the practice of brainstorming follow the ideas expressed in this chapter about where idea power comes from?

7. Next time you're in a meeting, take two consecutive ideas and try putting them together into a new idea, giving full credit to those who offered these ideas. How do the people who brought up the original ideas react?

8. Make a list of some problems you're having now. Now take two of those problems and put them together so that each solves the other. For example, you may be overweight and also not have time to exercise; you could put them together by spending your lunch hour taking a long walk.

9

The Vision

Where there is no vision, the people perish.

—Proverbs 29:18

Although ideas have a central place in problem-solving leadership, becoming a leader means shifting the focus from your ideas to the ideas of others. What makes an innovator want to encourage or organize other people to be innovative? What makes others want to adopt the leader's ideas as their own? These are essential questions about your transition to a leadership role, and the answers require perspective on your own life over a long period of time.

THE CAREER LINE

Your journal can help you get a short-run perspective on yourself, but sometimes it's hard to see yourself in the long term. The following exercise can help you gain that perspective by making a picture out of your entire career.

Take a large sheet of newsprint and a marker pen. Draw a horizontal line across the middle of the sheet; this will represent *time*, running from the beginning of your career to the present day. Draw a vertical line near the left edge to represent your *feelings*, running from high at the top to low at the bottom. Now draw a graph representing your *career line*, moving through the ups and downs of your career. If possible, do it in front of someone else while you relate the story of your career. When you're finished, stand back and look at the whole graph and give it a title. Then, try to extend the lifeline into the future.

You may want to sketch your own career lifeline before you read further.

We've studied the career lines of hundreds of problem-solving leaders. To understand some of what we've learned, let's start by looking at Figure 9.1, which shows a fairly typical career line, drawn by Tony, a computer programmer. Here are some of the things he said as he drew his career line:

(1) "Through high school, I enjoyed math and physics, but it wasn't too exciting. By my senior year, I'd taken all the advanced courses, so I only had social studies requirements to get out of the way. That year was real boring, so the line's way down to here.

93

The Rollercoaster

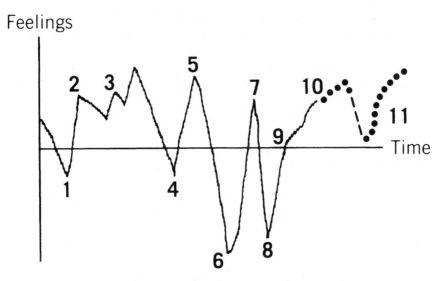

Figure 9.1. Tony's career lifeline.

(2) "In college, I took my first programming course, which shot me way up to here. I took every computer science course that was offered, but I started to taper off when I exhausted the challenge of my course work.

(3) "In my junior year, I got a part-time job in the computer center helping the users solve technical problems. I spent about eighteen hours a day at the computing center, and I was also seeing recruiters, which was exciting.

(4) "I took a programming job with a consumer electronics company, and I started with tremendous enthusiasm. But after three years, I became convinced that I was meant for something more meaningful than maintaining decrepit COBOL programs.

(5) "I quit and wandered in the woods for a few months, then I went to work developing an accounting system for a health food company. It was a wonderful place to work, and I met a woman there whom I married after we knew each other for three weeks.

(6) "After a year, the company went broke, and so did the marriage. I truly hit bottom at that time, but I recovered pretty fast. I

knew that I could never again work for a company where I couldn't contribute to something I believed in.

(7) "My next job was for the company I work for now. They're a very professional outfit producing a top quality on-line service, and they treated me with real respect for my abilities. I got two promotions in a year, and was chief programmer on the most critical part of my project. It was a happy time, kind of utopian, where I didn't let myself see any of the problems.

(8) "But the fact was that the project I was working on was very shaky from a marketing point of view. Just when we had something we were very proud of, the management scrapped the project late one Friday afternoon. So it was back down the roller coaster for me.

(9) "This time, it lasted only over the weekend. On Monday when I woke up, I realized that our system could be used for another application, with a small modification. I talked to my manager, and after a couple of weeks of struggling, I managed to sell the idea.

(10) "That brings me to right now. The first version of the project has been shipped, and now we're working on some enhancements. I'm happier with my work than I've ever been, but I've drawn the line wigglier because I now notice more what's going on. My happiness doesn't come so much from blindness, but from the satisfaction of facing and solving the problems that do come up.

(11) "The dotted line is the future. I've asked to be taken off this project and put on something new. I don't know what I'm going to be doing next, but I feel sure it will keep going up, with some more roller coaster rides, though I hope not such big ones."

THE EVENTS DON'T MATTER

Tony named his lifeline "The Rollercoaster," so he was surprised to find that most careers have ups and downs. Many people are surprised because in our culture, we don't talk much about these things. At least men don't. But once you do talk about them, there are lots of surprises.

One curious fact about career lines is that the same life events in different people's lives are associated with both peaks and valleys. For Tony the broken marriage was a depressing event, but for me it released me from an incredible burden. The only event I can think of that is almost universally a down is serious personal illness. Yet, for many people including myself, the deep depression of such an illness marks the beginning of a new and much higher period in their career. The same is true for other deep drops: losing a job, failing a test, messing up a project.

The first big lesson from studying careers is this: It's not the event that matters, but your reaction to the event.

CAN SUCCESS BREED FAILURE?

The dips can come from many sources: external troubles, for example, or our own shortcomings. Sometimes, though, there is nothing wrong at all; sometimes we just ride too high, and success changes the very conditions that made us successful. This was true for me in the Mercury project: Solving the big problems left me with only boring, routine work to do. The following examples illustrate some other common reasons for experiencing the same phenomenon:

For Frank, success changed his information system. "After being promoted for the third time in less than three years, I supervised more than a hundred people. Yet, I was feeling out of touch. Eventually, I realized that I'd been cut off from all my former sources of information—leisurely lunches with the people in the pits, coffee breaks, chance meetings in the john or in the corridor. I was such a big shot, with so many people depending on me, that I couldn't be allowed to have unprogrammed time. So I began to program in some unprogrammed time. It's not the same as the old days, but it's better than it was a few months ago."

For Iris, success led to pride, which led to defensiveness. "I was promoted because of my work in creating a system to operate the phototypesetter. Nobody had ever done anything like that before, let alone a woman, and I was truly proud of my achievement. But technology moves fast in the typesetting business, and within a year there were new developments that could have improved the system. When some of the people in my group suggested replacing part of 'my' system, I came down pretty heavily on them. At the time, I thought I was being perfectly rational. It was only much later that I saw through the smokescreen my own pride had created. In one year, I had gone from being the solution to being the problem."

Walston's success let him be seduced into staying too long with an obsolete system. "Over a period of five years, I rose from an unwashed college kid to the king of systems programmers. I had built such a toolkit of programs and techniques, I could make that system sing 'Waltzing Matilda' and dance to the tune. Then the company bought a new system, and I was asked to tend the old one during a one-year period of parallel operation, which eventually stretched to two. Obviously, I was the best qualified to do it, and the company made me a very attractive financial offer. Besides, I didn't really feel like giving up my top position and starting over at the bottom with a new system. The problem came when the old system finally went to the scrap yard. I had no place to go but the bottom of the new system, and everybody else had a two-year start on me. I decided to take a nontechnical position in operations. I don't particularly like it, though the pay is good."

The second big lesson from studying careers is this: Everybody has failures, if only because their success leads them to fail.

THE CENTRAL ROLE OF THE VISION

Many people imagine that successful people never experience downs, but life is no fairy tale for anybody. Virtue need not be rewarded. Wisdom sometimes produces blunders. Nobody succeeds every time. People don't become leaders because they never fail. They become leaders because of the way they *react* to failure.

The successful leaders I've known have the ability to bounce back and use their defeats as springboards to new successes. (Perhaps "bounce back" is too optimistic; sometimes "crawl back" would be a better description.) People who become leaders are those who do not just overcome adversity, but turn it to their advantage.

How do they do it? After twenty-five years of studying the question, I've come to the conclusion that people who become innovators do indeed possess a secret key. That key is a special kind of vision, a vision that *combines* an ordinary part with a special part. One part is the ordinary, run-of-the-mill mission in life. Any politician, preacher, or postal clerk can have this sort of vision. The second part is special, however, in personalizing the vision, tying it to the leader's obsession with the great idea.

In other words, there must be something worth doing, but it must also have a unique part that only I can contribute. That's the key to achieving the vision. Joining a mass movement may keep me going as a person, but it won't keep me going as an innovator.

Kathy is a typical, successful innovator, who describes her personal vision: "I always wanted to help the handicapped because my brother was born blind. I could see that computers had terrific potential for the blind, and I determined to go into computer science. When my algebra professor told me I had no mathematical ability, I knew she was wrong. I knew that I *had* to pass if I was going to do computer work with blind people. The second time I took the course, with another professor, I suddenly got it. From that moment, I got an A in every math course I took."

Kathy can relate her vision to a particular circumstance, her blind brother. But Steve, who just "knows" what's worthwhile, may be more typical: "Nobody believed that the project could be finished, but I knew we could do it. People would ask me how I could be so sure, since nothing like it had ever been built before, and I just said that I *knew*. I'm not sure why management kept funding us, but they did, and the system eventually made them a fortune. Then people asked me if I wasn't angry that I had done all the work and the company had made all the money, but I couldn't understand that. Long after they've spent the money, I'll still know that we accomplished something worthwhile that nobody else could have done."

Kathy and Steve, because of a personal vision, an image of a future when things will somehow be better, were helped along by *their* key ideas. The vision may be more important to them than money, or power, or prestige, or helping specific people. The third big lesson I've learned from studying careers is that every successful technical leader has such a personal vision.

WHY THE VISION CREATES AN INNOVATOR

A personal vision permeates the lives of star performers. For almost any occasion, the personal vision gives a reference point, a rule for separating the essential from the trivial. Each vision can be translated into a question that makes the separation. "Does it contribute to designing better operating systems?" "Will it be required if I'm to help the blind find useful work?"

The vision is what gives the problem-solving leader the necessary obsession with quality. With a vision, the work is important, and it is an extension of the producer. If the work is of poor quality, by extension the producer is either uncaring or inferior, or both. In such a state, the worker may not be able to tolerate criticism, unless the critic can demonstrate the connection between the criticism and the perfect realization of the vision.

For instance, computer programmers tend to resist finding errors in their programs because they want to believe that the programs are perfect. When they become convinced that someone else will eventually find those imperfections, resistance turns to enthusiastic cooperation.

In fact, the vision influences all interactions with other people. When people who are driven by a vision see something wrong, they might say to their teammates, "I feel bad because we're not building the kind of system we can be proud of. What shall we do so we don't feel this way?"

On the other hand, when someone has motives besides getting the job done—like wanting power, money, or prestige—the transaction is twisted. A leader can hardly say, "I feel bad because if this job doesn't get done, I'll get passed over for promotion and a raise. Couldn't you people work harder so I can get richer?" Such visionless people are usually clever enough to try to conceal their true motives, but few people are fooled. Studying many careers has taught me a fourth lesson: People without vision don't have much influence on other people.

Visions are contagious. Even misguided visions, like Hitler's, can sweep people along in their path. If people share your vision, you can lead each other to great accomplishments. The same cannot be said for most of the other reasons people want to be leaders. Only your mother cares if *you* get rich or famous.

FINDING THE VISION IN YOURSELF

Without a personal vision, no leadership skill or secret will do you any good. Without a vision, at the leading edge of technology, people and projects perish.

Someone once asked me what happens to potential leaders who don't have such a vision. I couldn't answer, because I've never met such a person. Even those who claim to be cynical about prospects for the future, or claim to want only money or power, have a vision, albeit hidden away under the protective shell of cynicism. Under the crust of callous interest in money and power, there's a fear that people will laugh at something as idealistic as a vision of a better world.

Perhaps I can see the vision in each of these people because I've studied so many people's career lines, but I wouldn't be able to see into those dark places if I'd never been there myself. I've seen my projects fail, and I've seen them turned to the very opposite of the purpose I had intended, causing me so much pain that I couldn't think beyond my own survival, let alone think of "making a better world." I've squandered many years of my life being swept up by the quest for money and power, trying to conceal the fear that I couldn't reach my higher goals. I've known these follies, but I'm no longer ashamed to admit it because I've learned that *most* people have known such follies.

I know the vision is in me, but I don't know how it got there. Psychoanalysts may know, but I don't think I want to find out. It's too important to me, and has a sacred quality that I know many other problem-solving leaders share. At the movies, I start bawling over any corny story of a bright young person who believes a better world is possible, and who triumphs over all the skeptical adults.

Cynics may label problem-solving leaders as "childish," scoffing at their "innocence" and "science fiction mentality." Perhaps only children can believe that what they do makes a difference in the world, but to me that quality is not "childish" but "childlike." Why would you do *anything* if you didn't think it would make any difference?

And, if it really doesn't make any difference, then it doesn't make any difference if you believe it makes a difference.

If you lack such a vision, perhaps it is merely misplaced. Somewhere in your past, you must have believed that something was important—that something you could do would make a difference in the world. Look for it, and welcome to the quest!

CHAPTER 9: QUESTIONS

1. Do you feel as comfortable working with people as you do in your technical work? If not, what do you intend to do about it?

2. Have you ever seen people so carried away with their own success that they became unpleasant to be with? Were you one of them?

3. Has your success ever changed the conditions that fostered the success in the first place? If you succeed at what you are now trying to accomplish, what will change? What are you doing about it?

4. Can you remember the worst time in your career? What was the hardest thing about it? How did you pull out of it? What did you learn from it? What would you do differently now if you reached a low point?

5. What difficulties are you now experiencing? What are you learning from them?

6. When you deal with other people, do they understand your motives? Do you want them to understand? How do you check whether they do or don't understand?

7. Draw your own career line. If possible, share it with a friend or friends as you draw and talk. Be sure to extend the line into the future. If it were a novel or a movie, what title would you give it? Who would you like to play you in the movie version?

Part Three
MOTIVATION

Some people become leaders to realize their vision, and for many, their vision is that they will help other people. They will show them, tell them, force them, coax them, or drag them, but one way or another, they will help them. Even when it's "for their own good," others aren't easily moved.

In the following chapters, we'll learn what gets in the way of influencing others, and what may be done to increase your influence.

10

The First Great Obstacle to Motivating Others

O wad some Power the giftie gie us
To see oursels as ithers see us!
It wad frae monie a blunder free us,
    An' foolish notion:
What airs in dress an' gait wad lea'e us,
    An' ev'n devotion!

—Robert Burns
"To a Louse"

$\mathbf{T}$he first great obstacle to *innovation* is self-blindness: the inability to see yourself. The first great obstacle to *motivation* is a different kind of blindness: the inability to see yourself *as others see you*. When Robert Burns saw a louse crawling up the neck of a vain young lady in church, he perfectly expressed this obstacle: We simply have no reliable way of anticipating the reactions of other people.

TESTING YOURSELF

It would be wonderful to have a simple question to help you determine your capacity for motivating others, something like this:

Can you see how you look to other people?

a) Yes.

b) No.

c) Sometimes.

d) How could I possibly know?

The problem with such a direct question is that every innovator will answer yes. Even though you can overcome the first great obstacle to innovation and see your own behavior, you still may not be able to see how *funny* it is to others. Innovators require a certain narrowness, egoism, and rationalization about their own behavior. The budding innovator needs to concentrate on one vision, to believe that vision is more important than anything else, and to be oblivious to what other people say or think. Innovators, therefore, tend to be unaware of the humorous effect their actions have on other people.

Top problem solvers tend to believe that they each have succeeded without the help of other people. Other people are invisible, or, if seen at all, are seen as obstacles. But when the individual star tries to become a leader, this lack of awareness of other people's reactions becomes the number one obstacle. Other people are welcome to work with the genius, so long as they stay out of the way and confine themselves to admiration and administration.

This type of leader is more like a chief surgeon than an athletic coach. People on the team are not there to solve problems themselves, but to serve as tools to streamline the surgeon's own work. It may be

107

permissible for some of them to learn useful things about surgery, if they do it without stealing the surgeon's time or glory. At best, this is a master/apprentice relationship. At worst, it is master/slave.

The master does not notice apprentices and slaves, unless they interfere with the master's work. Not only that, the master does not notice that the master does not notice. All of this makes it rather difficult to create a truly diagnostic question about seeing the effect of your own behavior on other people.

Fortunately, there's a much more reliable test question:

Are you willing to appear foolish in front of other people?

Since you can't reliably know your effect on other people, the best strategy is to learn to accept that you'll sometimes be the laughing stock. If you can't tolerate being a public fool, you're not going to succeed in a role where all your actions are studied in detail by your admirers. Ask any parent.

AN INTERACTION MODEL

I wish I had the power to grant this "giftie" to others, but I barely have any of it myself. What I have acquired is from working with people outside my areas of expertise. I especially benefited from a model of pair interactions taught by the family therapist Virginia Satir. I find Satir's model particularly appealing to my technical background as a computer programmer, because it breaks down a seemingly complex process into a series of simple steps. This step-by-step analysis may seem tedious at first, but it can give you the power to understand why people react to you the way they do.

Let's start with the following interaction between Yetta and Sam. It was brief, but Yetta's reaction entirely mystified Sam.

> Yetta: "Someone has to set up the coffee."
> Sam: "I'm willing to do it."
> Yetta: (angrily) "If you're going to feel that way about it, I'll do it myself!"

At this moment, everyone in the room grew silent. One of the men in the room looked at Yetta and raised both eyebrows. "What's happening for you?" he inquired.

Yetta's eyes misted over. "I . . . I don't know," she stumbled. "It just came out of me."

We've all had that experience, when a reaction "just came out." How can we know how people will respond to us when they don't even understand their own responses? This kind of understanding is acquired by examining what goes on between the time Sam says, "I'm willing to do it" and Yetta screams, "If you're going to feel that way about it, I'll do it myself."

THE MANIFEST PART OF AN INTERACTION

In the fraction of a second it takes to respond, many things go on inside of Yetta's head. In any feedback interaction between me and you, there is the part that takes place within me, the part that takes place within you, and the *manifest part*, the part that takes place outside of both of us and that theoretically could be observed by others and even videotaped.

In the feedback diagram of Figure 10.1, the manifest part is represented by the two lines: the *behavior* and the *feedback*. It includes both verbal and nonverbal interactions. Though we often fail to pay attention to some parts of the manifest interaction, they are all at least theoretically available for study. They are also available for observation and comment by others.

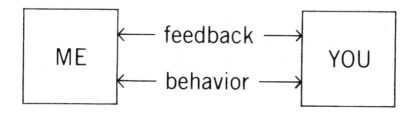

Figure 10.1. A model of interaction.

Sometimes we forget the difference between the manifest and the hidden parts. That's when we say things like, "I know what you're trying to do!" or "I'm sorry I hurt your feelings," things that to be true would require the ability for us to see the hidden part directly.

Yetta really believes she knew what Sam was feeling inside, but the only way she could have known was through clues from the manifest part of their interaction. Yetta *could* know about what's going on inside herself, if she learns to look.

THE HIDDEN PARTS OF AN INTERACTION

What does go on *inside* of me as a result of an interaction with you? These are the things you need to know about me if you are to overcome the first obstacle to motivation. Every interaction can do such things as

- open new possibilities
- reinforce old possibilities
- activate survival rules
- increase assaultiveness
- increase pain

Since all this goes on inside of me, it is unknown to you, and—more important for our present purposes—perhaps even to me.

Everything that you see or hear coming out of me is the *result* of my inner processes. At the same time, I am aware of a *mixture* of what's inside of me and what's outside, and I'm not always aware of what's inside and what's outside.

Sometimes, like Yetta, I'm not even aware of what I said, or my tone of voice, or my gestures. Even my own thinking goes by so fast that I frequently fail to notice the sequence, yet the more I'm aware of my inner sequence, the easier it is for me to be aware of what *you're* seeing in the manifest interaction.

SATIR'S INTERACTION MODEL

I find it easier to see what's going on inside of me when I use Satir's model of this lightning-fast inner process. The model has seven major steps that take place between the time you manifest something and I respond:

1. sensory input
2. interpretation
3. feeling
4. feeling about the feeling
5. defense
6. rules for commenting
7. outcome

Everything starts when you are manifesting something, to which I will respond. For instance, Sam manifests, "I'm willing to do it." Then things start happening inside Yetta.

Step 1: sensory input

Yetta's inner sequence starts with *sensory input* from Sam's manifestation. This input is not perfect but contains "holes."

Yetta may not be paying careful attention to Sam's words, she may not understand some term he uses, she may miss a significant gesture, or she may fail to catch a nuance in his tone of voice or stress pattern, such as "*I'm* willing to do it." She may miss the implication that he wanted to do it *himself.* Sam undoubtedly thought that this part of his message was perfectly clear.

We tend to think that our messages are perfectly clear, but you can generally assume something will be lost in every reception. The same applies when you are on the receiving end. You never get exactly what was sent.

So this step gives you at least two ways of improving your ability to understand how people react to you: You can develop your ability to see and hear more accurately, and you can choose to be aware of the possibility that someone may not be reacting to what you think they're reacting to.

Step 2: interpretation

Let's say that Sam sends message A and Yetta receives message B. Yetta's next internal step is to *interpret* B (not A, which she doesn't have) according to her past experience, which may be different from Sam's past experience.

So, for example, even if Sam said, "I'm willing to do it," and Yetta actually heard exactly the same thing, her past experience with Sam may cause her to *interpret* this as message C: "I'm willing to do it, but I'm not happy about it, and I won't really do it unless you force me to."

Yetta can make this kind of past interpretation even if she's never met Sam before. She might think, "My ex-husband always said he was willing to do it, but he never did it, and I always got stuck with the job."

Or she might not even be thinking of a specific person, but a general principle, such as, "Men always say that, just to try to make me like them" or "People always say that, but they resent me asking."

Awareness of the interpretation step gives you two more new abilities: First, you know that more than one interpretation is possible; and second, even when you think of several interpretations, you can be aware that your list may not include the sender's interpretation.

Step 3: feeling

At this point, only a tiny fraction of a second has elapsed, but Yetta is already two steps removed from Sam's manifest behavior, A. What she does now depends not on A, but on C, the meaning she attached to B, the part of A she observed.

Yetta reacts with a *feeling* about C, based on her own security needs. "Is it for me or against me?" she asks herself.

In this case, she might think Sam's reluctant willingness means D: "I'm afraid that you are trying to thwart me in my attempts to be a leader in this workshop."

There doesn't seem to be a lot of choice in this step. Once you've fixed on an interpretation (C), the feeling just appears before you know what's happening.

At least you have the choice of being aware of the feeling, and differentiating it from other feelings. It can help keep things straight if you know whether you're angry or hurt or excited or scared, and to know that other people can have these feelings, even in response to you.

Step 4: feeling about the feeling

Yetta now reacts to D with E, a *feeling about the feeling*. According to Satir, this is a crucial point, for this feeling-about-feeling depends on Yetta's feeling of *self-worth*.

If Yetta feels good about herself, she can accept that she is afraid of Sam trying to thwart her attempts at leadership. "I'm afraid, but it's reasonable to be afraid in such a circumstance." If Yetta's feeling weak and vulnerable generally, such a message will tend to frighten, hurt, or anger her.

This feeling (E) is probably associated with some *survival rule* (F) that Yetta acquired early in life. For example, she might have the unspoken rule: "If you show you're afraid of a man, he'll take advantage of you." This rule might lead to Yetta feeling afraid of being afraid.

Another typical survival rule might be, "I must be strong, and never be afraid of anyone." This rule might lead to Yetta feeling ashamed of herself for being afraid.

Knowing about survival rules makes you aware that people often respond to you based on experiences they had years ago. This understanding doesn't make their responses less real, but it does make it easier for you to deal with them effectively.

Step 5: defense

If Yetta's survival rule (F) says it is okay for her to have this feeling, then she will simply move directly to step 6 and start preparing her response.

But if her survival rule (F) says it's *not* okay for her to have this feeling, then she will call some *defense* into play. She might *project* by putting the problem somewhere else: "You are *making* me angry, Sam."

She might *ignore,* as by changing the subject: "Do you think it will rain tomorrow?

She might *deny* that she's really having that feeling: "I'm not hurt. Who cares what you think about my leadership?"

She might *distort* what she heard even further: "Sam didn't really mean what he said."

Obviously, Yetta has many choices here. First, she chooses whether to defend at all, and if she does decide to defend, she has many choices of what defense to use. It may be hard for you to believe that anyone needs to defend himself or herself against you, but you'd better believe it if you want to understand why your attempts at motivation don't always work.

Step 6: rules for commenting

Whatever her choice, Yetta has now produced an internal response (G), which is several steps removed from what Sam said. Suppose her inner response is, "You're making me angry, Sam, with your resistant attitude."

Even now, she has choices to make, for this is still an *inner* response. It's not G that Sam will hear, because Yetta must first apply her *rules for commenting.*

She might have a rule that says, "Always be polite." This rule could lead her to transform G into H_1: (smiling and gritting her teeth) "Thank you for being so helpful, Sam."

She might have a rule that says, "Be forceful with men." This might lead her to say H_2, "Don't think you can pull that stuff on me. You'll do it whether you want to or not."

Another rule might be, "Don't ever mention anger explicitly, but don't push men directly." In that case, she might translate G into H_3: "If you're going to feel that way about it, I'll do it myself!"

Step 7: outcome

The final step is the actual outcome. This includes Yetta's verbal utterance H, but it's likely that some residues that have accumulated along the way will be mixed in. For example, if taken at their face value, the words may sound more conciliatory than hurt or angry, but Yetta may let hurt leak through in her tone of voice and anger peek through in her finger, pointing at Sam in a slightly accusing manner.

Yetta has choices about this kind of leakage, but they're generally much harder to exercise than her choice of words. Even so, not all her actions fall into the category of leakage. Yetta can choose to hit Sam, or not to hit him. She can choose to walk out, or to stay. The more explicit her movements, the more choices she has.

People who say, "I had to hit him, I couldn't help myself," are either lying to themselves or very sick. You may not be in very good control of how you look or sound, but you can readily control what you *do*.

The outcome completes one cycle for Yetta, and because it is an outward manifestation, it starts a new one for Sam. The cycle probably all happened in less than a second.

On the surface, Sam said, sincerely, "I'm willing to do it." Yetta's response, in a hurt tone and pointing an angry finger, was, "If you're going to feel that way about it, I'll do it myself!"

UNDERSTANDING WHY COMMUNICATIONS GO AWRY

With such a long way from A to H, is there any wonder that people have so much trouble understanding their reactions to each other? If you examine many such sequences, you'll discover that there are five principal reasons why the transformations between A and H are so confusing:

Perception: Neither of us perceives even the manifest part in the same way, because we are different people and so have different perceptions.

Wrong time: The transformation refers to things in the past or future, things that have no logical bearing on the present communication. For example: "You used to behave in a certain way"; "You might not fulfill that promise"; or "A long time ago, I wasn't able to deal with angry people, so I can't deal with angry people now."

Wrong place: The transformation refers to some other context. "When nobody else is present, you can speak to me about these personal things, so you can speak about them when others are present." "You said you were hungry before lunch, so you must be hungry now, before dinner."

Wrong person: The transformation refers to some other person. "My mother used to point her finger at me when I had been naughty, and you're a woman, too." "My brother always lies to me about money, and you have curly hair just like my brother." "My previous three bosses never fulfilled their promises to me, so obviously you can't be trusted."

Self-worth: My feelings about myself have a powerful influence on how I respond, but you have no direct access to how I feel about myself, either in general or right at this moment.

Under the circumstances, it's no wonder that Satir estimates that ninety percent of all communications are *incongruent*, inconsistent with what we truly want to communicate. Incongruent communication is deadly to motivation, which depends on the free and accurate flow of information about how we respond to one another.

A WAY TO START CLEARING COMMUNICATIONS

Virginia Satir's model helps to explain one of the great paradoxes of human interaction. People respond better to me if I devote attention to their problems, but one way of devoting attention to their problems is by being candid about *my* problems. As the interaction model makes clear, many of *their* problems arise from trying to deal with me, to understand why in the world I'm doing the crazy things I'm doing. They have no knowledge of my internal response sequence except through my own candor, so congruent statements about me become helpful to them.

Students and clients often pose problems that stump me. If I'm feeling stupid but I try to hide the fact by making *them* feel stupid, I'm not giving them the gift of clear, reliable information. Suppose I simply say, with good humor, "Gee, I'm having a hard time figuring that one out, and I'm feeling somewhat embarrassed to look dumb in front of you." This is a reasonably clear, straight comment about my internal response sequence.

Using this information, they now have a better idea of where I stand, and they also have a model of how they can behave as leaders when they are stumped. This opens many new possibilities for them, both as leaders and as followers, a gift that they can reciprocate by giving me accurate information about their own internal response sequences, or about their perceptions of my response.

As far as I know, the only place you can get this gift is from other people. If you don't have it, they may not want to bother giving it to you, unless you give them something first. My gift-giving technique can almost be reduced to a formula: Tell them what you *perceive*, how you *feel* about what you perceive, and if possible how you feel about that feeling.

Here is another typical example: "When I find myself asking you three times when you will finish this late assignment, I feel ashamed about acting like a dictator and not trusting you, yet I don't know how else to deal with my anxiety over the project schedule."

These are difficult things to say to other people. You are saying, in effect, "I am vulnerable, but I am confident enough in myself and in you to expose my vulnerability." By showing your vulnerability, you begin to open up a channel that might get you the information you need about yourself.

The risk is that the other person might use this channel to attack you. In my experience, it's not a great risk, but it definitely feels enormous the first few times you try it. It might help you to know that you're not really exposing yourself by revealing yourself, because the more you try to hide, the more easily other people can see your foolishness. The louse looked all the more lousy creeping up the neck of a woman who thought she was fooling the parishioners by her fancy dress.

I have found workshop settings a fine place to learn to see myself as others see me. Like all participants, though, I need a bit of courage to hear the messages I need the most—those that might drop me off my comfortable plateau into a ravine.

CHAPTER 10: QUESTIONS

1. Think back to some foolish thing you've done recently. How did you respond when you were found out? Are you getting more or less defensive as you advance in your career? What are you doing about your defensive behavior?

2. Recall a recent time when you were puzzled by an interaction. How were *you* involved?

3. What have you done recently that gave people a chance to understand where they are in relationship to you. For example, when you were distracted by another problem, did you let them know that your mind was elsewhere?

4. What was the most recent time you laughed at yourself? What was the most recent time you laughed with others who were laughing at you?

5. In a typical meeting, how much time do you spend observing yourself? others in your group? observing the interaction among members in the group?

6. Think of all the people you frequently interact with. Which of them would be most likely to exchange observations with you? What's keeping you from such an arrangement?

7. Arrange to have yourself videotaped, preferably in some natural setting where other people respond to you and you respond to them. Watch the videotape at least twice, noting especially those things you didn't see the first time. If possible, review the tape until you stop seeing new things. Then, put the tape away for six months and watch it again, to see what you notice now.

8. Possibly using some interaction you have on videotape, write down the steps of your internal process in detail. Try to share this with another person in the same interaction, until you can account for the entire manifest interaction.

9. Using a transcript of what you said in some interaction, write down for each sentence what perception, time, place, persons, and self-worth were implicit in the sentence. Do you see any characteristic patterns of yours?

11

The Second Great Obstacle to Motivating Others

When I'm in charge of a team that has a task to do, and the success of the task is threatened, I am likely to

a. put the task ahead of the people

b. put the people ahead of the task

c. balance the people and the task

d. escape from the situation

e. none of the above

$\mathbf{T}$he preceding question is adapted from a textbook on management. Put in plain English, it poses this familiar leader's dilemma: A task must be completed with certain results or by a certain time, or else something dire, known only to you, will happen. If you require everybody to work overtime or do anything else necessary to complete the task, you are putting the task ahead of the people. If you share with your employees the need for the task, thereby allowing people to decide for themselves how, or even *if* they'll accomplish the task, you are putting the people ahead of the task.

You may become an individual success without ever having to face this dilemma. As an individual achiever, you are the only person involved, so you necessarily balance the task and your needs, though you may be unaware that you are doing so. In that case when you start working with others, the conflict comes as a shock to you, and you may not handle it well.

In fact, you may be so overwhelmed that you fail to realize that there actually is no conflict. If so, you'll be in good company. Many people, even some textbook authors, think there is a conflict between people and task. They are trapped by the second great obstacle to motivating others.

It's an easy trap to fall into. In this chapter, I'll explore some ways in which people and task are related, starting with an unpleasant task I had to do alone, by a deadline.

AN UNPLEASANT TASK

Upon my return from a month-long trip, I faced a huge stack of mail. One envelope contained a batch of articles submitted for publication in a management journal, along with a letter from the editor asking me to act as a reviewer. The articles were trying to answer the question, Which leaders are more effective, those who put people first or those who put the task first? Although I was vitally interested in the question, the papers were boring, so I put off writing my reviews until the morning of the deadline day.

I woke up so early that I surprised a mouse making her rounds of my bathroom. She surprised me, too. If there's one task I like less than reviewing boring papers, it's catching mice. So I fetched Beverly, the cat,

121

and delegated the job to her. I withdrew to my wife's office with the stack of articles.

Lessons from a task-oriented style

The author of the first article favored task first. *My* task was reading it, a task I was having great difficulty putting first. My mind kept drifting back to the mouse and my personal safety. I found myself reading and rereading the same sentence, unable to grasp its meaning. It occurred to me that there was a lesson there, somewhere, so I wrote myself a note:

> Lesson Number One: When survival is concerned, there's no choice but to put people first.

People in fear for their lives can't do any task well, except a task devoted to their personal safety.

Part of my problem was lack of confidence in Beverly. Instead of guarding the door, she climbed into my lap and wanted to be stroked. Beverly can't catch mice, but mice don't know that, so she makes a good leader of mice. I noted another lesson about motivation:

> Lesson Number Two: If the job isn't highly technical, the leader need not be competent, but can lead by fear.

Beverly makes a good mouse leader when the task is to keep the mice out of my room, but would fail if the task was to train the mice to do acrobatics.

Putting Beverly back on the floor where she could do her task better, I returned to the article, but I still couldn't concentrate. Searching for some way of avoiding this onerous task, I proceeded to analyze X's writing style, rather than his content. When I realized what I was doing, I wrote a third note:

> Lesson Number Three: People with strong technical backgrounds can convert any task into a technical task, thus avoiding work they don't want to do.

To prevent this method of avoiding the task, leaders must have enough acumen to spot what they're doing and stop it.

The technical trick I used to avoid my reviewing task is called the "Fog Index." It measures writing difficulty based on the average length of sentences and the frequency of longish words. A Fog Index of about twelve is considered to be the limit for most technical writing, but X consistently surpassed thirty. The soporific effect was better than two sleeping pills, a glass of warm milk, and a late-late rerun.

Writers are leaders. A writer's task is to lead you through the subject matter, so writing style can be considered a particular kind of leadership style. I believe X's foggy style shows a total lack of concern for me, his reader; it was the style of a leader who is totally task-oriented. Armed with the evidence of the Fog Index, I decided to give X's paper the bum's rush and to write another note:

> Lesson Number Four: Leaders who don't care about people don't have anyone to lead, unless their followers don't have a choice.

Sharp problem solvers usually have a choice, lots of choices, so they won't stay around to be abused by an uncaring leader.

Is a people-oriented style better?

Writer X was a perfect example of the task-oriented author who didn't care about his readers. The second article, by Y, was a lot easier to read, with a Fog Index of around eight. Y really cared about getting his message across. The problem was he had nothing to say. I will be merciful and spare you a sample of Y's writing, just as I was merciful to myself by stopping after two pages.

As Kenneth Boulding once remarked, there are two kinds of people in the world: those who divide everything in the world into two kinds and those who don't. Y is one of the first kind, your typical bifurcator. Using this style, he can write volumes on any subject—and say nothing.

"Bifurcation" may sound like a sexual perversion, and perhaps it is. To me, it's a perversion of thought that turns me away in disgust. It also led me to write another note:

> Lesson Number Five: No amount of caring for people will hold your audience if you have nothing to offer but pretend you do.

Now, whose style is worse, X or Y? Personally, I think Y is worse. Whenever I read something like X's, I acquire a bad taste for the author, but from something like Y's, I acquire a bad taste for the *subject*. X turns me away from the present work, but Y turns me against further participation. To me, that's the ultimate sin of a writer, teacher, coach, or any other leader.

WEINBERG'S TARGET

When I write a book or an essay, or give a workshop, I measure my success by one simple test:

When I'm finished with them, do they care less about the subject?

If the answer is yes, I've failed. If it's no, I've succeeded and I'm happy for it. This is Weinberg's Target, the task to which I am oriented. Do you think my task is too modest? Think back over your own educational experiences: the courses you've taken, the books you've read, the films you've watched. How many have met Weinberg's Target? One in ten? From this answer, I derive another lesson:

Lesson Number Six: Task-oriented leaders tend to overestimate their own accomplishments.

This is a moral for all leaders, whether they're teaching a class of twenty, coaching a team of four, or laying plans for the lives of millions.

PLANNING AND THE FUTURE

As I wrote that note, the mouse darted out of the bathroom, past the sleeping Beverly. I suddenly thought about Robert Burns, who two hundred years ago came upon another mouse. When he turned up her nest with a plough, he told her those words we all know from his poem "To a Mouse":

> But Mousie, thou art no thy lane,   [not alone]
> In proving foresight may be vain,
> The best-laid schemes o' mice an' men
>   Gang aft agley,
> And lea'e us nought but grief an' pain,
>   For promis'd joy!

Leaders tend to be overly optimistic about the positive social impact of their work. Believing that their vision promises such joy to the world, they can't allow themselves to worry about what their leadership is doing to the workers. In my own experience, I find engineers and computer programmers are infected with this optimism, which drives the information explosion. In the end, though, the vision doesn't seem that important, leaving us "nought but grief an' pain, / For promis'd joy." Even in two hundred years, mice and men haven't changed that much.

Very few of the classic leadership studies have been done in environments even vaguely resembling the technical work situation. Many have been done in military situations, where the soldiers were supposed to be willing to die for the cause. For a programmer or engineer, even for a school teacher, this is a bit unrealistic. Following this idea through to its natural conclusion, I derived another lesson:

> Lesson Number Seven: Very little work we do is really so important that it justifies sacrificing the future possibilities of the people doing the work.

If you can't do the task without exploiting people, perhaps you shouldn't do it at all.

We can't deny that there are two sides to this coin. If you put people ahead of the work, you may hurt your chances of succeeding with your project; but the people will be around long after the project has been forgotten, doing other projects and affecting the lives of other people.

Then again, it's just possible that you may not be hurting the chances for success. Many of the studies of leadership style have been done on routine work, like assembly lines. Possibly the task-first people are correct about assembly lines, but the bifurcation of task versus people doesn't work for complex technical work. When things don't go according to plan, only the adaptability of people can rescue the operation. I've learned this lesson hundreds of times:

> Lesson Number Eight: When the work is complex, no leader can be absolutely sure that plans won't "gang aft agley."

In a complex environment, even the most task-oriented leader is forced to put people first, or the task won't get done.

THE SECOND GREAT OBSTACLE

All of these lessons lead me to believe that when talking about technical leadership, the best answer to the question posed at the beginning of the chapter is (d) none of the above. When the task is complex, I can't choose between people and task, because then I simply cannot separate people and work.

Whenever there is a task, even an individual task, there are people involved. We don't work for abstract profits; we work to make profits for certain people. We don't work for peace; we work so that certain people can enjoy the benefits of living in peace. The people involved in our task may be our customers, or our managers, or our constituents, or our board of directors, but even though they are not directly visible, they are people.

If we believe that the choice is between people and task, we are denying or distorting the real choice: between one group of people and another. We sometimes make that denial because it's easier than facing the true choice between groups. How much easier it is to say, "We can't implement your idea, because we have to stay within budget" than "We can't implement your idea, because our stockholders are dissatisfied with their dividends."

Unfortunately, this kind of distortion usurps people's problem-solving power by denying them the possibility of a correct definition of their problem. So, if you deny the human reality behind your work, you'll never be a very successful problem-solving leader. Which is really another lesson, one of the most important:

> Lesson Number Nine: To be a successful problem-solving leader, you must keep everybody's humanness at the forefront.

The belief in the task/people dichotomy is the second great obstacle to being a successful motivator because it pretends that tasks are as real as people, rather than deriving from people. You may motivate people once in a while with that false dichotomy, but eventually they will see through it, even if you don't. Once they realize you've been fooling them, you're finished as a motivator.

THE LEADER AS A PERSON

By this time, I noticed that I had enough lessons to write an article of my own, so I decided to stop denying my humanness, drop the reviewing, and take care of my own needs.

I looked up what Virginia Satir had to say about the humanness of leaders. She was writing for therapists, but you can substitute the word "leader" for "therapist":

> Using oneself as a therapist is an awesome task. To be equal to that task, one needs to continue to develop one's humanness and maturity. We are dealing with people's lives. In my mind, learning to be a therapist is not like learning to be a plumber. Plumbers can usually settle for techniques. Therapists need to do more. You don't have to love a pipe to fix it. Whatever techniques, philosophy or school . . . we belong to, whatever we actually do with others has to be funnelled through ourselves as people.
>
> In my teaching, I focus in depth on the personhood of the therapist. We are people dealing with people. We need to be able to under-stand and love ourselves, to be able to look, listen, touch and

> understand those we see. We need to be able to create the conditions
> by which we can be looked at, listened to, touched and understood.*

Somehow this passage made me aware of the people on the other end of those articles, waiting anxiously for their reviews. I decided to give the reviewing task one more try.

I reread the cover letter that came with the articles, in which the editor explained that the authors and I were being kept anonymous so "the reviews can be accurate and impartial." It suddenly struck me that this device ensured that we could not look, listen, touch, or understand each other—a complete separation of people from people under the guise of separating people from task. What was the task? In the editor's view, I was to *judge* the papers, to see which were the "winners" and which were the "losers."

Such anonymous reviewing grows out of the threat/reward model of human interaction. The authors are supposed to be so vindictive that they will try to damage me in some way if I give them an unfavorable review; I'm supposed to be so afraid of possible repercussions that I can't be honest unless I am anonymous; and I'm so biased that I can't give an honest review if I know who the authors are.

I quickly realized that I had been having trouble because I couldn't accept this threat/reward definition of the problem. Rather than continuing to play cat-and-mouse, I wrote a letter to the editor telling him that it was impossible for me to do my job under these circumstances. I offered to communicate personally with the authors if they wanted my help in making their papers better. Two of them accepted my offer. They produced two improved papers, and I gained two grateful colleagues as well as one further lesson:

> Lesson Number Ten: If you are a leader, the people *are* your work. There is no other work worth doing.

One more thing: The mouse also made a clever escape.

---

*V. Satir and M. Baldwin, *Satir: Step by Step* (Palo Alto, Calif.: Science and Behavior Books, 1983), pp. 227-28.

CHAPTER 11: QUESTIONS

1. When was the last time you tried to lead by fear? What happened?

2. When was the last time you tried to convert some task to a technical task of a type you were better equipped to do? What happened?

3. Have you ever made a choice of task over person that you now regret? Have you ever made a choice of person over task that you now regret?

4. How have people changed after they've worked with you?

5. How have people changed after they've worked for you?

6. What type of situation do you typically escape from? What is your typical escape pattern?

7. Would you be motivated by a person who acts the way you do?

12

The Problem of Helping Others

That people cannot do everything they want to do for others seems to be a well-established fact of life; it is nonetheless a very difficult reality for many counselors to accept and make operational in their own activities.

Counselors need to develop, for their own good, simple and reliable estimates of what they can accomplish in trying to help their clients.

—Eugene Kennedy
On Becoming a Counselor

The organic model says that leadership is the process of creating an environment in which people are empowered. This is an appealing definition because most people want to help people, and creating an empowering environment is one way of *helping* people. Creating helpful environments, however, is no easy task and in this chapter, we'll examine some of the reasons why.

HELP SHOULD BE NATURAL

We've seen how the problem-solving leadership style is concerned with process, the way things are done. In our society, the *content* of work is supposed to be difficult and reserved for specialists. The process, on the other hand, is something that everyone should know. Teachers are hired on the basis of their knowledge of subject matter rather than their classroom skills. Programming team leaders are promoted according to their technical skills, with the assumption that any normal person will be able to pick up leadership skills along the way.

This myth persists because once in a while, someone does seem to acquire process skills without visible effort. Just as some people learn to program computers without direct training, others seem always to know just how to be most helpful. It's wonderful for those people, but does that make them *better* than people who have to learn by conscious effort? The threat/reward model leads us to make such judgments, so we are ashamed of the effort we need to learn.

Our shame may explain why people start to believe that work can be separated from people. When we begin to realize, as Eugene Kennedy says, that "people cannot do everything they want to do for others," we are ashamed of our inadequacy. By pretending the work is somehow abstracted from the people, we can transform our *interpersonal* failure into a *mechanical* failure. It's much easier to say, for example, "We couldn't get the program working on time" than "I wasn't skilled enough to help Jack become a better programmer."

The myth of "natural helpfulness" creates a vicious circle. People who want to work with others generally get little practice, so is it any wonder that they know so little about helping? In this chapter, I hope to

131

fight that myth by presenting some lessons that technical leaders need to learn about creating helpful environments.

TRYING TO BE HELPFUL: AN EXERCISE

To give potential leaders practice at creating helpful environments for others, we designed the following exercise: Two teams are each assigned to create an innovative design and use Tinkertoys to execute, and then document, their design. What the teams don't know is that they later must exchange the paper designs (which can contain no pictures), each trying to recreate the other's design. Team members can communicate only through written messages, so that after the exercise, we can analyze the various attempts to help the other team.

In one such exercise, I recall, the Blue team had concocted such an abstract structure I worried that the Green team wouldn't have a chance. I wanted to make it easier on Green, without giving the whole exercise away:

"Perhaps a name would be helpful," I ventured. The Blue team worked on a name, eventually coming up with Inert Toky, an anagram of Tinkertoy. It was certainly creative, but I doubted that Inert Toky would enhance the environment for the other team. I shuddered to think what Green's reaction would be.

Later, after Blue and Green exchanged designs and Blue was working to reconstruct Green's Hurdy Gurdy Banjo design, Alex of the Blue team suddenly announced, "They're not going to be able to build our Toky."

"Why not?" asked Cassie.

"Because we didn't break the little green and yellow plastic blades off this waste piece left over from the mold."

"So?"

"Well, if you look at their banjo, you see that they've already broken their blades off the waste piece. There's no way to get them back on, so they can't build the Toky."

"Maybe we could send them our blades, in exchange for theirs." Cassie turned to me, seeking permission.

"You know the rules," I reminded her. "You can exchange written messages only."

"But can we exchange kits? Otherwise, it isn't going to be too helpful for them to know they don't have the right parts to build the Toky."

"All right," I agreed, wanting to be helpful. "If Green agrees to the exchange, in writing, then you can do it."

Alex and Cassie wrote the message, which I read as I carried it to the Green team:

Dear Green:

We are willing to swap parts with you, if we can. The Inert
Toky requires some esoteric parts.

Love, Blue

When Green received this message, they were a bit unsure of its
meaning. They had no particular objection to swapping parts, but they
had already started to work on the Inert Toky and weren't eager to break
up their hard work.

Nils turned to me and asked, "Why are they asking for a swap?"

"I'm just a messenger. What do I know?"

"Maybe it's our 'unidentified parts,' " Vinetta offered. "I told you
they wouldn't be able to figure out that those were the box top and the
rubber band."

"Let's not get into that again. It should be obvious to them once
they realize it's a banjo."

"Maybe they don't have a rubber band? The little sets didn't have
them."

"Okay," Nils said, "I don't think it's necessary, but I guess we
should be willing to help them out." He wrote his reply below Blue's
original message:

Dear Blue:

We are delighted to swap parts. The parts for 1 Assembly are
in the can.

Green

In their confusion over the meaning of the message, Blue didn't seem to
notice that Green had left "Love" off their message. "Do they want to
swap some individual parts?" Cassie asked. "Are we allowed to do that?"

"I think they're asking to swap the completed models," said Alex.
"Is that allowed?"

"No," I replied, "swapping models would defeat the purpose of
the exercise."

"Okay," said Cassie, "but time is growing short." She scribbled
another message below Green's message and handed it to me. Then,
she took a quarter from her purse and flashed it in front of my nose.
"There's a big tip for you if you deliver this and get back with their kit
in less than three minutes." It wasn't a big enough tip to prevent me
from stopping in the corridor to read the message:

Above messages not clear. We wish to trade Tinkertoy Kits.
Are you willing? If so, send your kit.

Evidently, Cassie in her haste had also forgotten to write "Love," but Green didn't notice. "See," said Vinette, "they don't understand that they've got all the parts they need. We can't trade whole kits now. We haven't got time to break up all this work and start over."

"Here," said Nils. "You keep working and I'll make it perfectly clear to them." Under the previous messages, he wrote

> Our Tinkertoy Kit contains parts for Hurdy Gurdy Banjo, all
> & only. We are interested in parts of Inert Toky, all & only.

Vinette read the message, then added a footnote:

> Note: Box top and rubber bands are "unidentified parts."

She probably should have left it off, because Alex reacted badly. "Do they think we're idiots? We figured that out in two minutes, but they'll never figure out that our blades aren't separated if we don't tell them."

"Maybe we should just give it up," Cassie ventured.

"No, it wouldn't be fair not to help them. I'll try one more time," Alex said as he scrawled the next message in the series:

> Impossible to separate at this point. You will not be able to
> complete the Inert Toky without this exchange.

I couldn't figure out exactly what this meant, and neither could Nils. "Are they threatening us?"

"I don't think so," said Vinette. "Maybe they don't think we're smart enough to build it?"

"In that case," Nils said, turning to me, "You can tell them to stick their box of Tinkertoys . . ."

"I'm sorry," I replied, "but it's not my job to deliver verbal messages. You'll have to put it in writing."

Evidently, Nils thought better of putting obscenities in black and white, so there were no more written messages. I did hear a few more opinions about ancestry and anatomy, but they wouldn't add greatly to the story.

SOME LESSONS ABOUT HELPING

As an isolated incident, these events are merely humorous, though the emotions of frustration and anger were real enough. Similar sequences happen to would-be problem-solving leaders every day. The details differ, but the pattern never varies. It begins with a sincere desire to help, progresses through some muddled communications, degenerates into emotional name calling, and finishes by making things worse.

The only thing unique about this case is the existence of the observer and the written record, giving us the opportunity to review the incident. When those who seek money, power, and other forms of personal gain are thwarted, it's easy to moralize about their motives. What can we learn from the plight of the Blue and the Green, who were only trying to be helpful?

Lesson number one is this:

> Wanting to help people may be a noble motive but that doesn't make it any easier.

Blue thought that since they were trying to help, it would be easy to succeed. As a result, they were careless with their initial message, which got the whole affair off on the wrong foot.

The second lesson to be learned is,

> If people don't want your help, you'll never succeed in helping them, no matter how smart or wonderful you are.

Had they understood the nature of their problem, Green might have welcomed help from Blue. Lacking that understanding, they misinterpreted Blue's offer, first as a request to help Blue, then as an insult to their abilities.

Blue's blundering start illustrates a third lesson:

> Effective help can only start with mutual agreement on a clear definition of the problem.

Interestingly enough, Blue considered Green's offer insulting, but they never dreamed that their own offer could be interpreted that way. Neither did Green. This is the most common motivational mistake among star problem solvers who find themselves supervising other people, offering help that they would consider insulting if offered to them.

You can prevent this error by asking yourself if you would want this help, but if you're not absolutely sure they want help, it's best to check it out. Since you can never be entirely sure that they want your help, or even that they understand the problem, lesson number four says,

> Always check whether they want your help.

The simplest way to check is by asking them if they want help, which neither team ever bothered to do.

As the two teams worked on the problem, getting further and further into the construction, the situation changed, and so did the problem definition. Also, when they discovered what the help would cost them, they changed their minds. So, a fifth lesson is,

> Even when people agree that they want your help, that agreement is not usually a lifetime contract.

It's all right to admit you failed in your generosity, especially if it helps you stop before you make things a lot worse.

This sixth lesson seems especially hard for some leaders to accept. Once they offer to help, they seem to feel that breaking the contract, even when there was no contract, is selfish. They don't seem to realize that *every* offer to help is intended to do something for the helper. There are very few living saints.

> People who want to help other people generally expect to get something for themselves, though they may not be aware of it.

When we discussed the incident, Blue realized they were afraid Green wouldn't rebuild their masterpiece, which meant that half the class wouldn't see it. Things might have gone rather differently had their initial message been this:

> We made a blunder when we built Inert Toky. Our blunder could cause you much difficulty because you'll need a special piece that you don't have. We'd sure like to see the Toky rebuilt, but the rules say we can't send you the piece unless you agree to swap kits. Do you want to help us out by swapping?

Of course, it's easy for me to say this, after the fact, but what about my own attempts to help? I had suggested they give the Inert Toky a name, and I had bent the rules to allow them to exchange kits, but I had never thought much about my own motives, which is a lesson in itself:

> Most people understand that helpers are selfish, but also think they are exceptions to the rule.

During the discussion, Green revealed that the name Inert Toky had contributed to the problem. "We thought they were trying to give us a hard time by being cute," Nils said. His reaction was completely typical.

> Attempts to help are often interpreted as attempts to interfere.

You can use this lesson two ways: one when you're trying to help and are meeting resistance, and another when you think someone is trying to interfere with your work. This may be the most important lesson of all:

> No matter how strange it may look, most people are actually trying to be helpful.

That doesn't mean that they are succeeding, or that you must accept their help, but only that you might be better off understanding where it's coming from.

HELPING AND SELF-ESTEEM

As I look back over the sequence of messages, I'm struck by the way that "Love" dropped off after the first message, both literally and figuratively. It reminded me of the Golden Rule, which I've seen expressed in two different ways:

> Do unto others as you would have others do unto you.

> Love thy neighbor as thyself.

The first version is often interpreted as meaning,

> Help your neighbor.

Based on my own experience with helping and being helped, I prefer to interpret it differently:

> Offer to help your neighbor only if you would want to be helped in the same situation, and do it in the way you would want to be helped.

How do we want to be helped? I don't want to be helped out of pity. I don't want to be helped out of selfishness. These are situations in which the helper really cares nothing about me as a human being. What I would have others do unto me is to love me—not romantic love, of course, but true human caring.

So, if you want to motivate people, either directly or by creating a helping environment, you must first convince them that you care about them, and the only sure way to convince them is by actually caring. People may be fooled about caring, but not for long. That's why the second version of the Golden Rule says, "Love thy neighbor," not "Pretend you love thy neighbor." Don't fool yourself. If you don't really care about the people whom you lead, you'll never succeed as their leader.

I cannot teach you to care about people, neither people in general nor particular persons, but I have learned that caring about other people is impossible if you don't care about yourself. The Golden Rule doesn't say, "Love thy neighbor even though you think you're a despicable worm." The ability to love others—and thus to help others, and thus to lead others—starts with the ability to love yourself.

As we've just seen, the attempt to help others is not guaranteed to succeed. When you run into difficulty as a helper, your own feelings about yourself will determine how you react. If you care about yourself, you'll be able to persist through difficulties and, if necessary, to abandon the project without destroying yourself. If your self-worth is low, you're going to have to protect yourself. You may abandon the help just when it needs persistence. You may persist long after the attempt has proved harmful to the other party, or even to you. Or you may project the failure away from yourself, blaming the very person you started out to help.

If you hold yourself in low esteem, it will thwart your every attempt to motivate others. Before you set out to help others, you'd better work on yourself first, which is the subject of the next chapter.

CHAPTER 12: QUESTIONS

1. Eugene Kennedy in *On Becoming a Counselor* (p. 14) talks about "how much harm has been done all through history by resolute do-gooders—that sturdy tribe whose heavy handedness with human beings cannot be compensated for by the virtuous gleam in their eyes. Do-gooders are defined as those persons who act on others in response to their own needs. It is clear, therefore, that doing good is not to be avoided as much as setting out purposefully to inflict good on others at all costs." Do you wish to be a leader so you can do good for others? In what ways do you know when you are doing good rather than inflicting good?

2. Recall some time when someone tried to force some help on you. How did you feel? How did you react?

3. Are you in a helping relationship now? If so, what is your contract? What is the other person's contract?

4. For some helping situation you've experienced in the recent past, what were you trying to get out of it? If possible, recall several situations and see if you can detect a pattern.

5. Think of some person you work with to whom you find it difficult to apply the Golden Rule. What is it in that person that you find hard to care for? How is that same quality manifest in you?

6. Recall a recent occasion when people seemed to be deliberately thwarting your work. Try to imagine how they might have been sincerely attempting to help you, even though the attempt may have been misguided. If possible, speak to the people involved and listen to their version of what they were trying to do.

7. The Platinum Rule says, "Do unto others as they would have you do unto them." How does this compare with the Golden Rule as a practical guide to helping? What if you don't want to do what they want?

13

Learning to Be a Motivator

Why read this book to find out how to win friends? Why not study the technique of the greatest winner of friends the world has ever known? Who is he? You may meet him tomorrow coming down the street. When you get within ten feet of him, he will begin to wag his tail. If you stop and pat him, he will almost jump out of his skin to show you how much he likes you. And you know that behind this show of affection on his part, there are no ulterior motives: he doesn't want to sell you any real estate, and he doesn't want to marry you.

—Dale Carnegie
How to Win Friends and Influence People

It's all very nice to talk about the importance of self-esteem in influencing other people, but what about *techniques?* Even if you don't like yourself very much, wouldn't you think there are guidelines that will give you power to make other people do what you want?

Perhaps there are, but as I sat down to write this chapter, I had trouble thinking of any that seemed important. Not only that, but I had trouble figuring out why I was having trouble. I tried a dozen tricks to get the chapter rolling, but none of them seemed to work. Finally, I decided to start by confessing to myself that I was having a lot of trouble. That broke the dam, and the chapter you are reading is the result.

ALWAYS BE SINCERE (WHETHER YOU MEAN IT OR NOT)

While searching for ideas for this chapter, I took a look at Dale Carnegie's *How to Win Friends and Influence People.* Undoubtedly the most popular self-help book of all time, it has been a best seller for more than forty years, spawning dozens of less successful imitations. What better place to turn for inspiration?

There was a copy of the book in our house when I was ten years old. At that age, I read everything in the house, so I read it. I wasn't impressed. Not only wasn't I impressed, but I was utterly disgusted. For forty years, I gratuitously expressed my contempt when anyone even mentioned Dale Carnegie or his book.

A few years ago, while holed up in a hunting lodge near the Rawah Wilderness of Colorado, waiting out a three-day rainstorm, I found a battered copy of *How to Win Friends and Influence People.* I decided it would be amusing to read it as a measure of how I had changed in forty years.

Eager for some quick results, I turned immediately to the lists of principles that summarize sections of the book. When I saw rules such as "Smile" or "Make the other person feel important—and do it sincerely," I became violently angry.

Why become angry? Those rules reminded me of a rule I was supposed to learn from the greatest hypocrite I've ever known:

Always be sincere (whether you mean it or not).

To me, people who learn to win friends or influence other people through memorized rules are practicing the lowest form of hypocritical deception, and I want nothing to do with them. The second worst thing in the world for me was to read a book that taught such rules. The worst thing, of course, would be to *write* such a book.

SURVIVAL RULES

I was so angry, I almost put the book down for another forty years; but since it was the only book in the lodge, I persisted. I'm glad I did.

What changed my mind was reading the book from the front, as the author had intended. The first thing I noticed was that regardless of the motives of his 15,000,000 readers, Carnegie himself was obviously sincere. Even though he never met me, he gave me the feeling that he really did want to help me win friends and influence people.

Apparently something in me had changed in forty years, because I didn't feel that way when I was ten years old. By the time I was ten, I had developed a powerful rule that said,

Don't trust people who say they want to help you.

Where did the rule come from? I don't know exactly, but I'm surprised I had such a rule. As we saw in Chapter 10 when we analyzed the dynamics of an interaction, everyone has some rules for dealing with other people. Some of these "survival rules" are learned explicitly when we are adults, like what sort of suit to wear if you're a banker, or whom to salute if you're a soldier. But most of our survival rules stem from an early age, some so early that we cannot remember learning them explicitly.

Rules come from a time when our survival really did depend on interacting properly, and so they are accompanied by strong emotions. And because they derive from a time when we weren't terribly conscious of the way the world worked, we tend to think of them not as *learned* rules, but as universal truths. Thus, it's easy to understand why I had another rule that said,

Beware of anybody who tries to teach you universal truths.

This rule was the source of much of the anger that interfered with my acceptance of Dale Carnegie's leadership.

META-RULES

A problem-solving leader is concerned with rules because they exert a strong influence on the flow of ideas. If you are trying to motivate someone to work in a new way, and that person has a rule about suspecting people in authority, you are going to run into trouble. Understanding about rules will help you figure out how to reach that person.

Certain rules are doubly important, like my rule that says to beware of anybody who tries to teach you universal truths. It's doubly important because it is a rule about rules, or a *meta-rule*. Meta-rules *control the flow of ideas about rules,* and thus determine how readily we can *learn* new rules, or unlearn old ones. Therefore, the meta-rules determine how easily we can change the way we interact with others.

By age ten, I was already in the grips of my meta-rule, so I never took well to Dale Carnegie's book, or his workshops, or to anybody else's books or workshops that deal with human interaction. Before I could change the way I interacted with other people, I had to learn how to unearth my survival rules and my meta-rules, and how to transform them—if I wanted to.

Survival rules can change even when we don't work on them explicitly, but without this explicit knowledge, the change can take an unbearably long time. It took me close to forty years to modify my rule that said,

Don't trust people who say they want to help you.

Long experience with other people gradually transformed this rule into,

You can trust some people who say they want to help you, because even if you trust someone by mistake, you can probably take care of yourself and survive.

This new rule allowed me to continue reading Dale Carnegie.

TRANSFORMING RULES INTO GUIDES

Suppose you have recently been promoted to lead a group of computer programmers. You think you're doing rather well until a survey conducted by management shows that the people in your group think you are "overbearing," "interfering," and that you "can't delegate a task." You are hurt and angry, and say to yourself, "I'm just trying to be helpful."

You could talk to the group members and explain to them that you're just trying to be helpful, but you realize that they could also interpret this as more interference. Perhaps there's something you can do about yourself. Perhaps your hurt and anger means that you are touching on some sort of deep survival rule that requires you to inflict help on people. This survival rule seems to be blocking you from being an effective leader, so you don't want to wait forty years for it to transform itself. Instead, you can apply a step-by-step transformation to produce a more effective version, a *guide* rather than a rule.

Step 1: State the rule clearly and explicitly.

> For certain men, this might be,

> I must help all women.

For other people, it might be,

> I must help all young people.

Let's suppose that your rule is,

> I must always help everybody.

This statement becomes the starting point for the transformation.

Step 2: Acknowledge the rule's survival value and strike a bargain with your unconscious mind.

Once you've stated the rule, "I must always help everybody," your first impulse might be to try to get rid of it, but even if you could do this, it would be a serious mistake. Let's see why.

For every rule, there is a reason. When you can clearly and easily identify the reason, it's relatively easy to change the rule. For instance, I have a driving rule, "Keep to the right." When I rent a car in England or Australia, I have some difficulty changing that rule to, "Keep to the left." Because the survival value is obvious, however, I'm driving like a native in a few days.

You would think that changing sides of the road would be more demanding than changing some other survival rules because driving on the wrong side even some of the time could be deadly. For most behaviors, the penalties for a partial change aren't nearly that severe, yet many people defeat their attempts to change rules by applying a meta-rule:

> I must change all or nothing.

If the reason behind the rule is not clear, this meta-rule makes change too risky. The reason behind the rule may be buried in the past, at a time when it really did mean survival. We don't think explicitly, "If I don't help Mommy put away the toys, she won't love me and then I'll starve to death." All those childhood reasons have been lost in the fuzzy past, replaced only by the strong emotions surrounding them, like the fear that something terrible will happen if we don't help everybody all the time.

So instead of spending seven years in psychoanalysis to unearth the reason behind the rule, you can simply say to yourself, "This rule has been valuable in enabling me to survive, so I have no intention of getting rid of it. I will keep it around for use when the proper occasion arises. I may add some new rules, but the old one will still be there if I need it."

This new idea becomes part of your unconscious mind, which is constantly at work taking care of you. For example, it can drive the car for you while you are talking or thinking of something else. If you've ever had the experience of arriving at your destination without being consciously aware of driving there, you know that your unconscious can indeed hear and understand directions from your conscious mind. But it won't ever compromise on your safety.

As you go through a rule transformation, it's important that every step be as safe as possible; otherwise your unconscious mind will resist, for your own good. As you go through each step in this transformation, your unconscious probably won't talk to you in words, but your body will respond with feelings that tell you whether it's okay to proceed to the next step.

Step 3: Give yourself a choice.

Once your unconscious is assured that there is always a safe path back to the old rule, you are halfway to establishing the idea that the old rule was *your* own choice, so that applying it or not in any circumstance is also up to you. What this means is that you now can transform the statement of the rule from one of compulsion to choice. For instance, the rule,

I must always help everybody.

carries with it the implication of omnipotence, that it could in fact always be followed. To some people, this rule implies, "Since I must always help everybody, if I can't help somebody, something must be wrong with me."

In step 3, transform the rule from compulsion to choice:

I *can* always help everybody (if I choose to).

Step 4: Change from certainty to possibility.

As you go through the steps in the transformation of one rule, you'll often come upon some other rule implied by the first. Nobody is omnipotent, of course, nor can anyone expect to be, but some people have the rule,

I must always be perfectly effective.

If you have a "perfection" rule, you're not going to get past this step in the transformation of your "helping" rule. In that case, interrupt the process and start a new process on your "perfection" rule, or whatever other rule is blocking your progress.

Once the implicit rule of perfection is dealt with, the next step of the transformation changes from,

I *can* always help everybody (if I choose to).

to

I can *sometimes* help everybody (if I choose to).

Again, this statement raises the issue of perfection, which leads to the next step.

Step 5: Change the rule from totality to non-totality.

Nobody's perfect all the time, so get rid of the universals, changing the latest rule to,

I can sometimes help *some* others (if I choose to).

Once you've accomplished this much, you can proceed to the relatively benign task of deciding *which* people, and *when.*

Step 6: Change from general to particular.

The transformation up to this point has served to make you aware that you have choices, so be wary in case you have another rule, the third great obstacle to innovation, that says, "There is only one right way." You want to avoid replacing one rigid rule with another, so try to make sure you give at least three examples, as in

I can help other people *when* . . .

> they ask me clearly for help
> I have the skills to help them
> I have the resources to help them
> it fits me to help them
> I choose to help them
> I will be able to tolerate failure to help

Since I learned this method from Virginia Satir, I've gone through this particular transformation myself, and I've also assisted dozens of leaders to make it. The results have always been a reduction in the accusations of interference and an increase in the ability to delegate effectively. I've also applied the transformation method to many other survival rules that commonly stop leaders from being effective with other people. It almost always helps, but as powerful as this transformation method is, it's not flawless. We all have the ability to forget things.

I find it helpful, once the transformation is complete, to have the steps written down in my journal. Then, when I've had a chance to practice, I can come back to the journal and see how well I'm doing. This fulfills the promise I made to my unconscious, and acknowledges that I'm not perfect. I may find, for instance, that I want to revise one of the particular conditions, or clarify it.

For instance, after some experience, I may be able to further particularize the statement,

> It fits me to help them.

into

> The two of us can arrive at an open, explicit, and limited contract for help, and I feel good about the contract.

BECOMING GENUINELY INTERESTED IN OTHER PEOPLE

Another of Carnegie's principles is a simple one:

"Become genuinely interested in other people."

Without this genuine interest, any action, such as smiling, remembering the other person's name, or making the person feel important, will be mere hypocritical gimmicks. I realize now that by the time I was ten years old, I had developed a set of survival rules that prevented me from being genuinely interested in other people. When Carnegie said "Smile," I couldn't take it seriously. I knew what an insincere smile looked like, and I wanted no part of it. I didn't want to remember the name of someone I didn't like, nor listen to people talking about themselves, nor try to relate my conversation to their interests.

Most of all, I didn't want to make them feel important because deep down, I didn't feel very important myself. Carnegie concentrated on others, but as Virginia Satir says, "Self-worth is at the center of our whole existence." Dale Carnegie may have missed this point because he seems to have had a strongly developed and unquestioned view of his own self-worth. Also, he seems to have had a survival rule about "selfishness," as evidenced by his approving statement that the dog has no ulterior motives. I know that my dog Sweetheart loves me, but I have no illusions about her desire to coax a Milk-Bone out of me, if she can.

Many of us carry a meta-rule that says,

Don't be selfish.

Because of this meta-rule, we feel guilty if we take time to develop ourselves in any way, be it reading a magazine, exercising, transforming our survival rules, or even just thinking about a particular conversation. But to become a problem-solving leader—that is, to empower other people—we must be "selfish" in just these ways. As the psychiatrist Nathaniel Branden observed,

> If one looks at the history of human progress, at all the steps which have brought us from the cave to our present level of civilization, and of the genius, daring, courage, and creativity that made this progress possible—one cannot help be struck by the fact of how much we owe to those whose lives were primarily given over to the task of discovering and fulfilling their own "destiny"—the artists, the scientists, the philosophers, the inventors, the industrialists whose life path was clearly one of self-actualization (self-development, self-fulfillment).*

WHY AND WHEN YOU SHOULD READ DALE CARNEGIE

If you already have well-developed self-esteem, you can learn a great deal about being an effective motivator by reading *How to Win Friends and Influence People.* You can also use Carnegie's book as a test of self-esteem. If you react negatively, as I did at age ten, somewhere deep inside you have a survival rule that says, in one form or another,

I'm not worth much.

---

*N. Branden, *The Psychology of Romantic Love* (Los Angeles: J.P. Tarcher, Inc., 1980), pp. 55-56.

If you feel that way, it will show, just as it shows on a dog that has been whipped once too often.

Such a dog doesn't greet you the way Carnegie describes. It doesn't love itself, and it has no particular reason to love human beings. So even if it makes a feeble attempt to charm you with its doggy wiles, you're not too inclined to give it a Milk-Bone. Some people will give a Milk-Bone to a whipped dog, out of pity, but is that really the way you want to influence others?

If you want to learn to motivate others, the best way is to transform your survival rules that make you feel as worthless and powerless as a whipped dog. You might start by transforming "I'm not worth much" into a sensible guide, such as

I'm exactly as precious as every other human being.

It really works, without gimmicks.

CHAPTER 13: QUESTIONS

1. Use your journal as a place for recording your survival rules as you become aware of them. Identify one of your survival rules and transform it into a guide.

2. In attempting to do the previous exercise, did you encounter any meta-rule? If so, transform it into a meta-guide.

3. Read Dale Carnegie's *How to Win Friends and Influence People* and identify what rules turn up for you. Transform them into guides.

4. As a leader, you may find yourself wanting to help people transform their rules into guides. Before you get too far into this kind of helping, find a friend with whom you can exchange lists of rules, and help each other transform some of them into guides.

14

Where Power Comes From

Even in war moral power is to physical as three parts out of four.

—Napoleon

Many people find it difficult to accept the idea that influencing others is not a problem, once they have their own self-esteem in order. People who lack power tend to believe that if only someone else would give them some missing ingredient, a secret key, they would suddenly become powerful. This is a dangerous idea, mostly because it blinds them and blocks their road to increasing their influence. It may even cause them to lose what little power they have when they make some change in their life, like assuming a leadership position.

In this chapter, we'll explore some of the things a problem-solving leader needs to know about power, especially where it comes from and where it goes.

POWER AS A RELATIONSHIP

The origin of power is both controversial and slippery. Mao Tse-Tung said that *all* power comes from the barrel of a gun, but Napoleon estimated that only twenty-five percent does. In the absence of artillery, however, everyone seems to disagree on where power comes from.

I recall once walking out of a tedious planning meeting because I felt powerless to accomplish anything. After the meeting, the chairman confronted me in my office and accused me of irresponsible use of power. *He* would never have the nerve to stand up and leave a meeting, no matter what was happening. To him, my leaving meant I possessed unimaginable power, while to me it meant I was powerless. To me, his being appointed chairman meant he was obviously the one who had all the power.

We were both wrong, because we both thought power was something we "possess." Power is not a possession, but a *relationship*. I saw the chairman as powerful because of my relationship to the organization that had appointed him. I was *dependent* on the organization. It could take away my livelihood, so it must be powerful. The less dependent I was, the less powerful the organization would seem. I don't feel that the National Roller Derby Association is a powerful organization, but then I don't skate.

The chairman felt I was powerful because he *projected* his own situation onto me, as if I were a movie screen. When I acted in a way that would have required power from him, he concluded that I was a powerful person. If a *woman* had left the meeting in the same situation, he might have seen her as "weak." Instead of identifying with her personally, he might have used her as a screen upon which to project one of his female stereotypes.

POWER FROM TECHNOLOGY

Technical leaders have their own special view of power. I especially recall an argument when a group of us were having dinner before a movie. "Power comes from position," Austin argued for the tenth time. "Until my promotion, I couldn't make things happen in my organization."

"Not so," Kevan said, "Before I was promoted, I could really accomplish things because of my technical skill. Now I can't even use that."

"I disagree with both of you," said Inabelle. "Technical skill may help when you're down in the pits, but unless you have personal power, promotion into the supervisory ranks won't do anything."

"Listen," I interrupted, "I'm going to use some of my personal power to call a time out. If we don't hurry, we'll be late for the movie."

The movie was *E.T.*, the tale of one extraterrestrial's encounter with Earthlings. As the movie began, I couldn't get my mind off the subject of power, which must have influenced the way I saw E.T.'s predicament. When his spaceship makes a hasty departure from Earth, E.T. is accidentally left behind, the perfect symbol of powerlessness.

E.T. is naked. He has no tools. He's lost in an alien environment light-years from home. All this is bad enough, but people won't leave him alone. The entire United States government is determined to capture E.T. so he can be dissected like a laboratory frog. And so the plot is set: a power struggle between the greatest nation on Earth and one lost, naked, strange-looking small creature.

E.T. is not a suspense movie. Right from the beginning, I was willing to bet my astrogator that the government never had a chance. I knew that, and every kid in the audience knew that. What made the movie so much fun was that nobody in the government knew that.

After the movie, we discussed the suspense angle. Austin was perplexed. "How did you know E.T. would win? I thought the government had all the power."

"Not against E.T.'s personal power," Inabelle replied.

"Not personal power," Kevan corrected. "E.T. had a superior technology."

"Personal power? Technology? I'd call it magic! It was unrealistic."

"Not unrealistic," I said, "merely unrecognizable."

"What do you mean?"

"It's called Clarke's Third Law: Any sufficiently advanced technology is indistinguishable from magic."

Kevan interrupted with a clarification. "It's just like managers and programmers. To my manager, my technical work is pure magic."

"Well, it works the other way, too," Austin defended. "We managers have lots of organizational power, which you programmers don't understand. We can mobilize resources to get things done. And don't you underestimate it!"

"Aw, you sound just like those bureaucrats in the movie."

"No name calling," I refereed. "Austin and his managers are frustrated because the programmers don't play by the rules of the game—their power game. The programmers aren't in a power struggle, they just want to write programs. E.T. is not in a power struggle, he just wants to go home. Once E.T. decides he has to go home, the government is powerless."

"But where does programmer power come from?" Austin wanted to know.

I explained that Victor Hugo once said that nothing in this world was so powerful as an idea whose time has come. In our time, the idea is technology, especially information processing technology. The programmer partakes of this technology power, in much the same way that E.T. tapped into some mysterious life force. The only difference is that E.T. knew what he was doing, while programmers usually do it unconsciously. The typical programmer takes technology power for granted—until it disappears.

"Like when they become managers," Kevan said, "and their brains go soft."

"Kevan, I think your view of power is too simplistic to let you understand why programmers often lose power when they decide to accept supervisory positions—'positions of power.' " I then proceeded to explain to them about power as a relationship.

EXPERTISE AS POWER

Kevan wasn't happy with this. "That sounds too abstract for me. You guys just don't want to admit that an expert programmer like me possesses something that you don't have."

"You do possess something, but it's *expertise*, not power. Any power you get from that expertise is based on a relationship between you and someone else. If you were the leader of a mountain-climbing team, your programming expertise would contribute no power whatsoever."

"But I'm not the leader of a mountain-climbing team. I'm the leader of a programming team, so my expertise *is* power."

"It may be, for your particular team, but it doesn't have to be for all teams. It all depends on the relationship of the leader to the other members of the team."

"Give me a for instance."

"Let me try," said Austin. "If your whole team consists of novice programmers, your expertise will give you considerable power; but if the other team members are also experts, they will attach less importance to your technical expertise. In that case, they'll pay more attention to organizational power, like the power to acquire an extra terminal, to extend the schedule, or to capture a more interesting assignment."

"I may owe you an apology, Austin. I'm beginning to see how we can both be right at the same time, but it sure is puzzling."

"The idea of power always seems to have this puzzling aspect," I said, "because people aren't used to thinking in terms of relationships."

"Like when I was promoted from team member to team leader? I definitely experienced a loss of power, which is why I came on so strong against Austin's argument."

"Exactly. Your expertise didn't change, but it no longer counted for so much because other people's expectations changed."

Kevan laughed. "You know, I really struggled to demonstrate to the team that my technical skill hadn't diminished, but all I did was convince them that I was a weak leader."

"Of course," said Inabelle. "If you really have power, you don't have to struggle to show it. That's what personal power is all about."

"Well," said Austin, "if that's what happens when we try to acquire power, how are we supposed to go about it?"

"Listen," said Kevan. "I don't care about acquiring power, but I don't want to lose what power I have. How can I get more responsibility without losing my power to get things done?"

KEEPING POWER

"Inabelle is on the right track," I said. "The first step in keeping power is to stop trying so hard to hang onto it."

"You always talk in paradoxes."

"It's not a paradox. It follows directly from the idea of power as a relationship. The desire for power is not a desire for a thing, but for a relationship . . ."

". . . and you don't keep or build relationships the same way you keep or build things!" Inabelle added.

"Exactly. Suppose you want something, but you haven't figured out what it is. You think you're dissatisfied because you don't have the power to get what you want, but the problem is that you can't visualize what you *really* want."

"So as long as I'm blinded by this illusion, I'm in danger of losing power whenever something changes?"

"If you don't know what you want, power is as useless to you as a Ferrari to a blind driver. You might accidentally steer along the track, but you'll probably crash somewhere."

"So if I concentrate specifically on what I want, power will come to me?"

"Not necessarily. I can see perfectly well, but I'd probably crash a Ferrari. Seeing clearly is necessary, but even when you see clearly, you may not be able to prevent the loss of power."

"Then what else do I have to do?"

"As long as you keep asking that, you're too blind to understand the answer. If you're seeking a promotion in order to obtain more power, forget it! Step away from the lure of power and learn more about yourself."

"That's what I meant by personal power," Inabelle said.

"That makes sense to me, now," said Kevan. "When I accepted a promotion, I really had no idea why I did it, but I sure was flattered by the idea of being made powerful."

"So when you see a chance for power, ask yourself what you want power *for.* If you don't know that, you're sure to falter and lose your way when your old power starts to crumble, as it must before your new power starts to grow."

Inabelle smiled. "That reminds me of E.T. He didn't want power, but because he knew what he really wanted, he beat the 'powerful' at their own game."

"I didn't understand the movie," Austin complained, "so that really isn't very helpful."

"Well," I said, giving it one last try, "E.T. really wanted to go home. What do you really want?"

CHAPTER 14: QUESTIONS

1. When you play games, how much are you interested in the score and how much in the play? When it is a team game, how much are you interested in the team's performance and how much in your own statistics? How does this affect your power to influence the outcome of the game? What about when you work in a group?

2. What is your principal source of power at work? What relationships is that power based on?

3. What power are you now trying to hang onto? What is the worst thing that might happen if you let go? the best thing?

4. What would you do if you won five million dollars in a lottery? What keeps you from doing it without the money?

5. When was the last time you gave away some power? What happened?

6. When was the last time you had the power to do something, but withheld it? What happened?

15

Power, Imperfection, and Congruence

A mature person is one who, having attained his majority, is able to make choices and decisions based on accurate perceptions about himself, others, and the context in which he finds himself; who acknowledges these choices and decisions as being his; and who accepts responsibility for their outcomes.

—Virginia Satir
Peoplemaking

The chief assumption underlying my own approach to personal power is that *everyone wants to feel useful, to make a contribution,* which of course derives from the seed model. Many of us know people who make this a difficult assumption to hold because they seem apathetic, uncooperative, or even destructive. If everyone wants so intensely to do good, how can so many people be doing such a miserable job?

Even worse, if *I* want so intensely to do good, why do *I* so frequently fail so miserably? Why do I say the wrong thing and think of the right thing two hours later? Why do I say the right thing at precisely the wrong moment? Where's all this personal power in *me* when I feel so inept?

A MECHANICAL PROBLEM

We know that low self-esteem underlies so many of these problems, but the relationship between the problem and the low self-esteem is not always easy to perceive. Many problems are *mechanical* problems, which don't appear to have anything to do with self-esteem at all. What I mean by a *mechanical* problem is one that may seem deep and complex, but turns out to be solved by something technical, a gimmick, with no great emotional or psychological turmoil.

The solutions to mechanical problems are more likely to involve physics than psychology. We all tend to solve problems using the type of solution we know best, which is why technical leaders tend to see the mechanical side of problems. For instance, when programmers are having a problem, their first attempt to solve it will almost always involve writing a program. Let me give an example.

When I wrote *The Psychology of Computer Programming,* I told the story of a young programmer who smelled so bad that other people refused to work with him. Over the years, I've received more letters about that story than anything else I've ever written. The typical letter says, "How did you know? Ralph works for me, and everyone is threatening to quit if I don't do something about his body odor. What should I do?"

On the surface, this seems to be a simple mechanical problem with a simple mechanical solution, like soap and water. To programmers, the first solution lies in a different direction: Design the software so that

Ralph's program connects in a minimal way with the other programs. That way, Ralph connects in a minimal way with the other programmers—a neat, mechanical solution.

Unfortunately, program logic doesn't always allow such a clean solution, which is why the programmers are eventually driven to complain to their manager. But the manager has access to a mechanical solution, too: soap and water. Just say to Ralph, "Several people in your group have told me that they get sick working near you because of the odor given off by your body. We like your work, but obviously we can't be a productive group if other people can't work with you. What can we do to solve this problem?" If the problem is so mechanical, why doesn't the manager do this? In fact, it's not even clear why the *manager* writes to me. Why don't the co-workers do this?

First, they are all embarrassed for Ralph because they identify with his situation. What if it were *me* who smelled like that? Well, what if it were? Does your value as a human being drop if your smell is not attractive to other people? Only if your self-esteem is low. Otherwise, you'll appreciate hearing the information, be sorry that you weren't aware sooner, and then do something about the situation.

In the one case where the manager took my advice and told the programmer directly, the programmer did just as I predicted. It turned out that his hobby involved tanning leather. The chemicals he used gave his hands a sickening smell—sickening, that is, to other people. He worked with the smell all the time and simply wasn't aware of it. He was grateful that his manager made him aware, and visited his physician, who prescribed a pill that changed the way his skin reacted to the chemicals—a mechanical solution if there ever was one.

Another reason programmers can't deal with this problem directly is that they just can't face what might happen if Ralph should react badly. They know that people do sometimes react badly if told an unpleasant truth about themselves. What they don't know is that this bad reaction emanates from a person's low self-esteem. If Ralph gets angry in response to information given out of genuine caring, it's not their problem. How can Ralph's anger harm them worse than the present situation? Would they prefer that he be fired, without knowing the reason, just to preserve their own minuscule self-esteem?

MATURE PATTERNS OF BEHAVIOR

Why is Ralph's mechanical problem so hard to handle? Once again, such problems are not caused by the event—the mechanical part—but by the reaction to the event. Using some patterns of behavior, we can make the event into a problem. Using others, we can make the problem disappear. The choice, as the saying goes, it to be part of the problem or part of the solution.

Behavior patterns that are part of the problem are called *dysfunctional* and characterize the immature person, with low personal power. Behavior patterns that are part of the solution are called *functional* and characterize the mature person, with high personal power. Of course, these are simplifications, because no person is equally functional in all problem situations. I've learned to deal rather effectively with the smelly programmer problem, but when a spider crawls up my pant leg, I'm not the model of maturity. Maturity is, rather, a statistical collection of behaviors, behaviors we can improve a little at a time.

Virginia Satir has composed a list of behaviors that help a person "deal in a relatively competent and precise way with the world." She says that such persons will

a.   be clear when they deal with others.

b.   be aware of their own thoughts and feelings.

c.   be able to see and hear what is outside themselves.

d.   behave toward other people as separate from themselves and unique.

e.   treat differentness as an opportunity to learn and explore rather than as a threat or a signal for conflict.

f.   deal with persons and situations in their context, in terms of how it is rather than how they wish it were or expect it to be.

g.   accept responsibility for what they feel, think, hear, and see, rather than denying it or attributing it to others.

h.   have open techniques for giving, receiving, and checking meaning with others.

This description of maturity emphasizes social and communication skills, which is why gimmicks are not terribly important. If you have these social and communication skills, you will soon invent or copy all the gimmicks you need. Let's see how that works in the case of the smelly programmer.

DEALING WITH YOUR OWN MECHANICAL PROBLEMS

First, suppose *you* are Ralph. You have all these social and communication skills, but you tan leather and can't smell your own hands. You would notice that other people were acting peculiarly toward you (c), and you would be able to check with others about what was going on (h). Because you would be acting in a straight, clear manner (a), without judgment of their reactions (f), chances are they would not be afraid to give you the reliable information you need but cannot obtain through your own nose. Once you have that information, you will be able to take responsibility for dealing with it, rather than blaming the others for not loving you sufficiently to put up with your odor (g).

Second, suppose you were *subjected* to Ralph's odor. You would see that Ralph was not you (d) and not a threat to you (e). You would be able to give him information in a manner that would likely be heard (h), and heard without accusation (f), so it would likely be acted upon.

Clearly, the presence of even a single mature person greatly increases the chance of a rapid, clean, and humane solution to this problem and others like it. In other words, the first step in creating a problem-solving environment is to work on your own maturity, but this can't be accomplished through gimmicks. Having a pleasant body odor is, in one sense, a communication gimmick. Many books on power and influence inform you of the importance of personal grooming. These books are correct, but how useful are they to the would-be leader? If you don't have a sense of your own self-worth and the more general social and communication skills, all the deodorant and perfume in Macy's won't hide your deficiency. If you do have them, you'll figure out soon enough everything you need to know about grooming.

For instance, a few years ago a client told me that even though I seemed happy underneath, I didn't smile enough, which made some people feel that I might be angry. I immediately realized that the sour expression on my face was a habit, left over from the days when I didn't like myself or others. I had changed my opinion of myself and humanity, but hadn't informed my face. So I worked on the problem, and now my smiles are a lot more congruent with my inner feelings— that is, I am more clear in dealing with others. My client's maturity made it possible for her to tell me clearly and without fear that she knew I was really happy, though not showing it for some reason. This in turn made it possible for me to increase my maturity—an example of the effect of her personal power.

Remembering to smile when you feel happy inside is a mechanical problem, like taking care of a bad odor on your hands. When I say I "worked a bit on the problem," I mean that I employed mechanical devices to help me remember what to do, just as the tanner might to remind himself to take his anti-smell pill. For example, I put a bandage on my thumb, and whenever I noticed myself fiddling with it, I remembered to be happy and smile because I wasn't actually wounded. Soon I reached the point where seeing a bandage on anybody reminded me to smile, and soon I was smiling at the sight of razor nicks on men's faces and women's legs. After a while, the smiling habit had replaced the frowning habit in seventy-five percent of the cases, and I could dispense with the gimmicks.

I must always be natural and spontaneous

While I was becoming more successful at remembering to smile, I felt a shadow over my successes. Eventually I tracked down this shadow to a rule:

> In dealing with other people, I must always be natural and spontaneous.

When applied to changing my interactive behavior, this rule became a crippling meta-rule. Whenever I would practice some gimmick to improve my interactions, I felt that I was insincere, wrong, and just plain bad. The rule was so powerful it often blocked me even from *thinking* about what I was doing when interacting with other people.

I acknowledged that this rule had survival value, and started to transform it:

> In dealing with other people, I *can* always be natural and spontaneous.

But when I tried to change this to

> In dealing with other people, I can *sometimes* be natural and spontaneous, if I choose to.

I didn't feel right about the transformation. I knew that I *could* always be natural (you may not be able to do anything else, but *everyone* can be natural). And that's the choice I *wanted* to make, always. So I was stuck.

I discussed this feeling with Susan, who works with little kids. When I said that I felt dishonest to practice smiling, she smiled and said, "What makes you think that it's *natural* to frown when you feel smiley inside?"

"It must be natural," I replied, "because I do it spontaneously."

"You also speak English spontaneously, but you certainly learned how to do that. I think you learned how to frown, too. You're confusing 'natural' with 'learned early in life, before I was aware of it.' In fact, what you learned was to be *unnatural*, because the natural thing is to be *congruent*, to show on the outside what's truly going on inside."

Susan's clue got my transformation back on track. I hadn't done the first step properly. I had failed to start with a clear statement of the rule, so I began again with

In dealing with other people, I must always be congruent.

I readily transformed this rule into the following guide:

In dealing with other people, I want to be as congruent as I can, which I can achieve by transforming old rules, and modifying habits I learned early in life, into rules and habits more congruent with the person I am today, and the person I want to be tomorrow.

This transformation felt terrific.

I must always be perfectly effective

Having learned that I want to be congruent, rather than spontaneous, I made rapid progress in learning to smile when I felt like smiling—until I reached a plateau at about seventy-five percent. I knew better, but I failed to *do* better. My old rule,

I must always be perfectly effective.

was making me feel very, very bad every time I forgot to show my interior smile.

With the help of some friends, I succeeded in relating this rule to the threat/reward model. The threat/reward model says that in any transaction I must be either a winner or a loser. If I fail to be perfectly effective, then I obviously can't be a winner so I must be a loser. And I felt like a loser.

The seed model is a choice model. It's true that I can choose to feel like a winner or a loser, but I also have a third choice: to feel like a *learner*. Even if I feel like a loser, I can also feel like a learner.

When problem definitions differ, learning is almost impossible. The only way I know to arrive at clear, common definitions is to concentrate on controlling the quality of communication. As always, the only leverage I have is on myself, but quality breeds quality. If my communications are of high quality, I'll receive high-quality communications—from which I can learn to do even better.

When I'm able to be congruent, then even if the communication is bungled, I'll have more reliable information to use in learning how to do it better the next time. Suppose I start a difficult interaction with Rod by shouting, "We would be on schedule if it weren't for your malingering? Why don't you get your act together?" When Rod shouts back at me, or clams up, I have no way of knowing whether he's reacting to the form or the content of my message. The interaction doesn't come out well, but I don't know whether it's Rod or me.

Suppose I start the same interaction with the more congruent statement, "I feel angry because we're not getting the job done on time, and I don't know why it's happening. When I look around for reasons, I notice that you've been absent six times this month. Do you feel that your absence is contributing to the schedule problem? Or is there something else?"

Rod now has an accurate problem statement to work with. Suppose the reply is "Gee, I didn't know we were having a schedule problem. Don't we have until next Friday?" Now you have several opportunities to clear up crossed wires.

But if Rod shouts back, or clams up, then I have a better idea that the problem does lie somewhere within him, not within me or my interaction with him. I could still be wrong—I may not have been as congruent as I thought—but I'm off to a better start.

THE PAYOFF FOR BEING CONGRUENT

As with any communication skill, being congruent is not something you ever learn one-hundred percent. But the payoff is so great, you don't have to be perfect. Even if one person manages to act once in a congruent manner when the rest of the group is acting in a twisted way, the results can be worth a thousand failures.

Many years ago, when I was teaching at the IBM Systems Research Institute in New York, several faculty members complained about a student who was "trying to get away with something." Steve, a student from Kansas, had failed to turn in any of his assignments for several weeks, and the outraged faculty members proposed sending him home. Steve wasn't in any of my classes, so I didn't get quite so emotional about the situation. When I suggested that perhaps we didn't understand the problem, I was forcefully reminded that all of the students had been carefully selected from among IBM's elite employees. Steve could certainly do the work, if only he was motivated.

Even so, I argued, sending him home would probably destroy his career, so we should be doubly sure that we understood the circumstances. They reluctantly agreed to allow me to speak with him, but I was to be his last chance. After an hour with him in my office, I felt we were getting nowhere. I thought I started out in a congruent fashion by asking Steve, "What's going on? Can you explain why you're not doing your work?" but Steve denied that there was any problem.

I noticed, however, that Steve didn't *look* like there was no problem. He sat stiffly in his chair, and couldn't seem to look me in the eye. I began to convince myself that he had something to hide, and that it wasn't something honorable. I was about to start accusing him of dishonesty when I realized that I was making inferences about what was inside him, rather than making statements about what was inside of me.

So I decided to try restarting the conversation on a more congruent note. "Steve," I said, "I'm sitting here getting angrier and angrier because I feel I'm trying to help you and you won't even talk to me about what's going on. You're telling me that there's no problem, but to me it seems that there is a problem. The other faculty members want to throw you out of the Institute and send you home. If that happens, you'll probably lose your job. To me that sounds like a serious problem, but you say it isn't. What am I missing that I need to help you?"

At this point, Steve's appearance changed from stiff avoidance to violent anger. He looked me in the eye and shouted, "Who the hell do you think you are? What makes you think you can help me? You think you're so big and powerful, but you're nobody! Nobody!" Then he stopped talking and turned away.

My first—my "natural"—impulse was to shout back at him, but somehow I realized that he was in terrible pain. Even though I didn't know what the pain was, I overcame my "natural" training, said nothing, and reached out and laid my hand gently on his arm.

Suddenly, he started shaking all over, then sobbing and uttering incomprehensible words. I sat there, my hand on his arm, until he recovered himself sufficiently to talk. Then he told me the whole story.

A week before he left for the Institute, Steve's wife had been diagnosed as having terminal cancer. She wasn't expected to live more than six months. He naturally decided he would not attend the Institute, but she insisted that he go, arguing that he would hurt his career by refusing this opportunity. After she was gone, he would be the sole support for their three children, so it was doubly important that he do well in his work.

To me, it was easy to see that he had made the wrong decision, but blinded by grief and unable to go against her expressed wishes, Steve went to school in New York. Under the circumstances, the homework assignments looked meaningless, and Steve couldn't bring himself to do anything but sit in his hotel room and weep. He was afraid to tell anyone, so his teachers assumed the worst.

When Steve attacked me for assuming I could help, he was exactly correct. There was no way in the world I could help his wife recover from cancer, which was a problem infinitely greater than his school-work. Had I not resisted my "natural" instinct to attack him when he attacked me, the whole story might have been an even greater tragedy. I couldn't help with his wife's cancer, but I could help him deal with his wife's cancer in a less destructive way.

Once the circumstances were understood, IBM arranged to send Steve home to Kansas, giving him a leave to be with his wife in her final days. A year later, he was able to return to the Institute and make a fresh start. You may have to succeed one hundred percent of the time to be perfect, but you don't have to succeed one hundred percent of the time to be powerful.

CHAPTER 15: QUESTIONS

1. Recall a situation when you knew what to do but forgot to do it. What was missing that might have made you remember at the right time?

2. Recall a situation when you didn't know what to do. What did you do? What would you do now if the situation arose when you didn't know what to do?

3. Think of a problem you're having because of another person's mechanical problem. Why can't you face it? What's the worst that can happen? Face it!

4. Recall how you felt in some group when you couldn't make a contribution.

5. What messages do you give yourself when you fail at something? What rules are behind those messages?

6. Recall a recent power transaction when you "lost." What did you learn from that transaction? What can you learn now by reviewing it in a new light?

7. What things are going on inside you that don't usually show on the outside? How can you change that? Do you *want* to change that?

8. What things are going on inside you that you're *trying* not to show? How do you know it's working? What would happen if you put that energy into something else?

Part Four
ORGANIZATION

Organization is usually the last component of the MOI model to be mastered by upcoming technical leaders. Innovators themselves, and capable of motivating others by example, technical leaders often regard organization as superfluous, or not quite nice to think about. They are quite blind to the role of organization in problem-solving success, so they stumble helplessly when organizational problems arise.

In the following chapters, we'll look at why organizational power is important, what can be done to convert existing power to organizational power, and how to learn to be an effective organizer.

16

Gaining Organizational Power

Indeed, if the mentality of the scholars of the various countries, as revealed by the recent war, often appears to be on a lower level than that of the less cultured masses, it is because there is a danger inherent in all power that is not disciplined and directed toward the higher aims which alone are worthy of it.

—Marie Curie
"Intellectual Cooperation"

Much of the ability to help other people arises from personal power, but it would be naive to assert that nothing else is required. In large organizations, there are many resources available to a leader— money to pay for training, support staff, office space, tools to make work more efficient, access to helpful people. Such resources are not evenly distributed, and one of the requirements for becoming a problem-solving leader is to acquire organizational power so as to obtain resources for other innovators.

Most innovators who move into leadership positions know little or nothing about organizational power. They face competitors who may lack technical talent but have more experience obtaining scarce resources for their people. Thus, the new leader needs new powers just when technical power is about to slip away. Since technical power doesn't disappear instantly, there may still be time to trade other goodies, if the new leader understands about *power conversion.*

CONVERTING POWER

I first learned about power conversion when interviewing Edrie, the top woman engineer at Faultless Computers. So she wouldn't be interrupted by phone calls, we were working at a table in the corner of the cafeteria. Unfortunately, Atwood from Personnel overheard part of the interview and invited himself to join us. While Atwood was getting his coffee, Edrie tried to console me. "Think of it this way. In the time it takes to drink a cup of coffee, you'll get the official view of a personnel professional. You'll see, Atwood will be only too happy to have an audience."

"But I don't want to waste more of your time," I apologized.

"Don't worry. If I didn't think I'd get some useful information about company policies out of Atwood, I wouldn't have let him join us."

When Atwood returned, I asked him what Faultless looks for in their leaders.

"Of course," he said, "many leadership qualities are intangible, but we can pick good leaders with high accuracy based on their experience."

"Really?" I said. "What kinds of experience are you looking for?"

"Well, it doesn't have to be any particular job experience. For instance, if a man is married, and possibly a father, he'll generally make a better leader than someone who isn't."

"Oh," said Edrie. "Then women who are mothers must really be good leaders, since the mother is usually the one who does all the work."

"I'm afraid I haven't much experience with mothers as leaders. You know that we have nothing against competent unmarried women like yourself, but *naturally* we have nothing to do with unmarried mothers. And we don't hire too many married women."

Edrie was seething, but didn't seem to want to speak, so I continued. "Why do you think fathers are such good leadership material? Because they have so much experience conning mothers into doing all the work with the kids?"

"I hardly think so. . . . Oh, I see, it's a joke. No, I'm afraid I can't tell you just what it is about fatherhood that makes a man a good leader. I'm a bachelor myself."

"Do you have many kids?"

"Well, *really* . . . oh, is that another joke? I certainly hope it is a joke."

Atwood and I didn't seem to be on the same wavelength, and Edrie wasn't even tuned in. After a long heavy silence, Atwood pleaded pressing business down in Personnel and excused himself. "Alone at last," I said, knowing Edrie appreciated my jokes. But she just stared at the empty doorway.

"Edrie? Are you there?"

"Oh, sorry. I was thinking about what Atwood said."

"About fathers making better leaders? Don't worry about it—I'm sure he's all wet."

"No, he's probably right."

"That surprises me, coming from an ardent feminist. Why should fatherhood increase leadership ability?"

"That's easy. It's a matter of power conversion."

"Power conversion?"

"Yes, you know. The ability to convert one form of power into another that you value more. Like converting water power from a stream into electric power to light your house."

"What does that have to do with married men being better leaders?"

"Well, in this country, married men have an advantage over single men. They have power over a woman, which they convert into services that support them in their work. Single men have much more work to do just taking care of themselves, so they are at a disadvantage."

"Yes, but those traditional married men have the burden of supporting their wives, don't they?"

"That burden is usually much less than the cost of obtaining the same services on the open market. So the married man converts a small part of his money power along with a large part of his traditional male dominance power into time and other services that help him advance in his career."

"So that's what you mean by power conversion: You use power you have in one form to gain power in some other form you want more."

"Exactly."

"A lot of men would see it differently. They would say that the married woman is converting her sexual power over the man into money power—a guaranteed lifetime of support."

"It's hardly a guarantee these days," corrected Edrie, "but, yes, some women see it that way, too. There's no contradiction in both people using power at the same time and converting it into something they both want more."

Edrie's examples of power conversion

I asked Edrie if she could give me other examples of power conversion from her own career.

"Sure, dozens. From the moment I was born, I converted my parents' love for me into their support for my proper upbringing, which helped me to become an engineer."

"There's nothing wrong with that, is there?"

"No, not at all. I didn't say there was anything wrong with power conversion, though some conversions are looked on with disapproval."

"Like male power into money power?"

"Some people disapprove of that, yes. But even more disapprove of trading sexual power, say, for positional power in a company. That's why rumors about women engineers sleeping with their bosses are so harmful. The society in general disapproves of that particular power conversion."

"Did you suffer from rumors like that?"

"Not that I know of, but others have. My career has progressed steadily upward."

"You've been lucky."

"Not so much lucky as adept at converting what power I had into more useful forms. I mean I was lucky to be born bright, which I converted into scholarships—money power. More recently, I've done the reverse conversion—money power back to brain power."

Edrie explained that when she took our Problem-Solving Leadership Workshop, her manager had refused to pay her tuition or give her time off. She told him she'd pay for herself and use her vacation. Her manager knew that his manager would find out if she paid her own way, and that he would be called in to explain. He really didn't have any good reason for not paying, and the official company policy encourages attendance at courses like PSL, so he paid. She used the power of the company hierarchy to force her manager into paying.

"Nice going!" I said.

Edrie chuckled. "It's funny, isn't it, how everybody I tell admires that particular power conversion. But if I told them that my boss sent me to the class as a reward for sleeping with him. . . . "

"I guess you have to know the culture pretty well to play this game."

"It's not always so risky, but you do have to know what power you have. If I want to go to a workshop now, I can simply sign my own voucher. I can convert my own position power into more technical competence for myself, without anyone asking questions. But lots of people here can do that and never take advantage of it."

"Perhaps they have things they value more than the technical competence."

"Yes, a lot of them use their spending power to go to boondoggle meetings that may be fun, and may enhance their sense of importance. But I personally think they're wasting their position power on something that has no further conversion value."

Collecting points

"Maybe they're buying points with upper management."

"Ha! Don't talk to me about points. When I first came to work here, I was their token woman engineer. They kept giving me the unimportant assignments that none of the men would do. Then, when an important new assignment came along, my boss would tell me that I didn't have any experience working in critical situations. When I complained that I could never get out of that loop, my boss said I was accumulating points. After two years of that, I must have had a few million points, not counting interest."

"So what did you convert them into?"

"Nothing. Points don't convert. At least, I've never heard of an authenticated case of anyone converting points into anything useful. Points are just a fiction that people in power use to keep those below them doing stupid things. I know. I wasted two years collecting points."

"Well, if you couldn't convert your points, how did you get anything besides unimportant assignments?"

"When I finally realized how dumb I'd been, I took an inventory of what power I had to convert. I realized that if I had been working on something crucial, I could have threatened to quit and leave them holding the bag. I was pretty sure my only course was to quit and start again at another company."

"But I know you didn't quit. What happened?"

"It was our friend Atwood who gave me the idea, right here in this cafeteria. I asked him confidentially about the company policy on pay for accumulated vacation when you resign, and he went into a tizzy. It turns out that he was going to get into a lot of trouble over affirmative action if I quit, something I hadn't realized. So after thinking it over, I just went up to my boss and told him that if I didn't get a better assignment, I was going to resign."

"And you got it?"

"He tried to tell me there was nothing available right then, but that if I was patient, he would be sure to have something in a month or two."

"So you waited?"

"You must be kidding! Once I knew that I had all the power, I just insisted that if I didn't get it that day I was leaving. Then he 'remembered' something—a design job on our hottest project. *That's* power conversion at its finest."

"Yes, but at what cost? What if you had screwed up the assignment?"

"Oh, sure, if I couldn't do it, then I shouldn't have been there in the first place. Maybe they were keeping me around as their token woman engineer, but that's not why *I* wanted to be kept around. I wanted to be known as a *competent* engineer, not a *woman* engineer. The conversion only worked because *they* were playing that woman engineer game."

"Was that the same boss who tried to keep you out of PSL?"

"Yep."

"Well, I know you don't believe in points, but perhaps your conversion accumulated some *negative* points?"

"Oh, I *do* believe in negative points."

"Well, it sounds like you accumulated quite a few with your boss."

"True. But then they were all canceled when I converted all my technical competence and took his job!"

USING POWER

Ever since I met Edrie, I've used the concept of power conversion whenever I'm asked to help identify potential leaders among the technical rank and file. I first look for personal power, which can be converted into almost anything. Next, I look for power conversion experience, which can be translated from obtaining power for one's own use to obtaining power for the use of others. These things take a long time to learn, but they are needed immediately when one joins the ranks of appointed leaders. They are hard to teach, and some stars never learn to use them.

There are, of course, many other necessary attributes, like unselfishness. Studying Edrie's tale, you may get the impression that she used her power tactics to advance her own career. Such a person might not use this talent to help others. Once Edrie became a team leader, she did apply her personal power and power conversion skills to obtain resources for her team members, but not every new team leader makes this switch.

Some new team leaders merely continue to use their tactics to obtain what *they* need, not what their team members need. Some are foolish, some are selfish, but most don't yet understand the leader's role, to create an environment in which *everyone* is empowered. Only in that way can they discipline and direct their power toward higher aims.

CHAPTER 16: QUESTIONS

1. How many different kinds of power do you hold in your present environment? What are you doing to convert them into more usable forms?

2. What are you going to use it for?

3. How does your present environment support the things you are trying to accomplish? How can you convert it into one that will be more supportive?

4. How much power do you lose from your age, height, sex, skin color, language, religion, attractiveness, education, or personal habits? What can you do about it?

5. How many points do you hold with your boss? What do you expect to buy with them? When are you going to cash them in?

17

Effective Organization of Problem-Solving Teams

What is the best way to organize a team for solving problems? Rather than answer the question directly, I prefer to use an exercise to explore the question through simulation. Although the following exercise simulates decision making, the results apply equally well to any problem-solving task undertaken by a team. You may wish to try the exercise yourself before reading further.

Ranking World Records

Rank the measurements of the following items by size, as listed in the *1980 Guinness Book of World Records*. Use integers 1 through 10, once each, to rank the items, with the smallest measurement ranked 1 and the largest, 10.

_____   Tallest tree

_____   Longest banana split

_____   Tallest chimney

_____   Longest jellyfish

_____   Tallest fountain

_____   Largest Ferris wheel (diameter)

_____   Tallest mobile crane

_____   Longest Frisbee throw

_____   Tallest dam

_____   Longest bar (for selling drinks)

185

$\mathbf{W}$hen our workshops use this simulation, the same decision is made in several ways, so that we can compare different organizations that a team can use to solve problems: individually, by voting, with a strong appointed leader, and by consensus.

- *Individual:* The first step is to have every member of a team rank the ten items, working alone. These individual rankings provide a base line for later comparison with the various team rankings.

- *Voting:* Once the individuals on a team are finished, they take a vote, without discussion, to pool the team's knowledge in a second ranking. Voting without discussion is the simplest possible method of pooling information to make a common decision. It is a mechanical method, avoiding all psychological issues like differences in personal power.

    After the votes have been collected, each team organizes itself to solve the problem as a group. We assign a different organizational form to each team.

- *Strong leader:* One team form uses an appointed leader whose job is to listen to each team member's opinions, privately, and make the final ranking decision according to personal preference. (We labeled this form "strong leader.")

- *Consensus:* In the consensus form, everyone on the team must agree totally with the team's ranking.

A SPECTRUM OF ORGANIZATIONAL FORMS

Many other forms have been used, but these four—working individually, voting, strong leader, and consensus—form a good spectrum for discussion. When teams are allowed a free choice of organization, they generally adopt some form that can be analyzed as a combination of these forms.

Finally, after the team finishes ranking the ten items in their particular manner, all rankings are scored on a scale of 0 (random) to 100 (perfect). (At the end of this chapter are the correct rankings and a scoring procedure, in case you want to find out how well you did.)

Individual scores and voting

The individual scores provide a standard of comparison for the other organizational forms. If the group method cannot do better than the individuals working alone, then the best group method would obviously be to have the members work alone. The exercise is designed so that nobody will be an "expert" with perfect knowledge, but almost everybody will have some partial knowledge available for sharing.

In the voting, partial information from each participant flows into the "ballot box," a computer that tabulates the decision mechanically. No discussion is allowed, so this method measures information, rather than the influence of one persuasive member on the result. Voting almost invariably produces a ranking between the best and worst individual on the team. If we examine the *average* of the members' scores, voting usually improves this average by about ten points.

Under what circumstances would voting prove a good choice of organization? If predictable time is important, voting is a superior method, as long as people understand and accept the balloting procedure. Voting may be helpful if we need assurance that we won't make a really poor decision, but to obtain this assurance, we will generally sacrifice any possibility of obtaining a superior decision. In other words, voting can be a way of ensuring no worse than a mediocre-plus decision.

Voting may be preferred, for instance, over some kind of strong leader method when one or more of the following are true:

- politically, it wouldn't be a good idea to appoint one member over another
- we may not know in advance who is the best-informed person
- we may not know who would be the most effective leader
- we may fear and suspect coalitions that could sway an open discussion
- nobody is willing to take individual responsibility
- it is important to make everyone feel a part of the decision

Voting is a consistent method. It generally works better than a consensus decision if the consensus breaks down. It is superior to a strong leader if that leader is poorly informed, or when the leader is moderately informed but unable or unwilling to use information from other team members. On the other hand, voting almost certainly produces a worse decision than other strategies when a team works even moderately well.

Another drawback of voting is that no information flows from one member to another. After the decision process, people are just as well or as poorly informed as before. To the extent that the decision process is supposed to be educational for the participants, voting fails.

The strong leader

The strong leader structure may or may not teach the participants more than they knew when they started, depending on the leader's style. The quality of the decision also depends on a combination of the leader's style and knowledge. Leaders who resist changing their own opinion may do well if they are the most knowledgeable members of their team, but may do terribly if they are the least knowledgeable. With such stubborn leaders, we have seen team scores as low as 5 (when the leader's score was 3) and as high as 95 (when the leader's score was 90).

Less stubborn leaders can be influenced by information from the team members. They typically produce a pattern of scores that resembles the consensus scores, consistently higher than the voting score. Such leaders can have a personal score of 0 yet produce a team score of 85, and leaders with a personal score of 50 can produce a team score of 95. In some cases, however, the leaders allow themselves to be influenced against their own judgment. We once had a leader with a personal score of 88 who listened to some less knowledgeable teammates and produced a team score of 57.

Consensus

Our method of consensus requires that each group member agree with each item's ranking before it becomes part of the group decision. For people not experienced at consensus decision making, this method can at times be both time-consuming and frustrating. It appeals to problem-solving leaders, however, because it typically produces high-quality decisions. For this to happen, though, participants have to follow certain guidelines:

- Keep in mind that not every ranking need meet everyone's complete approval in every detail, but that every team member should agree in principle with each ranking.

- Avoid arguing for your own opinions, just because they are your own. Instead, back up every position you take with logic and facts.

- Avoid changing your mind *only* to avoid conflict. Encourage others to give you facts and logic on which you can base a change of opinion.

- Encourage others to use facts and logic before changing their minds.

- Avoid techniques designed to reduce conflict, such as voting, averaging, or trading votes. Use facts, no matter how insignificant they may seem.

- Consider differences of opinion as helpful, as long as they can be supported by fact or logic.

- Don't withhold information just to be nice.

- If necessary, use your intuition, but make clear that you're doing it. Intuition is a valid fact to add to an argument.

Once a group learns to work in this way, the consensus approach can produce very fine results. Typically in the exercise, consensus scores exceed their team average by thirty points or more.

Once in a while, though, the consensus process breaks down, producing a very poor score. In such cases, there is no actual consensus, but a lot of arguing, trading off, and backing down, just to get finished on time. When this happens, however, it's obvious to everyone. Some teams wisely decide to discard any decision that is made under such conditions, even if it means not completing the assignment. Decisions made under breakdown conditions will not only be faulty, but will not be accepted by everyone, and thus will be easily undermined.

One great potential advantage of the consensus approach is the sharing of information. Everyone hears what everyone else has to say and can ask questions. Participants learn about substantive matters and about each other, which is excellent preparation for future teamwork. Consensus teams may be slow when they first form, but tend to become superfast once team members get to know each other.

One reason for this improved performance is that consensus team members share responsibility for the work. Voting also shares responsibility, but in an anonymous way that may not encourage individual responsibility ("Well, *I* voted against it!"). The strong leader may also encourage responsible behavior, but it's easy for the team members to sit back and let the leader take the credit—or the rap. When a true consensus has been reached, the team is much more likely to proceed to the next problem fully accepting responsibility for what has been done. If not, the team has probably not achieved a true consensus.

MIXED ORGANIZATIONAL FORMS

We rarely see a real team using a pure form from our organizational spectrum. Most typically, the team embellishes one form with an aspect from one or more of the others to eliminate the form's weaknesses. If team members are afraid the discussion might turn into campaigning that could result in a decision overly influenced by one individual, they might vote first and campaign afterward.

Obviously, the success of the strong leader form depends on the correct combination of ideas and motivation *within the person chosen as leader*. For this form to succeed consistently, there must be a consistent method of choosing a leader with the right qualities. Voting is a swift and moderately safe method of choosing a leader. Consensus is much more reliable, but takes longer.

After inheritance, probably the worst method of choosing a leader is to have one strong leader choose another, though that is the method used in most organizations. It works only if you start with a truly effective person at the top, someone who also has the full confidence of the people to be led.

Once in a while, the expertise in a group using the consensus approach will be so low that there is not enough information to make consensus viable. When consensus fails for lack of expertise among the participants, we may not observe it, unless we notice how little confidence exists when people offer information. In such cases, the consensus organization can be improved either by preceding it with a phase in which all team members work independently to inform themselves, or by putting together a more expert team.

Even within a pure organizational form, there are dozens of variations. For example, even though voting is a mechanical procedure, the group may decide to adopt a weighting scheme, or a two-thirds or three-quarters voting rule.

We've already seen how different appointed leaders interpret their role, and within each form, there are different roles that individuals can adopt. For instance, some groups work with official recorders to write down the group's partial decisions. Other groups use unofficial recorders, or let the leader record, while others use no recorders at all.

Consensus, of course, offers the most scope for organizational variation according to the problem, the participants, and the conditions. For instance, an experienced person might emerge to take a strong leadership role in a team that was not familiar with consensus decision making. Consensus does not mean "leaderless." It means that any leading is constrained by consensus guidelines, concentrating not on the *content* of the discussion, but on the consensus *process* itself. At the other extreme, the entire meeting might take place without any identifiable leader, as long as the consensus guidelines are followed.

Notice that for any of these mixed organizational methods to work, the people who are affected must agree they will use that organization. Essentially, this agreement must be by consensus, though the consensus may never be openly discussed. In most organizations, most of the time, the consensus is by inertia. Someone may suggest a vote to decide some issue, and because this type of vote is familiar to the group, they acquiesce.

For the organization to attempt a new form, someone has to reopen the question of this implicit consensus. Such an act is more than likely to cause a stir, so nobody would even attempt such a change unless that person thought the new organization would be better. Which brings us back to the original question: What is the best way to organize a team for solving problems?

FORM FOLLOWS FUNCTION

For participants in the "Ranking World Records" exercise, the most important lesson is that there is no organization that is *always* best for a team to use in making a decision. Although the exercise simulates decision making, the same lesson applies to organizing for *any* problem-solving task. The architecture of the group is guided by Frank Lloyd Wright's architectural dictum: "Form follows function."

What is the function of a problem-solving organization? The purpose of the organization is to create the proper environment for people to

- understand the problem
- manage the flow of ideas
- maintain quality

If the current organization isn't furthering these goals, the problem-solving leader starts looking for some new form.

To raise this awareness in our workshops, we sometimes repeat the previous exercise with ten new items to rank. We also introduce a slight change in goal and let the teams choose their own best organizational structure. For instance, we might tell them that the ranking is worthless if it takes longer than ten minutes or they score less than 60. This goal might bias them toward some form of vote.

If the minimum score is raised to 75, their previous experience tells them that a vote is almost certain to miss the mark. The teams often gamble on appointing a leader who did well on the previous exercise, then answering this leader's explicit requests for information. This organization succeeds about half the time, but voting almost always fails.

If the minimum score is raised to 90, but the time limit is relaxed to thirty minutes, the teams generally adopt a consensus format. Using their improved understanding of consensus, they can achieve a score of 90 about seventy percent of the time. Of course, if they felt they had an expert in world records, they might opt for a strong leader, with extended discussion on a few weak points, but there seldom is such an expert.

Sometimes, we introduce the new goal after the teams have already begun to work on the problem. The trick is not to know *the* best method, but the best method *under the present circumstances.* If circumstances change, the organization needs to change. No organization is best all the time, and no organization even *remains* best for very long. The most effective leaders are the ones who help the team to recognize when circumstances change and to find a new organization that fits.

APPENDIX: SCORING THE RANKING

In case you tried the ranking yourself, here are the actual rankings as found in *The Guinness Book of World Records*. They're arranged in the form of a scoring sheet, so you can compare your ranking skills with the numbers given in the chapter.

Ranking World Records—Scoring Sheet

Begin the computation by posting your own rankings to column B. Then compute each squared difference and post in the right-hand column. Add these squares to obtain the value of x, which you can use to derive y, z, and q, your quality score.

		(A) actual	(B) decision		$(A—B)^2$ difference
366ft	Tree	4	_____	///	____
5577ft	Banana split	10	_____	///	____
1245ft	Chimney	9	_____	///	____
245ft	Jellyfish	2	_____	///	____
560ft	Fountain	6	_____	///	____
197ft	Ferris wheel	1	_____	///	____
663ft	Mobile crane	7	_____	///	____
444ft	Frisbee throw	5	_____	///	____
935ft	Dam	8	_____	///	____
298ft	Bar	3	_____	///	____

sum of squares = ‗‗‗‗

COMPUTATION

1. x = sum of squares   _____
2. $y = x / 165$ _____
3. $z = 1.00 - y$ _____
4. $q = 100 \times z$ _____ = QUALITY SCORE

CHAPTER 17: QUESTIONS

1.   Think of some group to which you belong. How many different forms of organization does this group use? How does each form relate to the tasks it's used for?

2.   Recall the last time you used voting to make a group decision. Was it a device for avoiding conflict? Did it work? How could the voting algorithm have been modified to work better?

3.   When you are making decisions for other people in a group, how do you know if you are doing a good job? Do you write down your decisions and review them later to see if they proved to be wise? Do you ask the people in the group how the decisions affected them? If not, why not?

4.   When working in a group without an appointed leader, do you ordinarily select a leader implicitly or explicitly? by what method? Try to alter that method in a way that will encourage fuller participation. Make notes of what happens.

5.   Next time you're working in a group, ask the other members' permission to be a *process observer* to the group. If they agree, you will take notes on the evolving organization of the group as it works through various phases on its task. Every so often, at agreed-upon intervals, you will report to them on what you observed. If they don't agree, ask yourself why they didn't. Take the notes anyway, but don't report on them, except to your journal. Then, find another occasion when you can get the group's permission.

6.   Next time you're in charge of a group, select someone to be a process observer, as in the previous exercise. Ask the observer particularly to observe and report on your work as appointed leader.

7.   Organizations use different terms to designate the person who leads a meeting. Some common terms are leader, chair, moderator, and facilitator. Which term does your organization use? Why? What does the term mean to you?

18

Obstacles to Effective Organizing

In any of the ordinary emergencies of everyday life, do you prefer to

a. give orders and be responsible
b. take orders and be helpful
                              —Personality Test Question

Suppose you wanted to know if you could be a great organizer. One way of approaching this problem would be to take a personality test. I recently took such a test, where I found the preceding question. It led me to think about what were the *true* obstacles to effective organizing. The instructions at the start of the test said

> Do not think too long about any question. If you can't decide the answer to a question, skip it.

Taking those instructions to heart, I skipped 114 questions out of 166. I would have skipped more, but I didn't want the psychologist to think I was indecisive. It didn't matter, of course. I would be labeled "wishy-washy" or something worse, like "uncooperative."

Actually, I *am* rather cantankerous and do hate making decisions, so perhaps the psychologists know what they're doing. As a potential organizer, "uncooperative" would certainly put me in last place; "wishy-washy" would put me out of the race entirely.

FIRST OBSTACLE: PLAYING THE BIG GAME

To be an organizer, some people believe, you have to be a manager. If you believe that, and if you're not a manager, you've already encountered your first big obstacle. To be a manager, so these people say, you have to be a decision maker. As a management text might put it:

> A manager's entire orientation is toward solving problems and making decisions rather than toward personally performing the actions necessary for implementation; usually the actions are carried out by others.

In this model of management, there are two kinds of people:

a.   those who organize
b.   those who are organized

If you want to be an organizer, you'd better answer (a) to the psychologist's question posed at the beginning of the chapter, for you'll have to "give orders and be responsible." On the other hand, you'd better work in an organization where most of the other people answer (b), "like to take orders and be helpful." This kind of organization might be difficult to find. I've seen many organizations full of people who like to be helpful; I've also seen organizations where most of the people take orders; but I've never found one where people *like* to take orders.

In fact, I've rarely found people who like to *give* orders. What I have found is people who don't like to take orders, and who believe there are only two choices: order or be ordered. This false dichotomy leads to what Virginia Satir calls "the Big Game":

Who's got the right to tell whom what to do?

The Big Game is played without any rules except "do anything you can get away with." Some people play by trying to make others feel guilty, or shattering their self-esteem. Others play by rubbing up to strong players, hoping some of their "right to tell" will rub off. Some play the "I'm so helpless you have to take care of me" strategy; some play "I'm so smart (old, experienced, male, white, rich, . . .) you must listen to me"; and others play "I'm so unpredictable, you're sure to regret giving me orders." One of the most effective Big Game strategies is the psychologist's ploy: "If you don't answer the questions the way I think you should, I can label you 'indecisive' or 'noncooperative' or 'sociopsychopathic'."

The Big Game is a big obstacle to effective organizing. In many organizations, as in many families and other human relationships, people are so busy playing the Big Game that they don't have time to do what the organization was designed to do.

SECOND OBSTACLE: ORGANIZING PEOPLE AS IF THEY WERE MACHINES

Underlying the Big Game is a model that regards people the way programmers regard computers, not as intelligent decision makers who can interpret an order in various ways. You don't ask a new computer

When executing a program, do you prefer to

a.   tell the programmer what to do

b.   follow the programmer's orders

The question is certainly important, but you *expect* that all machines will follow orders. Machines always lose the Big Game. That's why we like to use machines.

If you're a computer programmer, you're accustomed to having your orders carried out invariably. If they are not carried out, you've learned through bitter experience that the problem is usually not a broken machine. More likely, your orders are not correct. You've said something that didn't mean what it seemed to say, but the machine interpreted it literally. Perhaps you said STOP, but didn't mean "stop instantly," but, rather, "stop as soon as you come to a place where my files won't be destroyed by stopping."

Unlike machines, humans are capable of interpreting a STOP command in various ways. This is fortunate in those circumstances where your files are saved, and frustrating in those situations where the STOP is too slow. People who play the Big Game take their good fortune for granted when someone understands and follows their orders. On the other hand, they do notice the frustration when they are misinterpreted, which makes them feel that other people are trying to beat them at the Big Game.

People who don't play the Big Game can accept the idea that other people can't always understand them perfectly, which is a small price to pay for the ability to recognize stupid orders and refuse to follow them. If they need perfection rather than good judgment, they get a machine for the job, if a machine can be programmed to do it.

The problem with the Big Game as a guide to organizing is that players are likely to respond to frustration the way they would with machines—by trying to make their decisions and orders even more rigid and precise. Regarding people as if they were machines is another big obstacle to effective organization.

Although this approach may sometimes be effective, when carried too far it leads to ever-expanding books of standards and procedures as the basis for organization; and as these books grow in precision, they diminish in effectiveness. Nobody ever takes the time to read them, let alone follow them. The leader who is busy organizing through written procedures and memos soon loses touch with the people who are supposed to be following them.

THIRD OBSTACLE: DOING THE WORK YOURSELF

Many people see the Big Game as an obstacle to effective problem-solving leadership, but some innovative problem solvers go much further and actually hold Big Game players in contempt. These independent souls regard taking orders as harmful to their creative spirit, and if they are sufficiently innovative, they can get away with not playing. This drives Big Game players into a blind rage, much like my golfing friends when I refuse to count my strokes.

Such innovators often have a difficult time creating environments in which others do the work. One reason is that they refuse to offer suggestions, lest their ideas be mistaken for orders in the Big Game. They may fail to understand that people don't follow orders the way computers or concrete mixers do. People respond to orders, but they also respond to suggestions, praise, hints, ideas, encouragement, recommendations, and clear feedback on their progress. Organizing work for other people requires different methods of making decisions and issuing orders.

The lack of effective communication methods is a relatively minor obstacle, one that can be overcome by training and experience. A bigger obstacle arises when the innovator perceives that the other people are having trouble doing some task. No matter whether the reason is poor communications, lack of skill, inadequate motivation, or a different idea of how the job should be done, the innovator's first and strongest impulse is to step in and do the work for them. Why? Because, in fact, the innovator *can* probably do it better. In such cases, the greatest obstacle to organizing other people for problem solving is *your own previous success as a problem solver.*

Why is this kind of intervention such a great obstacle? Isn't it the purpose of problem-solving leadership to get the problem solved by whatever means necessary? The fallacy in this view lies in the definition of "the job." The leader's job is usually not to solve a single problem, but to create an environment in which many problems will be solved, not just for today, but for the future.

Of course, there may be no future unless this problem is solved, in which case it may be necessary to step in and solve it. A surgeon who is training an intern obviously cannot just stand by and let the patient die; the intern can learn on the next patient. Similarly, a project manager cannot simply let the project fail if the company will go bankrupt. If that happens, nobody will have a job anyway, so what's the point of creating a great team for the next project?

Is the problem really life-and-death? That may be the leader's most difficult decision.

FOURTH OBSTACLE: REWARDING INEFFECTIVE ORGANIZING

Perhaps I'm indecisive and consequently poor leadership material, but I believe the *best* leader is the one who *rarely, if ever, gets into a position of having to make a decision,* let alone a life-and-death decision. When faced with the choice of moving or not moving the bleeding victim, there's always the risk of a poor decision.

Of course, if you've avoided the accident in the first place, there's no decision to be made by anybody, and thus no risk at all. So perhaps a better leadership question is this:

If you had to take a trip with someone else driving, would you prefer a driver who

a.   has never had an accident, but would likely be indecisive if an accident occurred

b.   has had an average of one accident a week, but was very adept at making decisions in emergency situations

Sad to say, many people seem to prefer (b). That's why Armistice Day has been replaced by Veterans Day. Peace is more difficult to organize, but war is more heroic. Really good organizing seems to lack drama.

Why is it that we reward programmers who work all night to remove the errors they put into their programs, or managers who make drastic organizational changes to resolve the crises their poor management has created? Why not reward the programmers who design so well that they don't have dramatic errors, and managers whose organizations stay out of crisis mode?

Organizing is not about solving problems, but avoiding them. Once you're in the throes of the problem, it's too late to do really effective organizing. Perhaps the biggest obstacle to effective organizing is *our eagerness to reward ineffective organizing.*

ORGANIC ORGANIZING

In a typical psychological test, there are many questions like the one that heads this chapter. Obviously, such a question wouldn't be very useful if everyone gave the same answer, and psychologists design their test so that approximately half the people will select each alternative. Therefore, the *existence* of the question says that approximately half the people who take the test will say they prefer to give orders and the other half will say they prefer to take orders.

This result is surprising if you believe in the Big Game. Doesn't everyone want to give orders, to be a winner? Perhaps people are answering at random, because they don't believe in the Big Game. Perhaps they don't even know what the question means.

One way out of this dilemma is to notice that there's a third possible answer to the question:

c.   stop playing games and take care of the emergency.

I hope I'm never hurt in an auto accident, but if I am, I sure hope the spectators won't stand around playing the Big Game. I hope, instead, that they're sufficiently mature and trained to do what's necessary. I may not be in very good shape to manage the process myself, so I'd much prefer people who are capable of managing themselves, without orders from me.

Problem-solving leadership is based on this sort of model of organization. According to the organic model, most everyone likes to organize some of the time, and perhaps be organized some of the time, depending on the situation. Giving orders and taking orders are merely means to an end, not an end in themselves. In the most effective organizations, *everyone* is solving problems and making decisions, as required to get the job done. In this model, organizing is done by anyone who takes the lead, and a better definition of the leader's job is

> A problem-solving leader's entire orientation is toward creating an environment in which everyone can be solving problems, making decisions, and implementing those decisions, rather than personally solving problems, making decisions, and implementing those decisions.

In this model, organizing is not creating a set of rigid rules; organizing is not giving orders or taking orders; organizing is getting the job done.

CHAPTER 18: QUESTIONS

1. Have you ever been labeled "uncooperative" when you were actually trying to be helpful by pointing out that a group wasn't organized well? How did it feel? Was it effective in advancing the group's performance?

2. Have you ever labeled someone "uncooperative" when that person was preventing your group from getting on with its work? How effective was this approach? What other approach might have been more effective?

3. When was the last time you played the Big Game? Were you a winner, a loser, or a learner? Did you enjoy it? Did it advance the task at hand?

4. Do you ever write a memo rather than deal face-to-face with the people involved? Does it make you feel better? Does it make them feel better? How effective are your memos?

5. What can you do to alter an environment of orders, memos, uncooperative workers, and other symptoms of the Big Game? What *are* you doing?

6. When was the last time you stepped in to take over some job you had delegated to someone else? How did it make you feel? How did it make the other person feel? Did it get the job done? What effect did it have the next time you delegated something to that person?

7. In what ways are you rewarding or being rewarded for ineffective organizing? How can you create an environment that reverses this tendency?

19

Learning to Be an Organizer

This is the first prize of power for all of us who work in systems: *to be able to act in ways which enhance the capacity of our systems to survive and develop in their environment.* When we're able to do that, we know we're powerful. If we cannot influence systems in this way, then all the other trappings of power—control, dominance, perquisites, intimidation, revenge, hard-lining, bottom-lining—all of these are nonsense; they are power's second prizes (or booby prizes); they are *attempts* to feel powerful or look powerful; they are consequences of not being powerful. But the true bottom line of system power is this: Are you able to influence the system? Are you able to act in ways which help the system cope and prosper more effectively in its environment? You may be the chief executive of your organization, you may enjoy an astronomical salary and luxurious perquisites, you may be King or Queen of the hill intimidating and dominating all comers, but if you cannot influence the system so that it is better able to cope and prosper, you are working on second prize.

—Barry Oshry
Power and Systems Laboratory

How do you go after first prize? How do you learn to influence the system so that it is better able to cope and prosper? I have no integrated theory to answer this question, but I do have a miscellaneous assortment of ideas on the subject.

PRACTICE

The first idea is so obvious I should be ashamed to write it down. I should, but I'm not, because ninety percent of our students don't seem to know that learning to be an effective organizer takes *practice*. And more practice. Perhaps they are afraid to make mistakes with other people's lives, so they want to master the theory first. Theory is important, but it can't prevent all mistakes. There are many conflicting theories about how to organize people, and they cannot even be understood without practical experience as a guide.

How can you get practical experience unless you already have enough practical experience to qualify for the kind of job where you're given the power to affect the organization? If you use your imagination, there are a million situations where you can work with people in different organizational forms. In a single brief brainstorming session, a group of clients came up with the following list from their own activities:

- community work: raising money for charity, running a thrift store, working in the city mission, operating a recycling center, working in the animal control center, being a volunteer firefighter
- political work: supporting a candidate, running a petition drive, organizing a protest
- professional activities: computer user groups, professional societies, alumni associations
- work with children: scout leader, little league coach, youth hostel trip leader
- work with the infirm: hospital volunteer, nursing home volunteer, companion for the disabled
- voluntary associations: the Lions, Elks, Toastmasters, Masons

- church work: missionary work, lay counseling, committee work
- athletic teams: softball, bowling, basketball

On the job there is a similar wealth of opportunities:

- attend courses and organize a meeting to report back to your work group
- attend laboratory-based training*
- become an apprentice to someone, or take an apprentice of your own, or both
- be a trainer so you can practice organizing courses
- be a tutor so you can practice on one person
- lead technical review meetings
- lead team meetings, trying different styles

In short, get involved in any sort of activity that lets you experience what it feels like to be in different positions within different organizational forms. If you find yourself saying, "Ugh, I couldn't stand doing *that*," then that's the best place to start. You'll be filling up the biggest hole in your experience.

OBSERVE AND EXPERIMENT

Practice is the oldest method of learning, and even without special efforts to find organizational experiences, you'll find yourself involved in many different organizations every day. If these seem too familiar to teach you anything, you need to cultivate a more modern set of learning skills: the scientific method.

The scientific method is a fancy way of telling you not to be content to experience organizations passively: Science means *observe and experiment,* and it can mean something as simple as going to your weekly group meeting and observing where everyone sits, counting how many times each person talks, and noting who asks questions and who, if anybody, answers them. What will you learn from such observations? I really don't know, but I can assure you that everyone else who has tried this kind of simple observation of their everyday work environment has

---

*Barry Oshry's Power and Systems Laboratory is the best one for this purpose that I know; another good one is the Tavistock Workshop as led by Harold Bridger at NTL. Refer to the Bibliography for complete information.

learned something useful about the way people organize themselves for different activities.

Observing can be habit forming. Once you've tried it on the job, you'll begin to practice everywhere you go: Waiting for the elevator, shopping in the supermarket, and watching the Superbowl will all become new and richer experiences.

Once you've acquired some skill at observing, try some little experiments. You might come early to the next meeting and sit in a different chair. This will give you a different vantage point from which to observe, and will also give you a chance to see what kind of "musical chairs" develops. Or you might try rearranging the room from its usual pattern. Turn the table. Add a chair, or remove one. Bring in a flipchart, or take away all the pens.

These experiments are completely safe, because nobody need know you've done them. As you grow more bold, you may want to come out of the closet. During the meeting, you might grab a pen and start writing important points on the flip chart that's always been there but never been used. Or if you're always the one who's writing, offer the pen to someone else. Suggest a break when the interchange gets heated, or suggest that the seating be changed when the interchange is running out of steam.

Experimentation, like observation, is habit forming. When you wait for the elevator, you might see if you can induce your fellow travelers to board in a sequence that will avoid the problem of the people in back wanting to get out first. When you pack the car for the next family outing, you might see what happens if you let the kids make some of the decisions.

LOOK FOR INCONGRUENCE: THEY'RE DOING THE BEST THEY CAN

What do you look for when you observe the way a group is organized? One of the best guides to follow is to look for *incongruence,* a difference between the way things are and the way they look. For instance, novice observers usually mistake the formal power structure for the real organization. They see what they're supposed to see, rather than the incongruence between what is and what is supposed to be, between observation and assumption.

For instance, many people assume that the organization is what's on the organization chart. Test this assumption by noticing how the people really interact, as opposed to what the chart says. Does the leader of the meeting really decide who will speak next, or does some other member make the choice with a silent nod of the head? Do people really go through channels to get information, or do they have their own informal channels?

I have some favorite assumptions of my own about organization, based on the seed model. The most important of those assumptions is that *everyone wants to feel useful—to make a contribution to the organization*. This can be a difficult assumption to hold, in the light of actual observations. If so many people within an organization seem apathetic, or even destructive, something must be wrong with the assumption. If everyone wants so intensely to do good, how come so many people are so miserable all the time?

My friend Stan Gross has a useful device for dealing with his feelings that people are not trying to contribute. He says to himself:

"They're all doing the best they can, under the circumstances. If I don't think they are doing the best they can, then I don't understand the circumstances."

These "circumstances" are usually some incongruence between the organization and the task to be accomplished.

But *what* has gone wrong? It's not always easy to see the reason clearly when you're involved in the situation. When I'm closely involved, I try to look at things assuming that something has gone wrong with one of the three essential functions of problem-solving leadership:

- defining the problem
- managing the flow of ideas
- controlling the quality

Groups can be dysfunctional, just like individuals, with the wrong kind of organization for their current problem. I can often understand a dysfunctional group by making the assumption that the organization exists to solve *some* problem, though it may not be the problem at hand.

Frequently, the problem is like one that the group solved previously, so a little historical research may unearth what they're really organized to solve. For example, a group that needs a high-quality consensus decision might be organized around an autocratic leader because the group formerly solved problems in an environment that favored fast decisions over high-quality decisions. Once someone realizes how the group structure has been affected by their history, they can see that some other form of organization is needed, at least for the present problem.

LOOK FOR CROSSED WIRES

You obviously cannot study the history of a newly formed group. In a new group, the organization can simply be the result of a mistake, as the following analogy demonstrates.

After suffering needlessly through ten cold Nebraska winters, Dani and I broke down and bought an electric blanket. One of the reasons we waited so long was that Dani and I have very different concepts about what is the optimal sleeping temperature. The availability of dual controls convinced Dani that each of us could have our own private temperature, so she bought our first electric blanket. Even so, I was still suspicious that the newfangled thing would never work.

Sure enough, the very first time we used it, Dani froze while I roasted. I fiddled with the controls all night, and when morning finally came, I discovered that Dani had done the same thing. We indignantly brought the confounded blanket back to Sears and demanded that we get a new one that wasn't broken. The salesman showed remarkable restraint when he explained to us that, like so many other people, we had cross-connected the controls.

What happens when Dani and Jerry try to sleep under an electric blanket with crossed controls? The control settings ranged from 1 to 10. We started sleeping with the controls set at 5. At some time during the night, Dani decided that it was a trifle cool, so she reached out and turned up her control from 5 to 6. Unfortunately, her control was connected to my side of the blanket, so I started to feel a little warm. Eventually, I reached out and turned my control down to 4, which had the effect of cooling Dani's side of the bed. She then turned her control up to 7. I got hotter; I turned mine down to 3. She got colder; she turned hers up to 8. Eventually, her control was at 10, and mine was turned off. We had reached the point of maximum suffering.

Overall, the situation can be described this way: Dani and Jerry both want to be more comfortable at night. They agree to buy an electric blanket to try to solve this problem. They each operate the new blanket to the best of their ability, yet the result is misery for both. Nowhere in this story do you find the slightest hint of poor motivation. On the contrary, you could argue that it was their intense shared motivation for comfort that led to all the discomfort, given that the blanket was connected wrong.

Nor was this a case of differing problem definitions. Both Dani and Jerry wanted the same thing. What went wrong was their inadequate understanding of how the blanket was actually connected, the organization under which they were working. In other words, they had their wires crossed, which the salesman could determine by assuming that they were trying to do the best they could and observing their lack of success.

LEGITIMIZE DIFFERENCES

People don't have to be connected by electric blankets for their wires to be crossed, nor do you have to enter their bedrooms to observe them unknowingly working at cross purposes. Much of the trouble arises because people are different, yet their organizational forms are not designed to take those differences into account. For instance, the Jungian-based Myers-Briggs personality theory (see the Bibliography) says that people have different preferences in four major areas:

- social
- informational
- decision making
- action

On the informational dimension, for instance, the theory says that some people (the N's) prefer to get their information in an intuitive way, while others (the S's) prefer to have specific, concrete data. In a meeting organized by S's, the N's may be bored by "an overkill of data." If the S's interpret the N's reaction as poor understanding, they may respond by presenting even more data to prove their point. The N's become even more bored, and they're off on an electric blanket cycle.

A similar cycle can start in a meeting organized by N's. The S's will constantly plead for "more facts to support your conclusions," which the N's may interpret as attempts to obstruct the meeting. The only effective way out of such cycles is to recognize their existence, then develop an organization that acknowledges both needs as legitimate. For instance, you might organize the next meeting so that the S's will have piles of facts and figures in their hands before the meeting ever starts.

The Myers-Briggs model is an effective aid to observing what's going on between people in an organization, and guide to making adjustments that render the organization more effective. The would-be organizer would do well to study *Please Understand Me* or one of the other excellent books about this model.

USE YOURSELF AS A MODEL OF THE TEAM

Another place to go for insights on organization is inside your own head: Modern brain research tells us that our brain is not a single monolithic organ, but more like a group of interdependent brains, each with its own talents, preferences, and weaknesses. The more aware you become of your own internal processes, the more you'll be able to use them as a model of what's going on in groups.

For instance, the Myers-Briggs model says that people differ in where they prefer to recharge their batteries—from internal sources (I type) or external sources (E type). But you don't need the theory to tell you this if you pay attention to your own brain. Haven't you ever felt a conflict between the need to be alone and the need to be with other people? If so, you'll be better able to recognize such a conflict between people who want to work on a problem by themselves and those who wish to prolong the drama of a problem-solving meeting.

CHANGE AS YOU SUCCEED

Once you start observing what is going on around you, there is no shortage of ways to learn how to be an effective organizer. How can you discover those ways that suit you best? One way is to apply the group model of brains along with the idea of a group's problem-solving history. Instead of trying to reorganize your brain to suit the task, ask yourself what kinds of tasks your brain is best organized to do. Then choose a method that suits your own talents and preferences.

A group needs to change as problems change, and so do you. Learning about organizations can offer you great power to make changes, but change produces difference. One day you may wake to discover that you must revise your old image of being powerless.

Now you will be faced with the problem of living in the new environment created by your own power. As your personal power grows, so grow the consequences of your every little act. When you make a suggestion, people may take it as a mandate. When you express doubt, they may interpret it as a veto. When you smile, it's approval; when you frown, devastation.

With new powers comes the responsibility to learn new ways to use those powers. Paradoxically, the greater the power you have, the harder it becomes to do what you have to do to learn those new ways. If people consider you powerful, it becomes difficult to observe without influencing. Little experiments are no longer safe, because everything you do threatens to have great effects. Even when you think you aren't doing anything, people will be watching your every move. And testing your reactions.

As you grow in power, you close the circle. The observer becomes the observed; the experimenter, the subject. You may not like to think about it, but if you don't, power can become paralysis. Chapter 20 will look at what you can do about it.

CHAPTER 19: QUESTIONS

1. How much of your time do you spend thinking about or acting upon the trappings of power? Do you enjoy what Oshry calls booby prizes enough to justify this amount of time?

2. Make a list of all the opportunities you have to practice your organizing skills. Make another list of all the opportunities you could have, but aren't using. Is there some reason you can't pick one item from this list and go for it? Could that reason be overcome by effectively organizing *yourself*?

3. Make a list of all the opportunities you have to observe and experiment with organizing. Make another list of all the opportunities you could have, but aren't using. Is there some reason you can't pick one item from *this* list and go for it?

4. Recall some occasion when you were doing the best you could, but this was interpreted as "not trying to contribute." How did you feel? Did you try to explain yourself? What happened?

5. Recall one of the times you thought someone wasn't contributing. Try to explain that situation in terms of the person's doing the best possible job, under the circumstances. What problem was that person trying to solve? Is there some reason you can't check that out with the person the next time it happens?

6. When was the last time you got into a really good argument with someone at work? Is it possible that you got your wires crossed? How could you prevent that in the future? (What? You never got into a really good argument with someone at work? You're either a great leader or you're dead.)

7. Take some form of the Myers-Briggs Type Indicator, such as the self-test found in *Please Understand Me*. If possible, find out the types of your co-workers and discuss how your different preferences give you problems and opportunities in organizing your work.

8. Do you ever have arguments with yourself? Next time you do, write down the argument. Whom do the different sides represent? Does this same argument ever happen with other people?

Part Five
TRANSFORMATION

To become a technical leader, it's not sufficient to know what goes into leadership. No matter how much you know intellectually, you will find yourself sorely tested by the practical realities of changing yourself. To survive the transformation, you must, quite naturally, be motivated, organized, and innovative.

In this final section, we'll examine how other people will put you to the test as you try to change your behavior, how to test yourself as a way of anticipating difficulties, how to plan for change, how to find time to implement your plan, and how to obtain the support of other people when the plan goes awry.

20

How You Will Be Graded as a Leader

That the birds of worry and care fly above your head, this you cannot change; but that they build nests in your hair, this you can prevent.

—Chinese Proverb

Transitions are always difficult. There's a whole new set of rules to the game, and you don't get a rule book. For instance, we spend a lifetime being evaluated in school, so we study the rules and we learn how to cope with poor evaluations. Then we leave school. It's bad enough to get poor evaluations, but when we try to improve, we are devastated to find a different set of rules.

In much the same way, we spend a lifetime being evaluated as followers, only to learn that other people use very different rules to evaluate leaders. Think back to your student days and how you dreaded the first day of class. Then multiply by 100, and you'll have some idea of the problems you'll face when you start putting yourself forward as a potential leader.

THE PROFESSOR'S FIRST DAY OF CLASS

Why is it so difficult? In the first place, your new role is more like the professor's than the student's. Each student is responsible for one person's problems, but each professor feels responsible for many. This is the difference between the player and the coach. If you think students dread the first day of classes, you should live with a professor.

Each semester when Dani heads back to the ivy-covered halls, it's the same story over again: students in the wrong classroom, students with drop cards, students with add cards, students who bought the wrong textbook and wrote their name in it, students who don't have the prerequisites but want to be allowed in the course by special permission, classrooms too small with not enough seats, and windows shut tight with a southern exposure.

I always try to arrange a trip on Dani's first day of classes. One year, however, I made the mistake of returning home from a consulting assignment on that difficult day. In addition to all her other problems, Dani had to meet me at the airport. I wasn't looking forward to the mood she would be in, especially as my own day hadn't been exactly perfect. Half of the day had been spent with a group of newly appointed project leaders who seemed to be wallowing in self-pity.

As the plane approached the gate, I struggled to think of some clever and soothing first words, but my weary brain wasn't equal to the task. As we raced to greet each other with open arms, all I could utter was, "Did you have a nice day at school?" Evidently, this inane remark didn't do the job. We drove all the way home without exchanging another word.

The fatal question

About half an hour later, after collapsing on the sofa, Dani took a sip of her wine, gave a long, deep sigh, and said, "You know, I think I could tolerate all the other things that happen on the first day of school, if only they didn't ask that one fatal question."

"And what question is that?" I asked, glad to hear she had not lost her powers of speech.

"You know as well as I do. No matter what the course, no matter what the level, someone always says 'Professor Weinberg, how will we be graded?'"

"And why is that so terrible?"

"Because they don't seem to think of anything but grades. Don't they care about what kind of education they're going to get?"

"Oh, I don't know. I think it's perfectly reasonable to be concerned about grades. If you don't want them to be concerned about grades, why do you grade them?"

"Oh, it's not that I don't think it's reasonable, it's just that the questioning never stops. If I give them an idea of how they'll be graded, they want a more detailed idea. If I tell them the grade depends partly on the final exam, partly on the paper, partly on the homework, and partly on attendance, they want to know how much does it count for each thing."

"So what do you tell them?"

"I tell them I don't know. I can't say it's exactly thirty percent for this, and twenty percent for something else. Besides, I can't add that well so it probably wouldn't come out to a hundred percent."

"Maybe that's your problem."

"Maybe what's my problem."

"That you try to get their grades by adding."

"Well, how else would I do it?"

"Well, I had the same question today where I was consulting. The project leaders wanted to know how to do performance appraisals, so I suggested they use multiplication, instead."

"I don't understand," Dani said. "They already complain that grades aren't like the real world."

"That's exactly my point. In the real world, you shouldn't get graded on your job by adding up all the parts, but by multiplying. If you're an eighty percent performer on each of four parts of your job, you're not an eighty percent performer overall." I took out my calculator and computed $0.8 \times 0.8 \times 0.8 \times 0.8 = 0.4096$. "You see, that amounts to about forty percent as an overall performance."

Multiplicative grading for leaders

Over the years, I've learned that Dani is never too impressed with theories, particularly mine, so I was prepared for her next question. "Is that the way it works in the real world?"

"I can't really tell you that's the way it works in formal appraisal systems, but it's certainly the way it works informally for people in positions of leadership," I replied. "Especially technical leaders. Do you remember Waldo at Minimaxi Software? He was without a doubt one of the most highly qualified technicians I ever met. He knew everything about the computers he worked on and the languages and the operating systems they used."

"But he had an uncontrollable temper," Dani said.

"Precisely! He might have scored one hundred percent on technical knowledge, but every once in a while he went berserk and completely negated any credit he might have gotten for his technical skill. No amount of technical skill could compensate for the lack of trust that the rest of the group had in Waldo, because of his nasty temper. To evaluate him, you would have had to multiply his technical skills score of one times his emotional score of perhaps fifty, which would give you not an average of seventy-five percent, but a grade of fifty, which was a definite flunk."

"That's interesting," Dani said. "Does it go the other way, too?"

"What other way?"

"I was thinking of Phyllis on the same team. She was really a cool customer, but I don't think she knew much technically—perhaps a ninety percent on emotion and fifty, maybe sixty, on technical skill."

"Well," I said, "grant her the sixty, that would give her a score of fifty-four, which is another flunk but for a different reason than Waldo. Phyllis could do certain useful things for the team as a member, but as a leader, she couldn't command their respect because she didn't know much about what they were doing."

"It seemed a little unfair of them," Dani said.

"It may be unfair, but that's the way people react to other people who put themselves forward as potential leaders. Nobody said that life had to be fair, particularly when you're trying for more money or more prestige or more influence. It's the great American pastime to look for flaws in the leader's behavior. And, problem-solving leaders have twice as many areas to criticize—both content and process."

A STRATEGY FOR IMPROVEMENT

"You may be right," Dani said, "and that could account for another problem with the first day at school."

"What's that?"

"The teacher is a problem-solving leader, too. I have to conduct the class well, but I also have to have something to say, be reasonably authoritative. If I fall down on either count, the students bring my grade down by multiplying the two together. So maybe it's all right if I do it to them."

"That makes sense."

"That also explains something I've been trying to figure out. If I multiply two scores together, rather than add them, it gives me a different strategy for improving my teaching."

"What do you mean?"

"Well, suppose the score for my material is eighty and the score for my ability to handle the class is forty. Under an additive system, a ten point increase in either one would be equally good. I would probably choose to increase my skill score because that's easier and I know how to do it even better than I already do. But if I'm multiplying the two scores, a ten point increase in the lower score has a bigger influence on my overall score than a ten point increase in the higher one."

"That's right," I said. "It's forty instead of thirty-two. I wish I'd thought of that example today, to help me convince those new project leaders not to work so hard on improving their technical skills. Most of them were pretty good technically but they have a long way to go in improving their people skills."

CAN TEACHING AND LEADING BE LEARNED?

Dani looked thoughtful. After a minute of reflection, she said, "I think that new teachers are the same way. They tend to be much lower on their classroom handling than they are on their subject matter knowledge. Yet they tend to work on their subject matter much more than on their teaching. In fact, I think they believe there's something wrong with working on your teaching ability."

"Why is that?"

"They think that teaching is a natural ability rather than a learned skill. In some mystical way, every baby ought to know how to teach from birth. Somehow, if you have to be taught to teach, there must be something wrong with you."

"Yes, they were trying to tell me the same myths about leadership skills," I added. "They seemed to feel that everyone should just naturally know how to run a meeting or delegate work or . . ."

". . . or give grades or performance appraisals."

"Yep. But those aren't inborn skills. They're things you either learn or don't learn. But if you think they're natural abilities, then you might feel there's something wrong with you if you don't have them."

Dani looked thoughtful again. "And lack of self-esteem is a great barrier to learning. When you're afraid you'll fail, you're likely to be right. Like discussing grades on the first day of classes."

GRADING ON THE FIRST DAY

"I thought this conversation would distract you," I laughed, "but you still haven't forgotten it's the first day of classes."

"Perhaps I need more wine. It's going to be a tough semester."

"You say that every semester," I observed, pouring another glass, "but it never turns out quite as bad as you thought. Students are most critical of the teacher on the first day."

"I hope so."

"It was the same for my project leaders. They've just emerged from the ranks, and many people in those ranks are asking, 'What's this bozo got that I haven't got?' "

"That sure sounds like students on the first day of classes. They put you through a really severe test, like we used to do with substitute teachers. Probing for the slightest weakness . . ."

". . . which they can use to gain leverage on you. So, really, the multiplication might be too *easy* a grading method."

"Easy?"

"Yes, it would probably be more accurate to take the *minimum* of all the different grades."

"You mean that the students judge the teacher by her *weakest* area?"

"Certainly they do at the beginning, though later they may be willing to give her credit for her strengths. That's why my project leaders were under such pressure from their former peers."

Dani sighed. "So on the first day, when I have so many new things to do, I'm trying to make a good impression by emphasizing my strongest points. But the students are looking for my weakest point. No wonder I'm exhausted."

A POSSIBLE SOLUTION

Dani's glass of wine was now empty, and she seemed pensive. As I refilled her glass, she asked, "So you think I use the wrong system of grading?"

"No, I don't think that's what I was saying at all. There's nothing *wrong* with your system of grading, but it's your weakest point. That's why the students probe you so hard about it."

"If it's not wrong, then why is it my weakest point?"

"Because you *feel* it's your weakest point. Because you feel bad about yourself in that area, you get upset about it when the students bring it up on the first day of class. You don't get upset when they ask you about the class schedule, or the textbook. The weakness is not the system of grading, but your *feelings* about the system."

Dani laughed. "That's easy for you to say, but it's not so easy to control your feelings up there in front of the class."

"Don't I know! But because that's *my* weak point, I've learned to structure my classes to avoid my weaknesses, rather than emphasize them."

"Hey, I could do that! I don't have to *discuss* grading at all."

"Sure, you could give them a handout describing the system."

"No, you don't know the student mentality. But at least I don't have to discuss it at a time when I'm tired and overloaded, when the students are anxious and confused, and when neither of us knows the other very well."

"Sure. Ever since you took assertiveness training, you're always reminding me that I don't have to answer every question the moment someone throws it at me."

"But if I postpone the discussion of grading, won't the students get even more anxious?"

"Not necessarily. Suppose you tell them that grading will be discussed fully during the *second* week of class. In the meantime, you promise them that nothing they do in the first week will affect their grade."

"And that would give me a week of classes to lower their anxieties about my grading system. . . ."

". . . and to get to know that you're not the type of person who's going to betray them on their grading."

Dani began to smile. "I like it! At the very least, it would be one less thing to do on the first day of class, which couldn't possibly hurt."

"And it's not just any old thing; it's the thing that gives both you and them the most anxiety. Very few people are comfortable with the idea of evaluation, either evaluating or being evaluated."

"I thought it was just me."

"No, not just you. Those new project leaders couldn't talk about anything but appraisals. I wish they'd heard this discussion. I always think of these things a couple of hours too late."

Dani smiled. "Actually, dear, you didn't think of it at all. I thought of it, but feel free to use it the next time the subject comes up."

"How about if I write an essay on the subject?"

"Sure. Just so long as you let people know where you get all your great ideas."

"Why, you know I'd never steal an idea from you. . . ."

". . . unless it was absolutely necessary. That's all right. Just be sure to tell them that anxiety over appraisals only leads to more anxiety."

"Right. So their first job is to establish a comfortable environment, which means getting acquainted with the new job, and particularly doing things that give both parties a chance to develop trust for one another."

"And what will you tell them to do if trust never develops?"

That stumped me for a moment. "I suppose in that case any grading scheme they use is going to be rejected anyway, so I might as well try to build trust first. As long as I trust *myself*, I can accept the idea that I might fail to win *their* trust."

"In other words, none of the grading systems matter that much, as long as you can pass your own system of grading yourself."

"Precisely. And *that* system doesn't change when you start a new class or a new job. You carry it with you wherever you go, and only you can change it."

CHAPTER 20: QUESTIONS

1.   Recall your own reactions the last time some new leader was assigned to you, like a new boss or committee chair. How did you grade this leader? How did the leader grade you? Was there any relationship between the two systems of grading?

2.   Recall the last time a new leader was appointed over you. What were the first things you looked at in that person? How long did it take, if ever, before you trusted the new leader? What actions led to increased trust? What actions led to decreased trust? Did you work actively to integrate the new leader, or did you actively resist? Why?

3.   Have you ever taken a real test that measured your leadership potential in some way? How were the results presented to you? Were they used to enlarge your possibilities, or to constrain you? How could you use them to enlarge your possibilities?

4.   If you took a leadership quiz, what question would you like to see on it? How would you answer it? (Do this as many times as you wish.)

5.   What's your weakest attribute as a potential leader? What are you doing to strengthen it? What are you doing to avoid being tested on it?

6.   How do you feel about performance appraisals? Do you prefer giving them or taking them? or not being involved in them at all? What are you going to do about it?

7.   What's your strategy for entering a new group? What's your strategy for welcoming a new member into a group you already belong to?

21

Passing Your Own Leadership Tests

If you can keep your head when all about you
        Are losing theirs and blaming it on you,
If you can trust yourself when all men doubt you,
        But make allowance for their doubting too;
If you can wait and not be tired by waiting,
        Or being lied about, don't deal in lies,
Or being hated don't give way to hating,
        And yet don't look too good, nor talk too wise:

—Rudyard Kipling
"If"

Kipling set a tough test, but no tougher than you'll have to pass if you're to have a successful career as a problem-solving leader. I'd like to write a poem that would tell you what traits you'll need, but I'm no Kipling. Barring that, I'd like to supply scientific data, but I can't generally use a real organization as a test environment for experiments.

Since direct experiments on real leaders in real organizations are not practical, I have to find other ways to discover leadership abilities in a person. In a workshop, I can simulate real environments, but most of the time I'm not in a workshop. To use the rest of the time effectively, I must learn to do what the biologists and anthropologists do: to interpret people's reactions to smaller tests that arise naturally. I particularly like to interpret the way people solve problems.

A TOP EXECUTIVE TEST

A few years ago, on the Japanese holiday "Honor Old People Day" I was in Tokyo attending the banquet of the International Conference on Software Engineering. I was seated next to Koji Kobayashi, chairman of the board of Nippon Electric Company (NEC). Author of several popular books on computers and control, Mr. Kobayashi is bright, alert, and full of delightful stories. At age 75, he is truly an old person to be honored.

One of his stories went back fifty years: The Western Electric Company had sent NEC some equipment in a sealed box marked WARNING: DO NOT BREAK SEAL! Mr. Kobayashi, then a young and very curious engineer, felt he simply had to open the box and thus defy a culture that demanded conformity and obedience to authority. He found a simple circuit, which NEC could easily manufacture in Japan. And did.

Mr. Kobayashi, telling the story so many years later, clearly recognized that box as a crucial test of the qualities that eventually made him chairman of the board of one of the largest high-tech companies in the world—a true problem-solving leader. The person at the top makes the rules, which is another way of saying, breaks the old rules. Cowardly conformists don't make it to the top, but then neither do blind rebels. To become chairman, you must have the courage to open the sealed box, but you must also stick with the company for fifty years!

THE ABILITY TO WITHSTAND TESTS

I must confess to testing Mr. Kobayashi, as I do many executives, using him to learn more about the traits needed to become chairman of NEC. I'm confident that he wasn't offended by my testing, because one such leadership trait is the ability to withstand tests. As we've seen, once you reach a conspicuous position, you're always being tested. If you're not tested by Western Electric or by your dinner companions, you're certainly being tested by your followers. And by yourself, incessantly.

As a workshop leader, I've often experienced the same kind of testing. On the first day, somebody in the group is sure to come forward with some challenge to my authority. If I pass that test, I get another. If I flunk, I get ten more, and risk losing control of the entire operation. If I do well, after a while, they stop testing—explicitly. But they still have one eye open for interesting tests that arise by chance.

It's perfectly reasonable for people to test others who purport to be their leaders. Children, for example, constantly test their parents' rules for behavior. It's doubly reasonable if those would-be leaders are in a position to test *them*. Personally, though, I despise being tested, so whenever possible, I arrange the workshop to get myself off stage. I lead by organizing the environment so as to empower their learning.

My technique is simple. The participants want to learn to lead, so I let *them* lead the workshop. It may take a few days to sell this idea— while they test me to see if I really mean it, but it's worth the effort. After a few days, when I'm exhausted, the participants have taken over; all I have to do is sit back and let them lose their heads and blame it all on me.

HOW TO HANDLE AN INTRUDER

At least, that's the theory. In practice, I can't create a perfect environment. Sometimes, situations arise that the students can't handle, or that I don't *think* they can handle. If I let them, they probably could handle them perfectly well, but I turn cowardly and step out of the background to intervene. When I do come forward, I fail another leadership test, because it would be undoubtedly better for their learning if I didn't interfere.

It happened again in a recent workshop. Without the slightest warning, the door was flung open, and a tight-lipped little man in a three-piece suit planted himself smack in the middle of *our* room. With hands on hips, he glowered at us as if he had walked into a teacherless kindergarten.

"What's going on in here?" he demanded. "Who's in charge?" It was fascinating to hear how loud he could talk with his teeth clenched, so I forgot to answer him. He repeated the question. "Who's in charge? I cannot allow you to disturb our meeting." He gestured toward the next room. "I want you to keep it quiet in here."

There seem to be a number of theories about the best way to stop people from making noise. Three-Piece's theory evidently was to make even more noise. Other people think that you stop noise by ignoring it. The class must have believed that, because everyone just kept building their Tinkertoy designs while the intruder kept screaming at us. In my opinion, however, neither of these methods is as effective as the move-'em-right-out-the-door method: out of sight, out of sound.

Unfortunately, I wasn't sure just how to put my theory into action. First I peered into his eyes over my bifocals and pointed to the door, but I don't think he even saw me, let alone my finger.

Next I tried speaking calmly, though I think my voice wavered a bit when I said, as politely as I could, "We're in the middle of an exercise here. We'd appreciate it if you'd allow us to continue."

But instead of leaving, he simply glared at me and demanded, "Are you in charge?"

Given the nature of my leadership of the workshop, I always have a hard time answering that question. I knew that Three-Piece would never believe me if I told him that *nobody* was in charge, so I didn't bother. I escalated instead. "This is *our* room, and *you* don't belong here. I'd appreciate it if you'd leave! Now!"

This didn't work, either. I was beginning to feel tested for my leadership ability in front of my leadership class, and I wasn't doing too well. I decided to try some dramatic body language. I stepped closer, hoping to back him out the door by invading his personal space. It worked for a few steps, until he realized he was getting close to the exit. "Stop pushing me!" he shouted. I wasn't pushing him, but evidently he thought I was. The next thing I knew, he had his hands on my chest.

Or maybe I put my hands on his chest. By this time I wasn't thinking too clearly at all. I may have failed my leadership test, but I would have earned an A+ in body-building. (Of course, I'm six feet two inches tall, and he wasn't more than five feet seven inches.) He was out the door in a moment, and soon all we could hear were muffled threats and curses fading in the distance.

Arnold's approach

In the workshop, everything that happens is grist for the discussion mill, especially a test of strength between the fearless leader and the mysterious intruder. Only two people seemed to feel I had done something wrong: One was Arnold, who was six feet six and weighed around three hundred pounds, and the other was Ramon, who might have reached five feet four and one hundred twenty pounds with lead weights strapped under his feet.

During the discussion, Arnold called our attention to the noises coming from *their* side of the wall. "They don't really bother me," he said, "but they make me aware of another way of looking at the problem. Our unwanted visitor thought that the problem was us, but *any* group makes a certain amount of noise. In our view, the problem was his belligerence, but that caused a problem only when he thought our noise disturbed his meeting."

"What's the point, Arnold?" I was still defensive about the way I'd handled the incident. "I tried to talk to him rationally, but he wouldn't have it."

"Look at this wall. If it had been thicker, none of that would have mattered. He wouldn't have even known we were here, and you wouldn't have had to throw him out."

The wall was one of those movable partitions that give hotels flexible meeting rooms. Like most such walls, it traded soundproofing for portability. In solving one problem for themselves, the hotel made problems for us. With a stronger wall, we wouldn't have needed such a strong leader.

"I agree, Arnold, but what good does it do? We could hardly ask the hotel to change walls just for our rowdy class."

"Of course not, but once we anticipated the problem with the wall, there might have been other things we could do, such as selecting a different hotel. Or a different meeting time, when there wouldn't be anyone next door. Or even by warning them in advance that there would be a few times when we might make a bit of noise. Noise is a lot easier to accept when it's not a complete surprise."

"What I don't understand, Arnold, is why you're being so reasonable. Of all the people in this room, I would have thought you would be the one to approve of my muscling him out. Heck, you could have pushed him out with one hand."

"That's just it. Sometimes little guys pick on me. They test me because my size is a threat to their machismo. The first few times that happened, I hurt them, real bad."

"So? What do you care? They probably deserved it."

"Maybe they did, but it didn't make me feel good about myself to hurt them. Sure, I take pride in my strength, but that made me even more ashamed. Why should I be proud of the fact that I'm bigger than most other people?"

I was feeling a little ashamed myself, so I changed the subject. "Okay, but suppose you didn't do any of those things in advance, and there you were in my position with this loudmouth messing up your class, what would you have done?"

"Oh, I would have pushed him right out of the room, a lot sooner and a lot more violently than you did! And then I would have been ashamed of myself for allowing that situation to develop in the first place."

"And that's why you favor a preventive strategy?"

"Right, because I can't handle the face-to-face situation very well."

Ramon's approach

Later, we were in the midst of a quietly intense problem-solving session, when the group next door started showing a loud movie. I rose angrily to do something about it, but Ramon gestured for me to remain where I was. He left our room and a moment later the sound from the movie was too soft to be heard. During the discussion period, I asked Ramon what he had done.

"Nothing, really. I just asked them if they would mind turning down the sound a bit."

"And nobody was offended?"

"No, they hadn't realized they were disturbing us. As soon as they understood, they were happy to turn down the sound."

Arnold looked at Ramon with wide eyes and said, "You're incredible! If I had gone over, there probably would have been a fight. You couldn't have paid me to go in there."

"That's the difference between you and me. I grew up in a rough neighborhood. As you can see, I'm too small to win fights. And also, I'm not a fast runner. So over the years, I learned how to keep everyone cool."

Two major coping styles for leaders depend on their emphasis on motivation versus organization. I call Ramon's style, based on motivation, the *personality approach*. Arnold's, based on organization, is the *planning approach*. Of course, there are many variations, but it's good to know where your major strength lies so you don't try to handle situations with somebody else's style. No textbook can tell you the right way to pass the intruder test, except to say, "Do what would work best for you, without making yourself feel bad about it."

WHAT'S THE RIGHT WAY?

Avoiding your weakest style is never sufficient, however, because of a paradox: In order to avoid your weakest style, you first need to strengthen it. Let's suppose both Arnold and Ramon are setting up classes. To avoid a face-to-face situation, Arnold proposes to plan some other arrangement with the hotel. But to convince other people to adopt his plan, he'll have to be able to handle them face-to-face. If he's not competent selling his plans face-to-face, Arnold will wind up in worse face-to-face situations in his classes.

Ramon, on the other hand, will do well in classes that are organized for spontaneity. Since most classes are not organized for spontaneity, Ramon must plan carefully or else he'll wind up in situations highly structured by other people—situations in which his personality approach won't be so effective. To get a chance to be spontaneous, Ramon needs to plan.

By and large, technical workers tend to be stronger on the planning side than the personality side. They often complain that they know how things should be run, if they could only get someone to listen. That's why computer programmers are so happy working with their machines: Personality doesn't influence computers.

At the higher levels of management, planning strengths also count heavily, so computer programmers might make terrific top executives, if only they had the personality strengths to get them through the intermediate ranks. Mostly, though, they just get shoved out the door.

USING AND ABUSING TESTS

Real tests are no fun and can even be dangerous. Tests can be used by personnel departments to label people for pigeonholing them. They can be used by managers to blame workers for their own failures as leaders, and they can be used as a smokescreen by workers who want to become leaders but are afraid to express their fears. I would personally be very happy if I were never tested again, but I'm not willing to give up my workshops.

If you really can't stand being tested, you should stay out of leadership roles. But if you want to become a leader, you can use the tests to your advantage. Tests can give you a baseline for development, letting you know what needs work. Your personal style can be changed, but only by long and difficult practice. The only way to get that practice is to put yourself in situations where you can work on your present weaknesses, as I do in workshops. When you become a manager, you can count on your staff to give you a thorough testing, that is, unless you punish them for testing you.

How do you test yourself for a new level you haven't yet reached? If you dislike testing, you probably avoid putting your staff or colleagues through difficult tests. For the same reason, your own management may not push you hard enough. They want you to succeed, so they can succeed. They will put you in situations where you are likely to do well, not situations where you *might* do spectacularly. With this sort of benign management, you will get little or no chance to strengthen your weaknesses.

You are free to choose this benign, or "plateau," strategy for yourself, avoiding situations that will really test your weakest abilities. It will make you better, but it will never get you up the next cliff.

How can you know if you're being properly prepared for the next climb? Ask yourself how many important tests you've failed recently. I start worrying if I don't fail at least five times in each workshop. If I haven't failed that often, I'm probably not testing myself very thoroughly. Suppose I never run into rude strangers or other problems I can't solve perfectly. Does it mean I'm a fully developed, well-rounded personality? It might. More likely, though, it means that someone is protecting me from growth. Perhaps it's me.

Will I pass my leadership tests? I certainly hope not.

CHAPTER 21: QUESTIONS

1. Are you more comfortable with planned or spontaneous situations? How did you endeavor to structure a recent situation to play to your strength?

2. Recall a recent situation you felt uncomfortable trying to handle. What did you learn from trying? What will you do the next time?

3. At work, have you ever peeked into closed files or fiddled with machinery you weren't supposed to touch? What does that tell you about yourself?

4. What's your emotional reaction when you know long in advance you're going to be tested, for instance, when you must take a driver's test or submit to an interview for a new position? How does this differ from your reaction when you suddenly find out that you're being tested? What can you borrow from each situation to help you in the other?

5. Think of some ongoing conflict at work. Can you think of three organizational changes that might make the conflict disappear? How about three interpersonal changes? Which list was easier for you to develop? Which do you feel more comfortable with?

6. How do you feel about testing other people? How do they feel about your testing them? If you don't know how they feel, why don't you know?

22

A Personal Plan for Change

I was always careful never to let my schooling interfere with my education.

—Mark Twain
from a letter to a friend

Where do people learn the things they need to become innovators? How do they maintain that learning once they are busy being leaders? Can they learn in school, or only in the school of hard knocks?

Even with the help of outstanding courses, it's hard to retain a grip on the *content* of your work, not to mention keeping up with new developments. Added to that, if you want to be a problem-solving leader, you must also master *process* skills. So how is it possible to be both a problem solver and leader at the same time? It seems to be an ideal that can't be accomplished by real human beings, but it's possible if you break down big learnings into a sequence of little ones, pay attention to the efficiency of your educational strategies, and become aware of your emotional reaction to learning.

AN EXPERIMENT

Are you interested in achieving something? Worried that you won't succeed? Don't know how to go about it? Here's an experiment you can do right now that will get you started on the right foot:

Step 1.	Prop up this book so you can read it without holding it in your hands.
Step 2.	Clasp your hands, fingers interlaced.
Step 3.	Take note of which thumb is on top of your clasped hands.
Step 4.	Reclasp your hands with the *other* thumb on top. Note how it feels to do this.
Step 5.	Hold your hands clasped in this new way as you finish reading this chapter.

THE MENTAL CLIMATE FOR CHANGE

How did it feel? If you're like most people, it feels strange to change the habitual way you clasp hands. For one thing, you are more *aware* of your hands. Doing something new heightens awareness, which is stimulating but also a little uncomfortable.

Most people cannot sustain their new handclasp long enough to read through this chapter. After a while, as consciousness of their

241

hands fades, they unconsciously reclasp their hands in the old way. I once gave a lecture in which I offered a dollar to anyone who could keep both hands clasped through the entire hour. I hadn't made this offer before, and I was really nervous about risking $120. I needn't have worried—only one of the 120 claimed the dollar. When he claimed his prize, he told me it was the most difficult dollar he had ever earned.

Why is doing something new so difficult? Sometimes there is financial risk, like my $120. Sometimes there is physical risk, like your parachute failing to open. And sometimes there's the risk of looking stupid, like losing to your eight-year-old daughter at PacMan. Even when you remove all financial and physical risks, a core of difficulty remains. After all, what's the risk in clasping your hands a different way?

My theory is that the difficulty is entirely mental, independent of the particular thing you're trying to do. I believe it is part of the hardware in our brain to resist new patterns of behavior. In the world at large, new things are generally dangerous, so whenever we try something new, the brain tries to protect us by

1.   putting us into a special state of alertness, so that we pay more attention to everything around us, not just the new activity, and

2.   trying to ease us back into the old, safe pattern whenever we stop paying attention.

The special state of alertness can be either exhilarating or debilitating. I take vacations to new places so I can sense the world with all my faculties. I love the feeling, but sometimes I'm so overwhelmed by the newness of my surroundings that I just retreat to the safe familiarity of my room at the hotel. The same thing happens whenever I try to achieve something new in my work.

The more I travel, though, the easier it gets to deal with the unfamiliarity without being debilitated. It's as if I have gotten familiar with unfamiliarity. The same is true with personal achievements. By practicing many small achievements, I learn how to deal with the unfamiliar feelings that might hamper me when I try for some big achievement. Sometimes the practice only has to be in my mind.

A PERSONAL ACHIEVEMENT PLAN

Bill Holcombe and I designed the following exercise, which exposes people to their own reactions to personal achievement:

Step 1.   Set a personal achievement goal, something that is safe, novel, and can be done by yourself. The achievement should have an immediacy, so that you will know right away what level of performance you have reached.

Step 2.   Establish a baseline performance on the first day, then record your progress each day in your journal as you practice at least once a day.

Step 3.   On the last day, be prepared to demonstrate performance and discuss what happened as you worked on your achievement.

The following reports are typical, and will give you an idea of the power of this simple exercise.

Russell: "My task was balancing these little cocktail sticks on a tennis ball. I learned that the surface of the tennis ball changed each day, probably because people were tossing it around the room. I never would have noticed that in a million years otherwise. As a result, I began to notice that *people* change every day, too, which requires a new kind of balancing each day."

Werner: "I was using the same tennis ball to balance a meter stick. Maybe it was too easy, or maybe it was because Russell was also balancing, but I changed my task on the second day. So the first thing I learned was that I could *change* a goal I set for myself, if it wasn't serving my purposes. My new task was writing three things each morning I wanted to practice while interacting with other people. And I did it! I was amazed at how easy it was, at the same time it was hard."

Renee: "I played Gorf, the video game. I'd never played a video game like that before, so I never really understood what I was doing. I didn't even understand what doing well meant on this machine. As a result, I set no explicit goals, so I didn't experiment, and I didn't learn much about Gorf. I did learn about what happens when I don't set goals."

Earl: "My task was juggling three very different objects: a roll of masking tape, a marker pen, and a die. I had juggled before and was pretty good at it, but the different sizes and shapes made juggling the three objects like managing three different people, which is what I do at work, but I couldn't see anything I could transfer from one situation to the other.

"By the third day, I had leveled off at a peak time of seventeen seconds. Jerry was watching me and asked, 'Do you always start from the same position?' I had never thought about it, and had actually been doing two different juggling sequences. Within five minutes of standardizing the starting order, my best time jumped to twenty-eight seconds! To me, this means that in dealing with three very different people, it will be a lot easier if I know where I've started. I'm going to try separating *my* issues from *theirs*."

Tanya: "I played PacMan. I'm a regular addict, and I hoped that playing in this new environment might help my game. I did play with new awareness. I found I was being too intense, so I tried to stay calm. I could for a while, then I fell back into the same pattern of excess intensity. I need something to remind me—to pull me outside of my own involvement at regular intervals."

Shih: "My job was bouncing a ball off the easel in a certain pattern, but I didn't like doing it very much. I found myself not doing it, so I thought, knowing me, that I would go back the next day and make up the practice I'd missed. That's what I usually do, keep punishing myself by sticking with something that I know is useless. But I surprised myself and didn't go back to it. I learned that I didn't have to finish stupid things, and that nothing horrible will happen!"

Peggy: "I decided to learn to keep time for five minutes without a watch, as accurately as I could. I was easily distracted. I learned that I habitually use half of my mind on one thing, half on another."

Derek: "Keying on an idea that Jerry said he'd tried, I decided to hold my speaking to the last in a discussion, to see if it would hurt me in any way. I learned to do it, and it wasn't that hard. I also learned that people seemed to hear me better when I spoke last."

CAN IT MAKE A DIFFERENCE?

An achievement plan is not just a way to practice balancing cocktail sticks on tennis balls, it's a way of learning how *you* achieve things. To find out about your own style of changing, you can start by setting up your own achievement plan.

The first thing you'll learn is your style of resisting suggestions that you try to learn something. If you have doubts about the usefulness of balancing cocktail sticks on a tennis ball, perhaps you're too well protected against change. Nobody said that the achievement had to be useless. Werner practiced new kinds of interactions with people.

"But," you say, "these are only small achievements. To become a leader, starting where I am now, I'd have to do something *big*." This argument sounds like the airplane passenger who reasons that if the failure of one engine produces a one-hour delay, the failure of all four engines will simply produce a four-hour delay.

Those who understand the structure of an airplane can predict that the loss of four engines will cause a crash. And those who understand the nature of change can predict that somewhere along the line, a series of ordinary, small changes will suddenly put you on the brink of something large and extraordinary. Those who understand themselves, and their reactions to change, have the courage to go to that brink and to take the plunge.

ELEMENTS OF A PLAN

Suppose, for instance, that you decide to embark on a course of formal education. In spite of the bad things that Mark Twain and I have said about them, schools offer real possibilities for efficiency in learning. Although college courses can be a good use of your time, you must know whether you, as an adult learner, can still tolerate the student role. This knowledge of yourself can also help you select courses, because some college courses are oriented to working adults.

Although colleges often suggest standard programs, you must ultimately choose your own sequence of courses according to your work experience and style of learning. Many management courses are full of theory that won't make any sense if you've had little experience in appointed leader roles. The experience makes the theory meaningful, though some people find that theory makes experience meaningful. Decide which type you are and choose your own sequence of courses accordingly.

Not everybody needs formal courses, but some need structure to motivate them. Sometimes, it's their boss who needs the motivation of a structured course. People who are not allowed to read a book on company time may discover that the same company will pay them for taking time off for a college course. You must know yourself, and you must also know your environment.

If you know your learning style and environment, the courses you take don't have to be in college. Many companies offer internal courses; some even have a company curriculum, taught by in-house instructors and outside consultants. Then, there are public seminars conducted by a variety of profit-making and nonprofit organizations. The trick is to find out what your organization considers legitimate, then take full advantage of it.

You are surrounded by thousands of opportunities for learning, but without a plan, you will miss most of them. Start your plan by brainstorming some ideas to add to those above, such as

Attend more conferences.
Use audio tapes of conferences.
Use video tapes at training events.
Watch video tapes in groups.
Spend more time discussing than watching the tape.
Organize a discussion group without the tapes.
Lead a regular discussion group at lunch once a week.
Read a book and discuss it in terms of real work.
Teach a class.

When your brainstorm dries up, seek the help of others. For instance, you might read Ronald Gross's *The Lifelong Learner* (New York: Simon and Schuster, 1979) for more ideas.

Whatever list you brainstorm, whatever advice you get from others, your personal plan for change all comes down to understanding yourself. Nobody else can do it for you, so how about setting up your first personal plan, right now? The first step in your plan should be this: Take responsibility for your own education.

By the way, how are your hands clasped?

CHAPTER 22: QUESTIONS

1. Pick a small skill and work on it for three fifteen-minute periods today. Write your reactions and observations in your journal.

2. Pick a slightly larger skill and work on it for five thirty-minute periods in the coming week, recording your reactions and observations in your journal.

3. Now do the same thing with a skill that you will work on three hours per week for a month. When you finish the month, review your journal and decide what you want to do next.

4. In what ways do you create obstacles for co-workers who are trying to change something about themselves? For example, do you laugh at their failures, or at the things they have chosen to change? What does this tell you about yourself?

5. How many hours of formal education have you had in your life? How much of that was directed to your technical abilities? How much of it was directed to your ability to work with other people?

6. How many hours of *informal* education have you had? How was that divided between technical and people training? Are these divisions appropriate? Are they serving your career goals?

7. Can you list three people who work with you and who can teach you things to increase your technical abilities? If not, why are you working there? If so, what are you doing to take maximum advantage of this resource?

8. What courses have you taken in the past year? What have they contributed to your progress toward technical leadership? What could you have done to get more out of each course?

9. What courses do you plan to take in the coming year? How are you preparing yourself to take maximum advantage of them?

10. What books have you read in the past three months? How has each contributed to your progress? What are you doing to make sure that the books you read in the next three months make a greater contribution?

11. Make a list of activities that contributed to the maintenance of your technical prowess, or the growth of your leadership abilities, in the past year. Can you add three items to the list? Why do you hesitate?

23

Finding Time to Change

When you sit with a nice girl for two hours, you think it's only a minute. But when you sit on a hot stove for a minute, you think it's two hours. That's relativity.

—Albert Einstein

When my clients are challenging me to back up my theories with practical examples, time goes slower than when sitting on a hot stove. I was having lunch with some clients recently, theorizing about planning for personal change, when Clayton said, "I'm so busy just keeping up with my job, how will I ever have time to make changes?"

Clayton's remark brought us dangerously close to a discussion of time management, a subject on which I'm a regular Einstein: long on theory and short on practice. I wanted to enjoy a leisurely lunch, so I tried to shut him up by remarking, "You don't *find* time, Clayton, you *make* time. You can make time for whatever you really want to do, so if you don't find time for it, perhaps you don't want to do it. Perhaps you should find a way not to do it."

I thought that would intimidate them and close the subject, but Melanie turned to me and said, "That's a great idea, but a little vague. Do you have any suggestions on how to make time?"

"A few," I lied, chomping on a carrot stick. "But there's no time to go into the subject right now."

"Sure there is—if you really want to," Melanie said. "Besides, these are the last few hours we have together. We have to make the most of our time."

I tried to change the subject by remarking that I was in a hurry, too, because I had to catch a plane that afternoon for Switzerland. Americans can usually be distracted from anything by telling stories about Switzerland: William Tell stories, Heidi stories, Einstein stories. I painted a picture of the ideal country: beautiful, efficient, clean, friendly, and well-governed. I explained how the Swiss regularly and universally display the kind of efficiency that makes you think every Swiss must be doing two things at once, yet everyone has time to offer polite assistance to a stranger. I was sure this would divert Clayton and Melanie, but it didn't work.

"How do they do it?" Clayton asked. "It sounds like I could learn a few things about time management from the Swiss approach."

STAYING ON TARGET

Looking at Clayton plucking his artichoke, I started to appreciate how Dr. Frankenstein must have felt. Clayton had been a responsive client, but now he was my monster, and I knew I would have to take

251

care of his needs. "Most people reveal a great deal in the stories they tell about themselves," I replied, hoping to distract him with a long-winded tale.

"Tell us a Swiss story," Clayton said, swallowing the bait, and I proceeded with one of my favorites:

> On a state visit to the tiny young Swiss Confederation, the Archduke of Austria was reviewing the troops. To test the true mettle of an army, he habitually singled out one ordinary soldier for questioning. "How large is your army?" he asked his current choice, an unshaven youth.
>
> "Five thousand men, Sir," came the proud, precise reply.
>
> "Hmmnh. Quite impressive. But what would you do if I should march across your border with *ten* thousand men?"
>
> Without hesitation, the soldier said, "Then, Sir, we should each have to fire *two* bullets."

"I get it," Clayton said when I had finished. "What a brilliant parable about time management. The Swiss secret is making each bullet hit the target or, as Kipling said, filling 'each unforgiving minute with sixty seconds' worth of distance run.' If you're efficient, like the Swiss, you have time to keep up with everything. But how to be efficient?"

Rather than give Clayton a lecture on a subject that isn't my best, I let the other people at the table contribute their favorite ways to escape time traps:

Don't redo work you've assigned to others. When you do, you pay several times for the same work: first with the time to explain it to them, then with the time to take it back without hurting their feelings (which really won't work), then the time to repair any damage they'd done, and finally the time to do it yourself. "Whenever someone showed signs of making a mistake—even of uncertainty—I grabbed the work back under the pretense of teaching them something," Margo admitted. "I've finally learned that you must let them make mistakes. It's part of the price you pay, and it's more efficient in the long run."

Avoid trivial technical arguments to prove your technical superiority. "As your career advances," Dirk said, "you have to let go of certain things. Arguing over minor technical points indicates you're still holding on. When I really am technically superior," he explained, "there isn't any long argument because I can convince people swiftly and easily."

Choose your own priorities and don't wait for a crisis to organize your activities. Linda admitted, "Suddenly, when I was appointed group leader, not only did I have to organize time for other people, but even worse, I had to organize it for myself. I didn't have any experience at that. When there was a crisis, I felt real good because the crisis planned my activities for me. It bothers me now to think that I may have even precipitated some of those crises because they made me look really well-organized. Now I feel that the true test of a leader is what she does when there's nothing to do."

DOING TWO THINGS AT ONCE

Everyone at the table had said their piece, which gave me time to enjoy my own artichoke. But Clayton wouldn't let me alone. "How about another Swiss story?" he demanded. Clayton was my creation, and he knew my weaknesses.

"All right," I conceded. "But this is the last one. It's the story of how Switzerland was created."

After creating all the peoples of the Earth, God created a country for each one in turn. When the first Swiss was asked what he wanted for a country, he replied humbly that anything would do. When God insisted he express his preference, the Swiss said, "Well, if Thou insisteth, I would like a few mountains, with snow on top, green grass on the slopes, clear lakes in the valleys, and a blue sky above with a few fluffy white clouds."

God granted this wish instantly, then asked if the Swiss had any other desires. After much protesting, the Swiss finally said, "I would be most grateful for a wooden house with a stone roof, and perhaps a few brown cows grazing on the grass."

God obliged, then asked the Swiss if there was anything else. "No, Thou hast already been too generous. I really cannot ask for anything else, but what about Thee? There must be something *I* can provide in return for all these wondrous gifts?"

"Well, actually," God said, "I am a bit thirsty from all this Creation. I'd be most obliged if you could give me a glass of fresh milk from one of your cows."

"I'd be delighted," said the Swiss, and ran off to get a glass of that wonderful, rich Swiss milk, which God drank thirstily.

Now God turned again to the Swiss. "Surely there must be something else you desire. All the other people of the world have asked for riches without end. What do you wish?"

The Swiss hesitated, then said, "Yes, there is one more little thing."

"Then tell me what it is, and it shall be yours."

"Well, if it's not asking too much, that will be one franc for the milk, please."

"That's terrific," said Clayton. "The Swiss are not just efficient, they're doubly efficient. Rather than ask for riches, the Swiss asks for something that will produce income, something that will continue paying in the future, even after God is no longer around to create or buy milk."

"I suppose you're right, Clayton," I replied. "And like the Swiss, successful problem-solving leaders seem able to create situations where they get a little more out than they put in. Yet at the same time, these situations seem to benefit everyone involved; nobody gets cheated."

"Can you give me some examples?"

"I'd rather go around the table again, so I can finish my lunch." And so they each gave an example:

Melanie: "I keep up with what's going on technically by leading technical reviews for other teams. It gives me a chance to practice my people skills. At the same time, I get the benefit of hearing our best technical people trade views about the very projects we're working on now."

Linda: "I also review, but in a different way. I read technical papers for journals and act as reviewer or editor. It forces me to dig into some good technical content, and I get lots of brownie points with management for doing it. It also improves my own writing skills."

Dirk: "We have all these technical courses on video tape, but everybody seems to hate just sitting in a little room and watching them. So I volunteered to tutor people who were taking the video courses. It sharpens my communication skills, my one-to-one handling of people, but even more, it gives me a chance to really learn the technical material in depth. I get far more out of it technically than any of the students do, yet I never spend more than four hours a week doing it."

Kingsley: "I got myself appointed as coordinator of our visiting speaker program. That means I get to attend every speech, seminar, or class that's done by an outside expert, if I'm interested. But better than that, I get to spend time with these visiting experts, time when I can discuss any subject I want. It's like having private tutoring from the smartest people that money can buy. And most of the actual coordination work is done by my secretary."

Merlin: "Our car pool is where I keep up technically. I spend two hours every day with our top designer and two of our best analysts. All I have to do is keep the conversation steered away from other subjects."

Kathryn: "I could never keep up with all my technical reading until three of us realized we had the same problem and decided to share the load. We each read something and report on it to the others. Sometimes, the first reader can tell them to skip half the material. Sometimes they can skip it all. I get three times the coverage now for the same effort, and I also have developed a special relationship with the other two in my group."

THE CHEAPEST TUITION

"You know, Jerry," Clayton said as we were returning from lunch, "I don't want you to take this the wrong way, but I think I learned more at lunch than I did from the rest of your consulting."

"I'm not offended," I said, trying not to show my devastation. "It's just another example of double-duty time."

"You know," Clayton smiled, "I was thinking of going to Switzerland for a few years to study some more about the way the Swiss do it."

"Yes, that's a nice way, but it can be rather expensive."

"Can you think of something cheaper that's not too awful?"

"I think you already know such a way."

"I do?"

"Sure. Instead of traveling to Switzerland, why not study the learning methods of the best people around you? Like you did at lunch today. They've already paid the tuition for you. All you have to do is listen, and that doesn't even cost you a franc."

Clayton handed me the notes he had taken during lunch. "I know you're writing a book on becoming a leader," Clayton said, "and your readers might put more value on these if they came from ordinary people like us." With that encouragement, how could I fail to give them? So here they are:

<u>Making More Time in a Day</u>

- Don't do things you've already assigned to others, even if you must let them make mistakes.
- Avoid administration like the plague.
- Don't waste time trying to prove your competence.
- Don't waste time arguing about wasting time.

- Pay attention to what you do when there's nothing to do.
- Get at least two for the price of one.
- Act as review leader.
- Act as editor.
- Be a tutor.
- Coordinate a speaking or training program.
- Use your car pool.
- Share the reading load.
- Have a good lunch, but a creative one.

and most important

- Listen to what other people have already learned.

To which I can't resist adding one more:

- Let other people show you how smart they are.

CHAPTER 23: QUESTIONS

1.   How are you affected by time pressures? What tactics do you use to relieve time pressures?

2.   During what activity of yours does time go by the fastest? the slowest? What does that tell you about these activities? about yourself?

3.   Give an example of how you do two things at once. Ask three co-workers to give you similar examples. Can you use any of them?

4.   What do you do when you don't have anything to do, as when an appointment is cancelled at the last moment?

5.   Are you able to "do nothing" some of the time? Do you have time to look around you and at yourself to discover why you don't have more time? If not, stop reading immediately and do it now.

24

Finding Support for Change

After the verb, "To Love," "To Help" is the most beautiful verb in the world!

—Bertha von Suttner
Winner of the 1905 Nobel Peace Prize
Ground Arms

P eople become leaders thinking they will help other people. Before long they realize that it's *they* who need help. They need help to see themselves as others see them, to carry them through their mistakes, to learn about other people, and to deal with the frustrations of trying to be helpful. The only way to learn to be helpful is by learning to be helped.

People who withstand the transition from individual innovator to effective problem-solving leader are usually supported by a large network of other people, although they don't always recognize the existence of this support system. Either they're lucky and have one, or they're unlucky and don't. If you'd rather your success as a leader didn't depend only on luck, you will want to take charge of designing, creating, and maintaining your own support system.

A SUPPORT SYSTEM

I've seen many strange information systems over the years, but one simple one stands above the rest. I first saw the system in action when Pete Woitach and I were developing a simulation model of a machine shop. Working with the client, Pete sketched a simplified model, then suggested we try computing a few cases by hand.

"We'd need a random digit to get it started," the client protested.

"No problem," said Pete. "I'll call someone on my Random Number Network." He checked his phone directory, dialed a number, then handed the phone to the client. "When someone answers, ask for a random digit."

After a moment, the client said, hesitatingly, "Pete Woitach says you'll give me a random digit . . . Oh, thank you." When he hung up, he addressed Pete with new admiration. "Five. He gave me a five."

Pete plugged the five into the model and ground through the calculations. As he worked, I saw that if an even number had been used, the model would have failed. Naturally, with the client present, I held my tongue. I figured Pete and I could work the bug out later, in private.

The client departed, happy as a kid in a candy factory, and I confronted Pete. "You know, the model doesn't work if the random number is even."

"Yes, I noticed that, too, but I was positive the client wouldn't notice."

261

"Then you were lucky he didn't get an even number over the phone."

"No luck about it," Pete said. "When you call that extension, you *always* get a five."

Pete's Random Number Network consisted of a group of consulting statisticians. They shared a need to impress their clients and couldn't risk real randomness in their rough models. Each person on the network had a preassigned digit to give in response to a phone call. Whatever digit you wanted, you called the appropriate phone number.

Pete was the greatest teacher I ever knew, and a great problem-solving leader in many other ways. Like many successful leaders, Pete maintained an extensive personal support system, of which the Random Number Network was only a tiny part. Everyone has some kind of personal support system, a system they can draw on to accomplish personal goals, though most people do it unconsciously and not very well. If you want to grow, you can hardly do better than to study and develop your own personal support system.

TECHNICAL RESOURCE SUPPORT

Each part of your personal support system serves different goals. Pete's Random Number Network was an unusual example of technical resource support, a supply of skills and resources to complement his own.

My own personal support system contains dozens of subsystems for technical resource support. When I need technical information that I can't find in my personal library, I can call upon either the city or the university library, but mostly I rely on a select group of individuals scattered all over the world. For information on human factors, I might call Ben Shneiderman, Tom Love, Sylvia Sheppard, Izumi Kimura, Bill Curtis, or Henry Ledgard. On software design, I might call Harlan Mills, Brad Cox, Tom Gilb, or Ken Orr. On programming languages, I might call Jean Sammett or Dines Bjorner, but I might also call Ben Shneiderman or Harlan Mills, because the systems are overlapping and interlocking.

In most cases, the support is also reciprocal. People stay in a supporting relationship if it benefits both parties. If one party gets all the rewards, the relationship is not likely to last.

Another reciprocal part of my technical support system consists of hundreds of former students, each of whom is a technical leader in some organization. If I need to know about the present situation with information processing in banks, for example, there are at least twenty people I can call to get an insider's view. If I want to know how programmers feel about fourth-generation languages, I could send a questionnaire to several hundred programmers, or call ten personally.

SUPPORT THROUGH CRITICISM

These parts of my personal support system supply me with information that I *may* be able to obtain myself in the library. I use individuals rather than books because their information may be more timely, more to the point, or more easily obtained. Other people in my personal support system provide services that I could *not* perform myself. For example, like any author, I find it difficult to criticize my own writing. I get reliable criticism from at least twenty people in my personal support system, often in exchange for criticism of their writing.

My toughest and best critic, though, is Dani. For instance, when she looked over the list of names a few paragraphs back, she said, "Sounds to me like you're name dropping." It was a tough remark because it was true. It made me examine my own motives and find that I was indeed proud to associate with such outstanding people. My own feelings of self-worth are reinforced by their willingness to associate with me, and I feel good enough about myself to put that in print.

Writers or not, we all need this kind of critical support to overcome the first great obstacle to motivating others. It's much harder to get than technical support. The person has to be close enough so we'll listen to the feedback without rationalizing it away. On the other hand, they can't be too close or they'll be unable to see clearly, or say anything that could possibly hurt our feelings.

SUPPORT FOR GROWTH

I may be rationalizing again, but I hope it wasn't merely pride that made me mention some of my famous supporters. I want every reader to understand that seeking support is a sign of strength, not weakness. Every top technical person I've ever met has an extensive and well-maintained support system. Only the weak technical people are afraid to admit they need support, and that's why they remain weak.

Unlike Pete's Random Number Network, my technical support system has a strong element of true randomness. Whenever I call for a specific piece of information, I often come away with a dozen other items that I didn't know I wanted to know. I tend to drop people who are *too* efficient at giving specific requested information. I like to grow, and growth requires the risk of exploration into the unknown. In designing my support system, support for growth is one of my highest objectives.

Many years ago, just after my first big promotion in IBM, my new boss took me to lunch. I don't remember what we ate, but I remember him telling me not to become too friendly with my co-workers. I was "on the way up," he told me, and someday they might be working for me. If we were friends, I might not be willing to do the unpleasant things that managers have to do. I remember deciding that if that's what you had to do to be a manager, I would be happier remaining in the pits.

He was right about one thing, though: Whenever you try to change, some of the people you know will try to prevent you from changing. Whether this is good or bad, of course, depends on the change. If you're drifting into a $200-a-week betting habit with your bookie, some of your friends may try to stop you, which is probably a good deed. Yet the same people may try to stop you from switching to a job that pays $200 a week less, even though the job offers you a chance to do the kind of work you've always wanted to do.

Some people in my support system want me to stay the same; these I call my *Conservatives*. Others want me to change; these are my *Radicals*. Both types have their own reasons, which are not necessarily the same as my reasons. It's up to me to learn to be clear about which things I want to change and which I want to preserve. Sometimes making my own goals clear to people causes them to leave my support system. Sometimes strong Radicals become arch Conservatives, once growth has passed a certain point, or changed direction.

Changes in your support system are seldom painless, but if you intend to grow, you cannot avoid some pain. Several times in my life, I've had a particularly wonderful relationship that I wanted to freeze, so it would never change. Each time I did that, I killed the relationship: The best relationships have been the ones with people who wanted both of us to grow, even if it was sometimes difficult.

SUPPORT FOR RECOVERY

Speaking of pain reminds me of my back spasms. To anyone who has ever had one, a back spasm is a problem that needs no explanation. To anyone else, it can't be explained. You aren't dripping blood, coughing, or even sweating, but any time you try to move, it's agony. To normal people, back spasms look like simple malingering.

Normal people, in trying to support the back sufferer, become Conservatives, unwittingly postponing the return to health. Instead of applying hot compresses, they apply social pressure. The victim responds by trying to be active, and thus aggravating the spasms. "Back people" generally go through this prolonged agony several times before they manage to build a group of fellow back people that supports the kind of changes needed for recovery.

My own "back group" includes my sister Cheryl, Bill Holcombe, Henry Ledgard, Charlene Morris, and Dani. We trade information about doctors, medication, and exercise, but mostly we exchange emotional support during attacks. We remind each other that the way to recovery is through resisting the social pressure and letting go of all those things that "must" be done. And we reassure one another that having back spasms doesn't make you a useless worm, regardless of what everyone else is implying.

When your back is in spasm, it's important to stay clear of ordinary people, which is difficult to do if you're married to one. For the first ten years of our marriage, Dani was on the other side of the fence. The first time she was immobilized in bed with a pillow under her knees, I had ambivalent feelings. I didn't want her to suffer, but I couldn't wait to add her to my back group. I knew how Count Dracula must have felt as he converted lovely young things to his support group of the living dead.

Like most American men, I was brought up to keep my problems to myself, at least until they got so great I collapsed. As a result, I've had a history of seemingly sudden collapse episodes. About ten times in my life, I've literally kept myself going until I had to be picked up and carried to the hospital. Very manly—and very stupid. My support system legitimizes discussion of problems before they become catastrophes. I still have back pains from time to time, but I've stayed out of the hospital for the past fifteen years.

EMOTIONAL SUPPORT

Like back problems, emotional problems don't draw immediate and general support from the people you pass on the street. Like most people, I suppose, I sometimes have periods when I can't cope very well with some of my responsibilities. My manly training tells me to keep such feelings to myself, presumably until I collapse and have to be carried to the funny farm.

Although nobody likes to be around a person who's always whining, I do have a part of my support system that can help me through periods when all is not rosy. For instance, I don't have to injure my back to get emotional support from Bill, or Charlene, or a number of other people who know me intimately from experiential workshops. And no matter how grumpy I am, my dogs always love me. Dani and my kids are almost as supportive, except sometimes when I direct my grumpy feelings at them.

Dani and I together have several other couples that support us when our relationship is under stress. One group, consisting of four couples and meeting monthly, was specifically organized to help cope with the strains on a two-career marriage.

SPIRITUAL SUPPORT

Even after you take away all the physical and emotional problems, there remains a residue that never goes away: like how to cope with a world where I eat well while millions of people are starving, or where a child has just been molested. Sometimes I need a special kind of support just to keep from going crazy when I remember that this surpassingly beautiful world is only one button away from nuclear destruction. At those times, I find great comfort in the silence of a Quaker meeting, seeking the light of God within me.

Others find their spiritual support while singing with thousands of others in a cathedral, or watching the waves pound upon the beach, or reading their Bible, or their Bertrand Russell. But whether the spiritual support is rational, mystical, or biblical, no support system is worth much without it.

SUPPORT TO MAINTAIN LEADERSHIP

With all this talk of physical, emotional, and spiritual problems, it would be easy to forget that most of the time, most of us are doing pretty well without any special help from other people. When my back is relaxed, I don't notice my back muscles, which is why I tend to neglect them. In the same way, when I am performing at top speed, I tend to neglect those parts of my support system that raised my speed in the first place.

We have one workshop exercise that's designed to show the participants just how much they rely on the support of other people. In the exercise, each team tries to score points by submitting combinations of letters to a computer, which then returns a score for that combination. The challenge is that teams don't know how the scoring works, so they must experiment with different letter combinations. Once a team finds something that scores reasonably well, they are forced to choose between sticking with that or risking new combinations to maintain their supremacy over the other teams. Then, the Radical and the Conservative in each player comes out in the open.

For instance, many teams quickly find that the combination of four Y's does quite well. This technological breakthrough puts them in the lead, for a while. Other teams surpass the all-Y's when they discover higher scoring combinations of letters, but by that time, the all-Y's have become hardened Conservatives. They find all kinds of excuses for not submitting new combinations, but as they sit and support one another in sticking with all-Y's, the other teams invariably discover better combinations and pass them by.

It's a devastating emotional experience to be caught playing all-Y's. As a result, graduates of our workshops form a worldwide network of support against the complacency that comes with success. Whenever a graduate gets locked into one way of doing things, no matter how successful, another graduate interrupts to say, "You're playing all-Y's again!" Many people, of course, can survive perfectly well by playing the Conservative strategy all their lives, but they aren't trying to be problem-solving leaders. In this business, it takes all the running you can do just to stay in the same place.

The paradox of problem-solving leadership is that you have to change in order to remain the same. It's awfully easy to fall into the trap of building a support system that's just like Pete's Random Number Network. Unconsciously, you seek support from those people who will give you the answer you want to hear. The worst part about that is that you are *unconscious* about it. Without knowing what you are doing, you slip into a fixed pattern: either hanging on desperately to what you have, or changing at every opportunity just for the sake of change.

Over the years, many students have asked me for advice about contemplated career changes. Many of them have told me, years later, that they followed my advice, and it worked out perfectly. The curious thing is that in such matters, I always act just like Pete's network. I don't give the digit five, but no matter what they say, I always say precisely the same words: "Do whatever you really want to do."

The Golden Rule says to do unto others as you would have them do unto you. "Do what you really want to do" is the advice I want, even though it sometimes frightens me. It's not the advice of the Conservative, who always wants you to do what will keep you the same, but it's not the advice of the Radical, either, who always wants you to change. Instead, it's the advice of the third and best kind of supporter, whom I call, simply, a Friend.

CHAPTER 24: QUESTIONS

1. Make a list of all the people in your personal support system. Think of some change you are contemplating and classify all the people in terms of whether they will support you in making the change or in staying the same. If you are contemplating more than one change, do this classification for each.

2. Using the list of people in your support system, describe what you are doing to maintain it in good working condition. Are there any areas in which it is deficient? What are you doing to add parts to remedy those deficiencies?

3. How has your support system changed in the last year? the last five years? How will it change in the next year?

4. Make a list of all the people you could go to for support if you lost your job? What kind of support would each one give you? What kind of support would you like to have, but for which there is nobody on your list?

5. Do the same as the previous exercise for the case where you were offered a new and better job, but in a new community.

Epilogue

I have now reigned about fifty years in victory and peace, beloved by my subjects, dreaded by my enemies, and respected by my allies. Riches and honors, power and pleasure, have waited on my call, nor does any earthly blessing appear to be wanting for my felicity. In this situation, I have diligently numbered the days of pure and genuine happiness which have fallen to my lot: they amount to fourteen. O man, place not thy confidence in this present world!
—Abd-el-Raham
(912-961 A.D.)

I've told you most of what I know about becoming a problem-solving leader, but the one thing I can't tell you is whether you're going to like it. Not everyone likes being a leader, but many are slow to realize that they don't. By the time they do, they've usually lost the skills or attitudes or illusions that would let them move back to their old status. They should have examined their motives *before* they made their move, but of course they didn't.

Although I've been a consultant to leaders for several decades, they remain a complete mystery to me. Why would any intelligent human being risk losing happiness for the questionable pleasure of organizing other people's lives? Is it that leaders are not as happy as they seem? or not as intelligent? Surely, after a thousand years, aspiring leaders with any intelligence would have learned that Abd-el-Raham wasn't kidding, wouldn't they?

People who won't listen to the great leaders of history certainly won't listen to me if I advise them to reconsider the whole idea of becoming a leader. Rationality can't erase a decision that wasn't arrived at rationally, so rather than be rational, let me tell you two more stories. These stories are about two remarkable leaders—Rosy and Dave—who helped me learn about my own motives.

ROSY'S RESPONSE

I met Rosy in a hospital when I was seventeen. The first moment I saw her, I knew why she was called "Rosy." I was lying in bed, after the operation, groggy from the anesthetic, but terribly curious about whether I was alive or dead. A distant, echoing voice asked, "Are you awake?" I didn't know the answer, and I wasn't sure I wanted to know.

It sounded like an angel's voice, which worried me no end. Then a pair of gentle hands shook my shoulders. My body struggled to return to sleep, but I had to know. Was she truly an angel? Was I really in heaven?

I opened my eyes and saw her fluffy coral hair encircling her face like a rusty halo. I had died, and she was my angel.

I was content. I smiled. She smiled back—and took my temperature. The thermometer informed me that I was alive after all, but I didn't care. I was in love, and she would take care of me.

The next ten days were filled with pain, discomfort, and embarrassment, but I wanted them to last forever. I wanted Rosy standing at my bedside, cooling my brow, holding my hand, injecting my morphine.

Every day I grew happier, and more in love. At bedtime on the tenth day, Rosy arrived with a dish of sherbet and a sleeping pill. She watched while I took the pill, then asked the familiar question: "Do you think you need another shot for pain?"

I gave the familiar answer, and for the first time in our short romance, her face wrinkled into a frown. "Do you *really* need it?"

"Oh yes," I implored. "I need it very much."

"In that case," she said, her angelic voice forever lost, "you'd better not have any more."

The next four days were a nightmare of incalculable proportions. I pleaded. I teased. I whispered. I shouted. I pounded on the wall. I screamed. I demanded. I begged. I wept. Rosy remained as remote as the heavens.

In four ruthless days, my undying love turned to unmitigated hate, a hate that I took every opportunity and avenue to express. But in four ruthless days, she cracked my incipient morphine addiction. When I left the hospital, I never wanted to see Rosy again. I never did. She saved me from a life of morphine addiction, and I'll always love her for it.

Rosy did more than save me. She taught me a principle that I've come to call Rosy's Response:

If you want something *that* badly, perhaps you shouldn't have it.

Throughout the life that Rosy returned to me, a few other people have had the courage to offer me Rosy's Response just as I was about to do something obsessive. Unhappily for me, I've *never* listened. If I hadn't been strapped into bed with a tube in every bodily aperture, I wouldn't have listened to Rosy, either.

DAVE'S DEVIATION

That's the trouble with Rosy's Response. It only works on people who don't need it, or people who are strapped to the bed. Obsessed people don't listen. If you're going to help them avoid injuring themselves, you've got to find another approach: like Dave's Deviation, which helped me conquer my obsession to become a manager at age 23.

I was working for IBM. The field of computers was wide open, and I had doubled my starting salary in less than two years on the job. I figured I knew about all there was to know about computers, and I itched for new worlds to conquer. Looking around, I decided there was only one way to really get ahead in IBM, and that was management.

In my semiannual appraisal, I expressed my eagerness to Dave, my boss. Dave was a district manager who had risen through the IBM ranks. In my eyes, he was cool, powerful, and rich. I wanted to be just like him, only more so.

"And just how far do you want to go in management?" Dave inquired.

"The sky's the limit! I intend to be president of IBM."

"And *why* do you want to do that?"

I hesitated. Why indeed? "Actually, I don't know why, but I know I want it, and I don't want to waste any more time twiddling with bits. That's not the way to the top. It's a dead end."

Dave waited patiently for me to finish. He knew there was no percentage to be gained in interrupting the obsessed. "What do you want me to do for you?"

"I want you to find me a job in management. As soon as possible!"

"I'll try to do that," he said, "but only after you've done something for me."

"What's that? I'll do anything."

"You're a good writer. I want you to sit down and write me two lists. The first list should be all the reasons you want to be a manager. The second should be all the assets and liabilities you have as a leader. When you bring me those lists, we'll discuss how we can get you a start in management."

Looking back, I understand now if Dave had offered me Rosy's

Response, I would have resisted, just as I resisted Rosy. Dave genuinely valued my technical contributions. He didn't want to lose me, but he must have been appalled at the idea of me leading even a Cub Scout den, let alone a team of IBM employees. Dave didn't have me strapped to the bed, and I could have left for any number of other jobs, probably at higher pay. I could even have found some manager stupid enough to give me the promotion I thought I wanted.

LISTING ASSETS AND LIABILITIES

Dave's diversion had the right effect. Instead of resisting, I rushed back to my office and started scribbling notes. I started with my reasons: respect, power, money. A good start, so I turned to my assets and liabilities.

My assets were mostly technical: I was quick to master complex ideas. I could write English that people could understand. I could compose computer programs that worked.

I hesitated a long time before committing my liabilities to paper. Sure, I knew what they were, but I didn't want other people to know. For one thing, I was young, and nobody seemed to respect me. For another, I couldn't seem to get anyone to do things my way, even though my ideas were terrific. Finally, my personal life was a big drag on my work, especially the constant bickering with a young wife bound to the house by two children in diapers.

Seeing my liabilities in black and white made me realize that I didn't look like a good bet to move into management. If Dave read this list as it was, my career as a manager would be stillborn. Perhaps I could conceal my weaknesses by cleverly rewriting the list.

As I worked on this rewrite, it occurred to me to relate my weaknesses to my other list, the list of reasons. I came up with the following:

1. I want the respect due a manager because otherwise nobody would respect someone so young and impetuous.

2. I want the power of a manager because I don't know any other way to get people to do things than by ordering them from a position of authority.

3. I want money because I can then get my personal life in order—hire a sitter, get a second car, buy a house.

It was the third item that finally cracked my thick skull. As I read it back to myself, an inner voice said to me, *"If you can't even manage your own affairs, what makes you think you can manage others?"*

That question killed my obsession. I reviewed the other items and realized that my answer to Dave's questions was too devastating to deliver. I would have to say, "Dave, I want you to make me a manager because I lack all the essential qualities of leadership. Most of all, I'm so out of control that I don't know why I'm doing what I'm doing, or what effect it has on other people."

I never gave Dave his lists, and for some reason, he never asked for them. In his own way, Dave had helped me more than Rosy had. He must have, because at the time, I was more furious with him than I had been with her. She had stopped me from hurting myself, but he had diverted me from hurting others. Each used the only method that would have worked under the circumstances.

TREATING YOUR OBSESSION

I find it impossible to finish this book without fulfilling a moral obligation to pass on what Rosy and Dave passed on to me. From Rosy, I learned that happiness doesn't come from outside through morphine. From Dave, I learned that leadership doesn't come from outside through appointment. Being appointed the leader is just like taking drugs: It may carry you through some pain of getting started, but it is more likely to deaden your senses to the very information you most need.

You'll never be much of a leader if you lack the ability to see yourself as others see you—something no junkie can do. Illusions about leadership can be devastating, but illusions about myself are the worst form of addiction. As a writer, I can expose some of your illusions about leadership, but only you can dissolve your illusions about yourself. The best I can do is tell you what sometimes succeeds for me.

Whenever I feel obsessed with the idea of taking the lead, the first thing I have to do is *notice* that I am obsessed. I might be about to say something clever in a meeting, or offer people advice on altering the course of their lives. It might be a wonderful thing to do, or it might be awful. What matters is how I feel as I think of doing it, and my experience with morphine helps me to recognize an obsession from the inside.

Having bought myself a moment of self-control and before I say or do something I may regret, I ask myself three questions:

1. Why do I want to do this?
2. What assets do I have to contribute?
3. What liabilities do I bring?

The questions have served me well, when I've asked them, and I recommend them to you. That's why you have a right to ask me why I wanted to write this book, and what assets and liabilities did I bring?

The assets and liabilities should speak for themselves through your experience with the book, but only I can speak for my motives. At various times, I've hoped this book would earn a lot of money, make me look brilliant, induce people to attend my workshops, generate consulting business, or force somebody to regret they didn't want to work with me. That's not the world's most noble list of motives, and by themselves wouldn't really justify the effort for me to write it or for you to read it. So why did I do it?

I think that I wrote this book out of gratitude, to Rosy and Dave and all the other people who have been my leaders. They would be best paid if I passed the happiness they taught me on to you, and if you, in turn, passed this happiness on to others. Besides that, what other reason really matters?

Bibliography

I've read hundreds of books on aspects of leadership, yet most of what I've learned about leadership has not come from books. Books are no substitute for experience working with people, so now that you've read this book on leadership, go out and interact with people before you read any more.

When you are ready to read more books on leadership, you may want to read some I recommend.

What specific book you should read next is difficult to say because there are so many books on subjects essential to the technical leader, but the following bibliography consists of books that our workshop graduates have found useful. I've annotated each listing to give you some idea of what you're getting into. None of them will waste your time.

Bolman, Lee G., and Terrence E. Deal.
Modern Approaches to Understanding and Managing Organizations. San Francisco: Jossey-Bass, 1984.

If you wish to pursue the organizational side of leadership, start with Bolman and Deal's clearly written text. They survey the important theoretical models of what makes organizations tick, putting each into perspective as only part of the picture. They achieve a synthesis of four major organizational models, none of which, however, adequately treats the role of innovation.

Bolton, Robert.
People Skills: How to Assert Yourself, Listen to Others, and Resolve Conflicts. Englewood Cliffs, N.J.: Prentice-Hall, 1979.

Other leadership qualities will be negated if you lack people skills. Every person, no matter how skilled a leader, could benefit from this down-to-earth review of the fundamentals.

Branden, Nathaniel.
> *The Psychology of Self-Esteem.* New York: Bantam Books, 1971.

> *Honoring the Self.* Los Angeles: J.P. Tarcher, Inc., 1983.

Self-esteem is at the heart of leadership. Branden is one of the most popular writers on this subject.

Carnegie, Dale.
> *How to Win Friends and Influence People.* New York: Simon and Schuster, 1936.

The general principles of leadership haven't changed in fifty years, or even five thousand (though there is a revised, modernized edition of this self-help classic). If you find you cannot tolerate Carnegie's rather ordinary rules, you're probably not ready to be a leader of rather ordinary people.

Doyle, Michael, and David Straus.
> *How to Make Meetings Work.* Chicago: Playboy Press, 1976.

Doyle and Straus have developed the "interaction method" for organizing and operating meetings of all types. Using this method, clearly described in this book, dozens of my clients have converted their meetings from the worst of times to the best of times. (For specialized technical meetings, see also Freedman and Weinberg.)

Freedman, Daniel P., and Gerald M. Weinberg.
> *Handbook of Walkthroughs, Inspections, and Technical Reviews.* Boston: Little, Brown, 1982.

Many technical meetings take the form of critical reviews of work in progress. Technical reviews can be a source of either technical growth or great anxiety and conflict, depending on how they are led. We feel that our handbook, with its question and answer format, is an essential guide for all people who spend time in review meetings. (For other types of meetings, see Doyle and Straus.)

Gause, Donald C., and Gerald M. Weinberg.
> *Are Your Lights On? or How to Figure Out What the Problem Really Is.* Boston: Little, Brown, 1982.

This friendly little book on problem definition will help you if you are generally uncertain about where you want to go next. It also teaches the kind of thinking that is essential in technical leadership.

Gordon, Thomas.
Leader Effectiveness Training: The No-Lose Way to Release the Productive Potential of People. New York: Wyden Books, 1977.

Gordon is the author of the tremendously popular and helpful *Parent Effectiveness Training.* Gordon's "no-lose" approach will appeal to technical leaders who want to step out of the Big Game.

Gross, Ronald.
The Lifelong Learner. New York: Simon and Schuster, 1979.

This is an essential handbook for those who take responsibility for their own learning; it is full of ideas, suggestions, and specific resources for self-renewal.

Hart, Lois Borland.
Moving Up! Women and Leadership. New York: AMACOM, 1980.

Almost all of this book would be just as interesting to men as to women, which is not a criticism. A special feature of this book is the great number of self-assessment charts.

Hollander, Edwin P.
Leadership Dynamics. New York: Free Press, 1978.

This book offers a good entry point to the theoretical and experimental results about leadership. The references are thorough, but inconspicuous, so that you may start with ideas and move to sources if you wish.

Josefowitz, Natasha.
Paths to Power: A Woman's Guide from First Job to Top Executive. Reading, Mass.: Addison-Wesley, 1980.

This book plots a woman's entire career in terms of power issues. Although it covers more than leadership issues, my informants assure me that this book has more information specifically useful to women leaders than, for example, Hart's book.

Kennedy, Eugene.
On Becoming a Counselor. New York: Continuum Publishing Co., 1980.

People who are seen as leaders often find themselves in the role of counselors to people asking for help. Kennedy's book is directed to those who are not professional counselors, but who often find themselves in this role and at least want to know how to avoid doing harm.

Oshry, Barry.

When it comes to understanding the systems aspects of power in organizations, Barry Oshry has no equal. Unfortunately, those of us who have learned from his Power and Systems Laboratory are still waiting for Barry to publish his definitive work. For the present, you can obtain information about the workshops and short articles from

> Power and Systems
> P.O. Box 388
> Prudential Station
> Boston, MA 02199

Larry Porter, ed.

> *Reading Book for Human Relations Training.* Arlington, Va.: NTL Institute, updated annually.

Many of my workshop graduates want to learn more about how they interact with other people. I often recommend that they take NTL's Human Interaction Laboratory, and this is the book of readings that they take home from that lab. The full address of NTL is

> P.O. Box 9155
> Rosslyn Station
> Arlington, VA 22209

Progoff, Ira.

> *At a Journal Workshop.* New York: Dialogue House Library, 1975.

If you want to learn more about keeping a journal, here's a whole book on the subject.

Reps, Paul.

> *Zen Flesh, Zen Bones.* Garden City, N.Y.: Anchor Books.

Some readers have suggested that my book should have been titled *Zen and the Art of Technical Leadership,* but Zen is only part of the story. Even so, those who would transform themselves into technical leaders should be aware of the Zen approach, and Paul Reps was probably the first author to popularize Zen in the West. This book is primarily a collection of Zen teaching stories.

Rogers, Carl.
  On Personal Power. New York: Dell, 1977.

If you are interested in power and leadership, read this book before you do anything else. Other books by Carl Rogers that will help you on your path to effective leadership include these:
  On Becoming a Person. Boston: Houghton Mifflin, 1961.

  A Way of Being. Boston: Houghton Mifflin, 1980.

Russell, Bertrand.
  The Conquest of Happiness. New York: Signet Books, 1951.

Unhappy people are not leaders. Nobel Prize-winning philosopher Bertrand Russell tackles the ancient question of how to be happy, and succeeds.

Satir, Virginia.
  Conjoint Family Therapy, 3rd ed. Palo Alto, Calif.: Science and Behavior Books, 1983.

  Peoplemaking. Palo Alto, Calif.: Science and Behavior Books, 1972.

  Self-Esteem. Millbrae, Calif.: Celestial Arts, 1975.

  Making Contact. Millbrae, Calif.: Celestial Arts, 1976.

  Your Many Faces. Millbrae, Calif.: Celestial Arts, 1978.

Obviously, I have been greatly influenced by the work of Virginia Satir. I first became aware of her radical approach to life through *Peoplemaking,* which is a good survey of her approach to how we learn to interact with others. *Conjoint Family Therapy* is more of a comprehensive textbook aimed at therapists, but like all her books, it is written without academic pretension. For a lighter introduction to specific topics of importance to leaders, try one or all of her little books from Celestial Arts. For information concerning her books, workshops, and videotapes, contact her at

  Avanta Network
  139 Forest Avenue
  Palo Alto, CA 94301

Shah, Idries.
  The Subtleties of the Inimitable Mulla Nasrudin. London: Octagon Press, 1973.

In many ways, my approach to leadership and teaching has been deeply influenced by Sufi ideas. I believe that anyone who aspires to be a leader should be familiar with the Sufi approach. Most of what is popularly known in English about the Sufi has been brought to us by Idries Shah. This is but one of his collections of Sufi teaching stories, but any other will do as a starting point.

Weinberg, Gerald M.

Understanding the Professional Programmer. Boston: Little, Brown, 1982.

Before you advance to bigger and better things, it helps to understand where you came from and where you are now. If you come from a programming background, the preceding book should help. Another book to read is

The Secrets of Consulting: A Guide to Giving & Getting Advice Successfully. New York: Dorset House Publishing, 1985.

As I assembled this bibliography, I realized that I have been writing about problem-solving leadership for a long time. Even though *Becoming a Technical Leader* is my first book to cover the subject as a whole, other books develop the three major concerns of problem-solving leaders. *Are Your Lights On?*, with Don Gause, addresses the subject of understanding the problem. *The Handbook of Walkthroughs, Inspections, and Technical Reviews*, with Daniel Freedman, deals with controlling the quality. *The Secrets of Consulting* is the latest in this series, and is aimed at the third major area: managing the flow of ideas. Its subtitle is what it's all about.

Index

Abd-el-Raham, 269
All-Y's strategy, 266-67

Baldwin, M., 127
Big Game, 200-204, 277
Bolman, L., 275
Bolton, R., 276
Boulding, K., 123
Branden, N., 150, 276
Bridger, H., 210
Burns, R., 105, 124

Carnegie, D., 141, 143-52, 276
Career line, 93-96, 99
Carroll, L., 25
Cat/mouse story, 121-27
Central dogma:
    of psychology, 8-9, 70-71, 85-86
    of problem-solving leader, 85-86
Change:
    conservative and radical strategies
        for, 264, 266-67
    environment for, 19-22
    excuses for resisting, 49-55
    leaders and, 11-12, 19-20, 37, 217ff.
    models and, 11-12, 37ff.
    MOI model and, 19-20
    personal plan for, 241-46
    success and, 215
    support for, 257-67
    time for, 251-56
Chinese proverb, 68-69, 219

Clark, C., 276
Communication:
    congruent, 165-69
    exercise, Tinkertoy, 132-34
    methods, 202, 211-12
    theory, 108-16
Consensus form of organization, 187,
    189-92
Curie, M., 175

Dave's Deviation, 270-74
Deal, T., 275
Decision making:
    Myers-Briggs theory, 214, 216
Dessert and dieting example, 63-65
Doyle, M., 276

Education plan, for leadership,
    241-46, 255-56
Einstein, A., 249, 251
Electric blanket story, 213
Environment, technical, 8, 12, 227
E.T., 156-59
Expertise:
    maintaining, 241-46
    power and, 157-58

Feedback diagram, 109
Ferber, E., 61
Fog Index, 122-23
Freedman, D., viii, 276, 280

Gardner, H., 15
Gause, D., *vii-viii*, 277, 280
Gordon, T., 277
Grading system for leaders, 221-27
Gross, R., 246, 277
Gross, S., 212
Growth, 42-44
  support for, 263-64
  theory of, 37-44
  ways to avoid, 49-55

Hacking, 27, 31
Hart, L., 277
Helpful environments, 132
  exercise to create, 132-34
  lessons, 135-38
Holcombe, B., 242
Hollander, E., 277
Holmes, O., 35
Horse-man problem, 69-70
Hugo, V., 157
Human Interaction Laboratory, 278

Ideas, 18-21, 29
  managing, 21, 27-31, 51, 144, 192,
    212
  strategies to develop, 85-89
Innovation, 18-21, 51-52, 59ff.
  power and, 177
  role in leadership, 13, 21, 27-31
  vision and, 97-100
Intruder test, 232-36

Josefowitz, N., 277
Journal, personal, 75-80

Kennedy, E., 129, 131, 139, 278
Kipling, R., 229, 231, 252
Kobayashi, K., 231-32

Lao-Tse, 3
Leader:
  (see also *Problem-solving leader*)
  appointed, 49-51, 182, 187, 189,
    199, 274
  as decision maker, 199-202
  as person, 126-27
  being graded as, 221-37
  strong, form of organization, 187,
    189, 191
  technical, 21, 27-32, 122, 131,
    157-58, 224-25

Leadership, 7-12
  change and, 11-12, 19-20, 37
  coping styles of, 235
  decision making and, 202
  defined, 12
  interaction with others, 109-16
  models of, 7-12, 19-22, 37-44,
    108-15
  power and, 54-55, 155-59
  self-esteem and, 114, 137-38, 150,
    155, 200, 225
  style, 21, 27-32, 107-108
  technical skills and, 21, 52-53, 59,
    131, 157-58, 224-25, 241-46
  vision and, 22, 97-100, 103, 107
  workshops and, 78
License plate problem, 65-67
Linear model of leadership, 9-12
  threat/reward model, 9-12, 22

Maccoby, M., 49
Mechanical problem, 131
  smelly programmer, 163-67
  smiling, 149, 166-67
Mensa IQ test problem, 69-70
Metacycle, 43-44
Meta-rules, 144-49, 167
Model, leadership, 7-12
  innovation and, 13
  interaction, 108-15
  development, 37-44
  linear, 9-12
  MOI, 17, 19-21, 53, 75
  organic, 9-13, 17, 49, 131, 163, 168,
    203-204
  plateau-ravine, 37-44, 116, 237
  psychologists', 7-8
  seed, 12, 163, 168
  threat/reward, 9-12, 22, 49, 55, 86,
    127, 168
MOI model of leadership, 17, 19-21,
  53, 75
Motivation, 17-21, 51-52, 75, 103ff.
  learning, 141ff., 245
  obstacles to, 107-16, 121-27
  personality approach, 235
  personal journal and, 75-80
  testing personal, 75-80, 107-108
Myers-Briggs theory, 214, 216
Myth of the appointed leader, 49-50
Myth of leadership skills, 224-25
Myth of natural helpfulness, 131

Napoleon, 153, 155
Networks for change, 261-67
  all-Y's, 266-67
  conservatives vs. radicals, 264,
    266-67
No-Problem Syndrome, 65-68, 71,
  86-87

Organic model of leadership, 9-13,
  17, 131, 203-204
  appointed leader and, 49
  seed model, 12, 163, 168
Organization, 18-21, 51-52, 75, 173ff.,
  235
  forms for problem-solving teams,
    185-93
  incongruence in forms of, 211-12,
    215
  manager and, 199-204
  methods for learning, 209-15
  obstacles to, 199-204
  personal effectiveness and, 199-204
  planning approach, 235
  power and, 177-82
Orr, K., 262
  foreword by, xi-xii
Oshry, B., 207, 210, 278

People-oriented style, 123-27
Personal journal, 75-80
Personality test exercise, 197
Pinball example, 17-19, 37-41
Plan for change, 241-46
Plateau-ravine model, 37-44, 116, 237
Porter, L., 278
Power, 54-55, 155-59
  converting, 177-82
  organizational, 173, 177-82
  personal, 163-71, 181-82, 215
  threat/reward model and, 11
Power and Systems Laboratory, 207,
  210, 278
Problem, understanding, 21, 27-29,
  192, 212
Problem-solving environment:
  creating, 21, 28, 166, 192-93,
    202-204
  quality and, 31-32
Problem-solving leader, 21,
  27-32
  Big Game and, 200-204, 277

central dogmas and, 8-9, 70, 85-86
defined, 21
grading, 221-27
high-tech environment and, 51-55
ideas and, 29, 85-89
meta-rules and, 144-49, 167
motivation and, 17-21, 51-52, 75,
  103ff.
need for change and, 267
No-Problem Syndrome and, 65-68,
  71, 86-87
obstacles to, 63-71
organization and, 18-21, 51-52, 75,
  173ff., 185-93, 211-12, 215, 235
people or task orientation, 121-27
power and, 54-55, 155-59, 163-71,
  177-82
self-blindness and, 64-65, 71,
  75-80, 89
survival rules and, 144, 145
technical skills and, 52-53, 59, 131,
  157-58, 224-25
testing, 107-108, 231-37
vision and, 22, 97-100
workshop, 78, 179ff., 231-36
Problem-solving team, 7-8, 12, 21
  organization of, 185-93, 199-204
Process observer, 195
Progoff, I., 278
Proverbs, 91
Psychology, central dogma of, 8-9,
  70-71, 85-86

Quality, maintaining, 21, 27, 31-32,
  192, 212

Random Number Network, 262, 263,
  267
Reps, P., vii, 278
Rogers, C., 83, 279
Rollercoaster lifeline, 95
Rosy's Response, 269-70, 273
Rules:
  commenting, 113
  for grading leaders, 221-27
  for problem-solving, 204
  Golden, 137-38, 267
  meta-, 144-49, 167
  perfection, 148, 168
  Platinum, 139
  survival, 112-13, 122, 144-51, 167

transforming, into guides, 145-49,
    167-68
Russell, B., 22, 279

Satir, V., 149-50, 161, 279
    Big Game and, 200-204
    interaction model of, 108-15
    leaders as people and, 126-27
    mature behaviors and, 165
    theory of incongruent
        communication, 114-15, 165-69
Secretary problem, 69
Seed model, 12, 163, 168
Self-awareness, leadership, 75-80, 85
Self-blindness, 64-65, 71, 89, 107
    tool to overcome, 75-80
Self-esteem, 114, 137-38, 150, 155,
    200, 225
    threat/reward model and, 10
Shah, I., 279
Single-solution belief, 68-71
Smelly programmer example, 163-66
Smiling rule, 149, 166-67
Straus, D., 276
Support systems, 261-67
Survival rules, 112-13, 122, 144-51,
    167
Swiss time management story, 251-52
Swiss creation story, 253-54

Task-oriented style, 122-27
Task vs. people test, 119, 121, 125-26
Tavistock Workshop, 210
Teams, problem-solving:
    organization of, 185-93, 199-204
    productivity of, 50-51
Technical skills, 52-53
    maintaining, 241-46
Technology:
    leadership and, 27-32, 52-53, 59,
        131, 224-25
    power and, 156-57
Teddy Roosevelt image, 51-52
Tests, leadership:

Arnold vs. Ramon, 233-36
being graded, 221-27
intruder test, 233-36
Mensa IQ, 69-70
people vs. task, 119ff.
personal, 221-37
personality, 197
self-blindness, 107
top executive example, 231
Weinberg's Target, 124
worker payment, 85
Theory of growth, 37-44
    metacycle and, 43-44
Threat/reward model, 9-12, 55, 168
    anonymous reviews and, 127
    appointed leaders and, 49
Thumb exercise, 241-42
Time management, 251-56
Tinkertoy exercise, 132-34
Twain, M., 239, 245

Vision, role of, 22, 97-100, 103, 107
Von Suttner, B., 259
Voting, as organizational form,
    187-89, 191, 192

Weinberg and Weinberg workshops,
    78, 179ff., 231-36
Weinberg, D., vii, 20, 64, 213, 221-27,
    263-65
Weinberg, G., 276, 277, 280
    NPS and, 65-68, 71, 86-87
    pinball experience, 17-19, 37-41
    smiling rule, 149, 166-67
Weinberg's Target, 124
West, R., 47
Woitach, P., 261-62
Workshop, leadership, 78, 179ff.
    tests and, 231-36
World Record Exercise, 185ff.
    answers to, 194
Wright, F., 192

Yetta/Sam interaction, 108-14